PRACTICAL

BUSINESS
RE-ENGINEERING

PRACTICAL

BUSINESS RE-ENGINEERING

Tools
and
Techniques
for
Achieving
Effective
Change

Nick Obolensky

KOGAN
PAGE

First published in 1994

Apart from any fair dealing for the purposes of research or private study, or criticism or review, as permitted under the Copyright, Designs and Patents Act, 1988, this publication may only be reproduced, stored or transmitted, in any form or by any means, with the prior permission in writing of the publishers, or in the case of reprographic reproduction in accordance with the terms of licences issued by the Copyright Licensing Agency. Enquiries concerning reproduction outside those terms should be sent to the publishers at the undermentioned address:

Kogan Page Limited
120 Pentonville Road
London N1 9JN

© Nick Obolensky, 1994

British Library Cataloguing in Publication Data
A CIP record for this book is available from the British Library.

ISBN 0 7494 1408 1

Typeset by Saxon Graphics Ltd, Derby
Printed and bound in Great Britain by Biddles Ltd, Guildford and King's Lynn.

Contents

4 ■ Contents

Preface

Business Re-engineering in many ways is a natural evolution, and practical strategic application, of a number of management approaches that have recently made an impact on the way managers look at, and change, organisations. Such approaches include Total Quality Management (TQM), Time-Based Competition, Customer Focus and, more recently, Business Process Re-engineering (BPR). Business Re-engineering is a holistic approach which can provide a process to link the competitive strategy of an organisation to its people and processes, a linkage enhanced by using the information and communication technology available today. The difference that Business Re-engineering has from some other approaches is that it radically changes the way an organisation works, it achieves large improvements and it is very difficult to do well. Indeed, it is often quoted that some 80 per cent of proposed re-engineering projects fail. Business Re-engineering is thus a risky venture. Many of the books and articles currently published about Business Re-engineering do well to explain the 'what' but do not go into the detail of 'how'. And yet the risk of failure is mainly due to the how, and not often due to the what. This book is intended to concentrate on the how, and to increase the odds of success.

Business Re-engineering is here to stay, at least until the majority of organisations have moved away from the antiquated models of Adam Smith and Frederick Taylor. Adam Smith's eighteenth-century model proposes the efficient division of labour through functional specialism, while Frederick Taylor's turn of the century model proposes the effective control of labour through vertical hierarchies. Although their models are sound when based on the assumptions of their day, the world has moved on since the eighteenth, nineteenth and early twentieth centuries. Organisations are no longer served well by the conventional wisdom of the division and control of tasks and labour into functional specialities and hierarchical management tiers. We are living in times of change as radical as the industrial revolution, and organisations are finding that they need to change to remain competitive, to embrace the technology of the day, and to get the best out of the improved abilities of their people. They also need to achieve a state of continual change. Organisations which successfully manage to re-engineer themselves find that not only do they achieve dramatic short-term results, they also turn themselves into flexible organisations which can continue to change.

The people who should read this book are those who are in organisations which are facing the need for change, but do not know how do deal with it. The book is fairly extensive in that it will suit organisations which need a lot of change such as that achieved by Business Re-engineering, but the principles herein can also be used for smaller, discrete change projects. Throughout the book the words 'change' and 're-engineering' are used interchangeably. It should be stressed that the approach in the book is *a* way to implement Business Re-engineering, not *the* way. I doubt if one right way exists – the right way is the way that works, and the approach in the book should work for most organisations. However, as can be seen in Part 2, there are many ways to re-engineer. And some of the approaches are refreshingly different from the details of the approach suggested in the book! So the book is designed to be used like a manual. You can read it cover to cover, or, more likely, dip in and out to suit your own needs and circumstance.

∎ In Part 1:
  — Chapter 1 provides an introduction to Business Re-engineering and an overview of a proposed four-stage model explaining how to re-engineer an organisation ('Know what you want' – 'Make a plan' – 'Do it!' – 'Monitor');
  — Chapters 2 to 5 explain the four steps in more detail;
  — Chapter 6 details how to keep a re-engineering programme on track when the changes do not achieve the desired outcomes, and also explains how the organisation, once re-engineered, can move to managing continual change;
  — Chapter 7 outlines some change management techniques which can be used during all the stages;
  — Chapter 8 proposes some immediate things to do to start things rolling.
∎ Part 2 contains a number of outline case studies of organisations which have undergone, and are in the process of implementing, Business Re-engineering.
∎ In Part 3:
  — Appendix 1 describes a kit bag of analytical and process tools and techniques to help you 'Know what you want';
  — Appendix 2 details a fairly exhaustive way to approach change projects using project management planning techniques which can help to 'Make a plan';
  — Appendix 3 outlines some of the essentials of current information and communication technology which can help you 'Do it'.

Change can be a fearful thing. Sometimes it is imposed upon us, and sometimes we struggle to implement it ourselves. It is also very difficult to achieve, despite a whole variety of theories and supporting technologies. For example, a report by McKinsey quoted in the *Wall Street Journal* in October 1992 stated that 90 per cent of Quality Assurance programmes do not come up with the expected results. Another report by MIT stated that despite billions of dollars invested into information technology, little demonstrable benefit has accrued to the shareholders of US companies (although a more recent report suggests that this is now beginning to be addressed, with more emphasis on managing the process of change itself). There are hundreds of corporate and organisational examples of how easy it is to mismanage change. Most of the failings are due to five common pitfalls:

- the objectives and rationale of change are not fully understood;
- the change itself is not planned in enough detail;
- the 'human dynamics' (some would say politics) are not well managed;
- there is a general failing to set up a rigorous method to monitor progress;
- the pain of the change itself is greater than the perceived pain of the status quo and the perceived gain which the changes promise.

The techniques and processes outlined in this book are from a variety of sources. I have, wherever possible, given credit for merely repeating the ideas of others. In addition, the study of hundreds of case studies has yielded useful common lessons which can be effectively used. The techniques and processes detailed in the book are also gleaned from years of personal experience working with a variety of organisations grappling with change. These have varied from 'non-profit' organisations (such as charities and governmental public sector organisations), to businesses in many differing industries (from manufacturing and retail to banking and insurance) and in differing countries (including Western and Eastern Europe, the USA and the Middle East).

It seems obvious to say that it is people, not ideas, plans or processes, which get things done. One frequently sees organisations getting too involved in the 'what' of change and too little concerned with the 'how'. Typically, over 80 per cent of the effort to plan and implement radical change concentrates on the 'what', with scant attention to the 'how'. And yet 90 per cent of the problems in implementing change lie in the 'how', with a fraction of the problems lying in the 'what'. If decent ideas and rational plans are not matched with well thought-out participative processes, then too often the people involved in striving for change achieve nothing but severe frustration, depression and broken dreams.

The only thing that stops us achieving dreams is the limit of our own imagination. Learning from mistakes, and successes, is a good way to learn – learning from other people's mistakes and successes is a cheap way to learn. This book is based on learning from many mistakes and successes, my own and others. I hope that in reading it, and more importantly in applying the principles herein, you and your organisation achieve the dreams that are in the mind but not yet forged into reality.

Nick Obolensky

Acknowledgements

A variety of people have been involved in giving guidance, information and advice in the preparation of this book. I am particularly indebted to Roberta Kelly and Bob Maher (both seasoned change management consultants in the USA), and Professor Jaques Bouvard (IMD Business School in Lausanne, Switzerland). I am also indebted to the people from the organisations in Part 2 who have kindly given their time which enabled me to prepare the useful and instructive case studies. These organisations are in alphabetical order:

- *AT&T, Global Business Communication Service (USA):* Barbara Augun (Director Process Re-engineering) and Glenn Hazard (VP Process Re-engineering);
- *Banca d'America e d'Italia (Italy):* Andrea Giochetta (General Manager);
- *Birmingham Midshires Building Society (UK):* Lorren Wyatt (HR Director) and Mike Jackson (CEO);
- *Cigna International (UK):* Ian Fergusson (Systems Manager);
- *Digital South Pacific (Australia):* Maggie Alexander (Quantum Project Leader);
- *Ford Motor Company:* Richard Lindner (Manager Process Improvement Planning, Ford of Europe);
- *Kingston Hospital (UK):* George Kempton (Patient Focused Care Team leader), John Langan (CEO) and Carrie Shroter (Business Manager);
- *National Vulcan (UK):* John Pearson (Consultant) and Ken Sinfield (CEO);
- *Oticon (Denmark):* Lars Kolind (CEO);
- *Progressive Corporation (USA):* Peter Lewis (CEO) and Bruce Marlow (COO);
- *Siemens Nixdorf Service ITS (Europe):* John Loveland (Divisional Director BUITS) and Gerhard Radtke (Chief Executive BUITS).

I am also grateful to Peter Deering (Systems Director) and Rob Lees (Business Systems Planning Manager) of Somerfield Stores Ltd for their help in preparing Part 3, Appendix 3. Finally, I would like to thank Alistair Forbes for his suggestions, advice and humour.

Part 1

Making It Happen

1

Introduction

1. WHAT IS BUSINESS RE-ENGINEERING?

Change is not made without inconvenience, even from worse to better.

Richard Hooker

Although this book is very much about how to achieve Business Re-engineering, rather than an explanation of what it is, it is still necessary to afford some brief, high-level, definition. Business Re-engineering is what an organisation undertakes to change its internal processes and controls from a traditional vertical, functional hierarchy to a horizontal, cross-functional, team-based, flat structure which focuses on the process of delighting customers. Most organisations are similar to 'chimneys' with large, hierarchical functional departments working in isolation, with little, if any, cross-functional management below main board level.

A Business Re-engineering programme will typically move an organisation from a 'chimney' to a 'grid', where newly established process teams cut across the functions, but the functions still exist, albeit in a thinned down way. The next evolution would be to move to 'bubbles' – teams of people who bring their specialisms and abilities to bear to focus on specific processes, change projects or technical support projects. This broad evolution is shown in diagrammatic form in Figure 1.1 . Bubble organisations are very fluid, with teams forming and disbanding, and people working on more than one team in different roles at a time. A high reliance is placed on an open, informal culture, with excellent communications, backed by a high degree of information and communication technology. The teams are networked using IT, and the organisation links the strategy, technology and people into a triangulated model

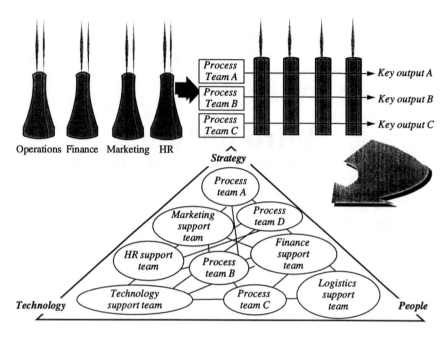

Figure 1.1 The aim is to move from 'chimney' to 'grids' and then on to triangulated networked 'bubbles'.

which ensures flexibility and responsiveness to change. Although it is rare for an organisation to move from 'chimneys' to 'bubbles', this is precisely what the head office of Oticon did in Denmark (see Part 2 for a full description).

The culture and leadership style in such organisations differ very much from the traditional approaches found in 'chimney' organisations, and thus the re-engineering often needs to include a large culture change programme aimed at all levels. The culture change will typically involve moving from top-down control to empowerment (allowing decisions to be taken at the point closest to the customers), the breaking up of traditional power factions, and the employment of networked IT systems. In some ways Business Re-engineering is a paradox, because it has to be started as a top-down exercise, but relies very much on bottom-up support and involvement.

Not only does Business Re-engineering typically achieve startling results, it also allows an organisation to become far more flexible, responsive and able to seize opportunities for change with relish. It is not an exercise which is easy, and in the initial stages of implementation can often cause an organisation pain and anguish. To succeed, a Business Re-engineering programme will typically need four variables to be right:

- **Pain of the status quo.** The status quo must be (or clearly about to be) producing pain to encourage people to move. Business Re-engineering is rather like jumping off a North Sea oil platform: it is not something you would want to do unless there was a very serious fire.
- **Gain of the future change.** The projected benefits of Business Re-engineering must be clear – and credibly so – to help an organisation maintain the will to keep moving forwards.
- **Perceived need for change by leadership.** If the leadership at the top does not believe in the need for change, then they will find it hard to show their visible support for it. And if the support for a change as radical as Business Re-engineering is not firm and visible at the top, any programme which tries to implement it will most likely fail.
- **Impact across the organization.** Business Re-engineering needs to have an impact across the organisation for it to yield the best results. Typically many organisations shy away from this, and just re-engineer one part of the organisation (often due to the political problems of 'invading' people's turf). This is not Business Re-engineering, it is more like process re-design using business process re-engineering (BPR) techniques. Business Re-engineering does not just re-engineer the processes – it re-engineers the minds.

Any change programme in an organisation will need an element of the variables above, but Business Re-engineering differs from other change programmes (such as quality circles and process re-engineering) as it typically demands a high degree from each variable, as shown in Figure 1.2.

If the variables do not score highly, then do not attempt to re-engineer! Instead work to make sure the basic circumstances are right for a Business Re-engineering programme to succeed. This is covered in more detail in section 3 below and also in Chapter 2, sections 1.2 and 1.3.

2. FOUR STEPS TOWARDS CONTINUAL CHANGE

Despite compelling potential gain, or an experience of status quo pain, most people dislike having to change. In fact it seems that the only time people really like change is either when *other* people change, or when outside circumstances change to the individual's benefit. The first step to making a change as radical as Business Re-engineering happen is to ask yourself 'How will I change myself?' It is only when you can answer that question, and get others to answer it for themselves, that you can really begin to structure a successful change programme. The reason why this simple question is always hard to answer, is that most people like to think that what they are doing is right, and that if they need to change it

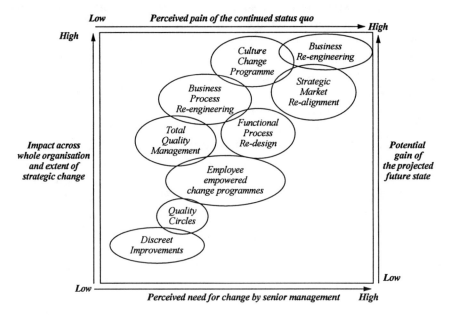

Figure 1.2 Business Re-engineering represents a large change programme.

is because they have been wrong – and nobody likes to think they've been wrong. The problem remains, however, that in this fast moving world, old actions frequently fail to meet new needs. This book outlines a process to make the radical change of Business Re-engineering happen, following the four simple steps shown in Figure 1.3.

The two additional steps in italics on each side are also important, and represent, firstly, the two options you have when the change you want fails to get the results you intended, and, secondly, how to improve continually and adapt to key stakeholders and market needs. This is important, as one of the main benefits of undertaking a radical Business Re-engineering programme is that it allows the organisation to become flexible, responsive and able to change and react quickly. Competitive advantage is gained not so much by *what* the organisation does, but by *how* it does it.

Behind each step there are tools and techniques you can employ straight away. The following chapters of the book go into more detail of each step, but it should be stressed up front that life is a bit more complex than simple management models, and the application of the tools and techniques which back each step up will differ according to unique circumstance. In addition, although the model in Figure 1.3 suggests a serial approach, there is a high degree of parallel activity and iteration. For

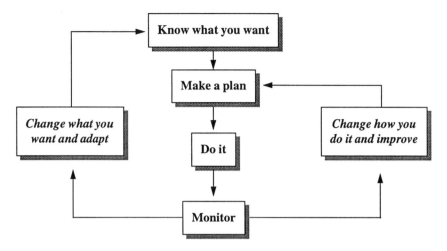

Figure 1.3 Four steps to Business Re-engineering.

example, one of the techniques described in Chapter 4, 'Do it', is to 'create and maintain dissatisfaction of the status quo'. Depending on circumstance, this might be the *first* thing you need to do, even before some of the earlier steps in the process. However, as a broad indicative rule you will need to do each of the four steps well in order to succeed in Business Re-engineering. You should not 'Do it' before employing a participative and high-quality planning phase, and it is pointless planning something you do not fully understand! Although the steps seem simple, one should always remember what Clausewitz said about war: 'In war all things are simple, but the simplest things are the hardest to achieve.'

Organisations vary, but they often share a common strand: they have objectives, and they employ methods and processes to achieve them. Organisations which generally do well are those whose objectives are clear, shared and defined, with well proven and efficient methods and processes, backed by a flexible and motivated workforce, using enhanced IT, focused on the customer.

However, even such organisations can be overtaken by changing circumstances, and they can find themselves doing no better than if they had unclear objectives and methods. So an organisation needs to be able to change rapidly not just once, but continually in order to keep up with the changing market. Although the initial re-engineering programme might be driven top down, subsequent change needs to be driven bottom up. The organisation needs to learn how to clarify and set objectives, and how to employ improved methods and processes to meet those objectives.

The first two steps ('Know what you want' and 'Make a plan') are aimed at moving an organisation from box 4, through box 3 to box 1, as shown in Figure 1.4. One of the main implementation problems of a Business Re-engineering programme is that it will tip an organisation which feels it is comfortable in box 1 into box 4, and chaos can quickly rule. That is why it is vital if such a large change is necessary to re-engineer in a measured and stepped way, to maintain control.

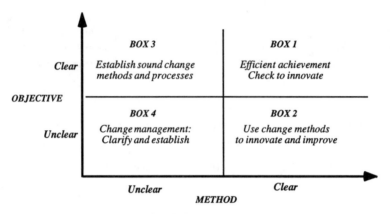

Figure 1.4 Clarifying objectives and methods.

Having started in box 4, and gone through box 3 to box 1 using the techniques in this book, the organisation will have learnt how to adapt and innovate. It will be able to cycle between box 1 and 2. In today's fast-moving, technologically evolving world, a Business Re-engineering change programme is only a medium-term solution. Change is not something an organisation needs to do just once: it needs to understand how to evolve rapidly in order to stay ahead in the fast-changing world in which we live.

Clarifying objectives and methods, however, is just half the story. They represent the first two steps which get you to the start line. The final two steps ('Do it' and 'Monitor') get you to where you want to be, and able to measure progress and the need for further change. There are a variety of tools and techniques which can be used in all of the steps.

3. KNOW WHAT YOU WANT

> Know yourself, and know your enemy, and you can fight a thousand battles without defeat.
>
> Sun Tzu, Chinese War Lord and philosopher, BC

Before any large organisational Business Re-engineering or strategic change is undertaken, you need to understand what it is you are changing, and why. This requires a fair amount of analysis, discussion and thinking. Analysis is sometimes seen as a boring activity, because most of us are action-oriented managers who want to get on with things rather than inspect our navels. However, if the action is not thought out, both the what *and* the how, the chance of failure is high. Many re-engineering programmes flounder because the target has not been fully defined and the reasons not fully articulated – and if people are not 100 per cent clear about the target and why they need to go for it, they cannot be expected to hit it! So you need to understand the organisation and what it is trying to achieve at the moment, and the technology and processes it employs, as well as appreciate the competitive environment within which it operates. Once that is done, you can start to understand the true nature of the competition, and where the opportunities for re-engineering really lie. It is generally pointless re-engineering a process when the output for that process is not wanted!

There are three stages to this first step of 'Know what you want':

■ Clarify the need for, and the organisational ability to, change.
■ Clarify how to serve the needs of stakeholders better.
■ Construct a 'Framework for Success' to assist communication and planning.

Bearing in mind the four variables needed as a background for a re-engineering programme (see figure 1.2), you need to analyse how much the organisation is willing to change, and how much pain is associated with the status quo. This will help formulate tactics later on. You need to understand how well the organisation has managed change in the past, and if lessons have been learnt. This will help decide what, if any, outside consultancy help you may require – and see what the likely support for change is going to be across the leadership. If such support is not there, it needs to be built up either by lobbying, or by generating subjective support for change using the objective findings from the stakeholder analysis as a catalyst.

The next step is to form a cross-functional team to analyse the needs of the key stakeholders of the organisation. These are typically:

■ customers;
■ employees;
■ suppliers;
■ shareholders.

There are various tools and techniques for analysing stakeholders' needs (and how the needs are currently being met), and these are discussed in Chapter 2 and detailed in Part 3, Appendix 1, sections 1 to 5. The process for gathering this information should include small cross-functional project teams from the organisation who can work and share together their findings, and lay the foundation for decision-making. The project teams should include not only the key decision-makers, but also some of the people who will likely be involved in future implementation. Getting these people 'on board' early in the process will pay dividends further down stream. Exactly how you do this is discussed in section 8 below and in more detail in Chapter 7.

During this stage of analysis, take a high-level look at the key processes which the organisation employs to meet the needs of the customer. They probably cut across functional boundaries. You will need to understand how much effort is spent on the activities which make up the process, and how long the overall duration of the process is. Simply walking around a process is a good way to get a high-level look – this simple technique was used by the managing director of National Vulcan (see Part 2). One will probably find out that although it might take only a few days of effort to complete the activities, the duration could be very much longer. How much of the effort is 'value added' (i.e. directly serves the customer) versus non value added (i.e. administrative routines)? Do the outputs of the process meet the needs of the customers? Are all the inputs necessary? One can either do such analysis by using process mapping techniques ('brown' fields approach), or by identifying the required outputs and starting with a clean slate ('green' fields approach), or ideally by using a mix of both approaches.

The analysis of the key stakeholders should give a clear answer to 'Where are we now, and what direction are we heading in?' The next question to answer is: 'Where *should* we be going?' To do this some additional analysis on the external environment needs to be done – competitors' strengths and weaknesses are key. Their strengths can give clues as to what you can achieve – ask yourself: 'If they can do it, why can't we?' Their weaknesses can give you a clue how to attack them. Frontal assaults should be avoided – go around your competitors instead of attacking them head on. The only inevitable result of a head to head clash is a headache! By now the analysis will give some indications where change is necessary, and what potential solutions may be.

Before delving too deep into the details, stand back and formulate a mission or vision statement. Examples are shown in Chapter 2. From this statement you should be able to formulate strategic goals to serve the key stakeholders. These strategic goals can be broken down into general initiatives, with each initiative broken down further into detailed objectives. These detailed objectives form the basis on which to plan the change projects which will implement the re-engineering programme. The change projects should be prioritised and phased. It is also vital at this stage to have an idea of how the action and the results will be monitored and measured, and what process will be in place to do this. It is important to get the optimal balance in meeting the needs of the various key stakeholders. At the same time, consider using a values statement to communicate the needed behaviours of the future state. While mission statements help focus an organisation onto the 'what', value statements help focus individuals onto the 'how'. Examples of value statements can be found in Chapter 7, as well as in some of the case studies in Part 2.

By the end of this first stage you should have a full understanding of your organisation and its environment, and the overall mission, strategic goals, general initiatives and their detailed objectives. You should also have a good idea of what future behaviour is needed by individuals in the organisation to move from the current state to the future state. This is the basis of the change that needs to be carried out. No doubt you and your team have become restless for action, and wish to charge ahead. Unfortunately, there is still some more preparatory work to do – that's part of the discipline needed for successful Business Re-engineering. The next step is crucial, and is one which many leave out – planning the action in detail.

4. MAKE A PLAN

If you fail to plan, you plan to fail.
Anon

The required output of the planning stage is a clear direction to guide effective action. Action gets results. This may seem obvious, but there it is. For some reason people forget to do the planning, and go straight to the acting – and then get frustrated that the action does not achieve the required result. Actually the reasons why people so frequently fail to plan are all fairly clear, but often diverse. And the annoying thing is that most of the reasons are good. For example, there is enthusiasm: the time spent in analysing what needs to be done is boring and frustrating – people just want to get on with it. Or there are outside pressures that dictate a tight time scale – no time for talking or thinking, just get on with it. The problem is that even more frustration results, and even more time is consumed, if things are not planned and thought out. Don't let any change project forge ahead if it lacks a coherent, written and well presented plan! Beware of the 'Sucker's Leap' – leaping straight from the first stage ('Know what you want') to the third stage ('Do it') without going through the discipline of making a well thought-out plan.

So how does one get such a plan? The first place to start is with the broad goals set in the first stage, and attack the problem in the same way one would when faced with the task of eating an elephant, i.e. one bite at a time. There is no problem big enough, and no change programme wide enough, that you can't break down into digestible chunks. Organisations which fail to do this end up with indigestion!

During the first stage of the change process ('Know what you want'), you will have defined an overall mission or vision statement for the organisation, backed up by strategic goals to meet the needs of your key stakeholders. Each goal will have been broken down into general initiatives, with each initiative supported by detailed objectives. These objectives should be '**SMART**' – a mnemonic for Specific, Measurable, Achievable, Results-oriented and Time deadline.

The second stage of the change process ('Make a plan') is to detail the action and resources which are going to turn these objectives into reality. Each objective should be backed up by a project plan. Each project plan should be drawn up by a small core cross-functional project team given the responsibility and authority to deliver the change, led by a project manager. The team should be trained in project management, as well as in team dynamics. Each change team should have a sponsor at the highest level. The best approach the team can use to plan the implementation is to employ project management planning techniques, possibly backed by a simple computer programme such as Microsoft Project. They should also use workshops and meetings with those affected to ensure the implementation gains consensus. Each project should have a strict definition which should include a specific project objective, clear deliverables, measures of success and definition of completion. The project plan should include tasks, deadlines, resource schedules, a critical path analysis, a budget, a clear programme and a 'work-to list' for those involved to follow. These detailed plans should be drawn up by those people involved in delivering the project, and they should be formed into project or project teams. The plan must be signed off and agreed by all concerned to ensure that everyone has a full understanding of what is going on. The project management planning techniques the project teams can use are discussed in Chapter 3, and detailed in Part 3, Appendix 2.

Each team will require a specific project manager (who may need some training in project management techniques), as well as a project director (who should be at the highest level and can act as a senior mentor to the overall planning process). These project teams should ideally be cross-functional, as many of the changes they will work on will have an effect across the traditional organisational boundaries and hierarchies.

Although working part-time on projects can work, better quality is often assured if the teams have a full-time component. Once the project delivers, the team can either disband (with some suitable recognition/ reward), or continue with the ongoing implementation of a newly designed re-engineered process as a new cross-functional process team. If the team is employed just to get the change started, it must include people from those areas of the organisation which will be expected to take the new policy/product and run with it into the future. Ideally the team should not number more than six, to aid teamwork.

There should also be a clear understanding regarding the cost of the project, and the budget should be agreed in advance. Again too many re-engineering programmes or projects run out of steam because no one had the courage to nail the costs up front.

As there may well be several projects running at the same time, a transition team can be formed to oversee the planning, and subsequent implementation. More about this team follows in section 5 below. Suffice it here to say that the transition team must include a manager of the highest level to manage the overall change programme.

The danger of the methodical approach described so far is that too many projects get started at the same time, and then grind to a halt when the organisation realises that it has bitten off more than it can eat. The transition team can assist senior management in making decisions regarding priorities, and then help to phase the projects.

Change requires action, and action requires people. If all these people for the project teams and the transition team come from within the organisation (and they should – consultants are expensive and should be used sparingly), then you need to understand what action should be *stopped* to release the people. Too often re-engineering programmes fail because all the time is spent planning what should be done, and no thinking is devoted to what should *not* be done (or what current activities should be stopped immediately to release resources for the change teams).

At the end of this planning stage, it is worth having a 2–3 day workshop with the project managers and their senior sponsors to check that everyone is singing from the same hymn sheets. Workshops are useful ways to both plan the change and deliver training to give people the skills they need to implement the change – more of this in section 8 below.

At the end of this stage the action is planned, and all the players are in place. Next comes the hardest part – doing it!

5. DO IT!

Whatsoever thy hand findeth to do, do it with thy might; for there is no work, nor device, nor knowledge, nor wisdom in the grave, whither thou goest.

Ecclesiastes 9: 10

This section is split into two. The first part talks about the technical techniques that can be used to ensure some success in implementation. The second describes the cultural techniques that can be used to help the organisation deal with the trauma of change. Too often people focus on the first, only to see a re-engineering programme run onto the murky rocks of organisational politics.

Underlying both types of technique is the need for clear, sympathetic, courageous and committed leadership. The new behaviours which will be needed for the re-engineered organisation should be demonstrated by the leaders. Re-engineered organisations need a new breed of leadership due to their flat informal structures, use of flexible cross-functional process teams, open and technologically enabled communications, and customer-focused service delivery. The leaders of such organisations need to be enablers, coaches, mentors, supporters rather than top-down dictatorial mandarins. They need to get the organisation to deliver in a way which individuals feel they own, rather than have to comply to. Such leaders need to be good listeners, not just good talkers. They must walk the walk as well as talk the talk, and lead by such example that people say: 'Your actions are so loud I don't need to hear what you say!'

Such leadership inspires people rather than drives them, and needs to be demonstrated very early on in the re-engineering process or else the newly formed cross-functional teams will quickly loose motivation. This crucial aspect of leadership is considered more in Chapter 4, 'Do it!'

5.1 Technical techniques

The delivery of the change programme by project teams is an effective way of making it happen. Using senior executives as project directors/sponsors ensures that top management does not lose control, and that the project teams get the support they need. The Transition Team should be tasked with the day-to-day management of the change. This will include communicating progress (up, down and sideways), resolving conflict about resources, making decisions about changing the methods employed – in short managing the unforeseen exceptions to the planned approach which was established in the planning phase. The Transition Team should report to the highest authority group in the organisation (i.e. the board), and meet at least twice a month.

The important thing to remember is that the transition from the current state to the future state should be viewed as a *separate* state in itself. The use of a 'project coordination centre' (PCC) can also help success – there is more about this in section 6 below. The technical techniques involved are not magical, and are based on common sense. They are described in more detail in Chapter 4. However, they need a background to operate within to ensure that political behaviour does not upset the change being introduced. This background can be provided by the cultural techniques.

5.2 Cultural techniques

Any change programme will run into a series of issues revolving around *resistance*, *power* and *control*. These issues, and the processes of dealing with them, are summarised below and explained in more detail in Chapter 4.

The first issue revolves around *resistance*. Change causes uncertainty and fear, and (especially if it is imposed) it causes a perceived loss of autonomy. Although these may only be perceptions rather than reality, the important thing to understand is that, for an individual, perception *is* reality. Many change agents believe the reasons for resistance are all negative – this is a simplification. Many of the reasons for resistance are positive – for example, the manager who wishes to reach an annual target and so does not release resources for the change programme resists change for positive reasons, the desire to achieve. Change also affects the all-important (but too often forgotten) 'informal networks'. Reorganisations can upset these networks, and this too can cause failure in communication and a resultant increase of rumour and uncertainty. Loyalty to work colleagues, who may be seen to be mistreated, also causes a high degree of resistance.

Resistance should be overcome in a compassionate, empathetic and positive way. In order to combat resistance it is necessary to *motivate constructive behaviour*. This includes creating dissatisfaction with the status quo, generating 'new' training, involving and motivating implementation project teams in the planning, rewarding desired behaviour, and, in the extreme, punishing undesired behaviour. These techniques can be enhanced by having a process to bring resistance to the surface, such as informal workshops and attitude surveys to gauge reactions to the change. This will allow resistance to be positively and proactively managed rather than dealt with in a reactive way. If the changes are very radical, then resistance can also be overcome by phasing the implementation and using pilots to demonstrate success and feasibility (as well as to learn and fine tune prior to roll out).

The second issue is *power*. Organisations are political systems made up of individuals, groups and coalitions who to some extent all compete for power. Political behaviour is natural and to be expected. However, in times of change, the level of ambiguity and uncertainty increases, and individuals and groups take action based on their perception about how the change will affect their relative power in the organisation. In such a highly charged situation, emotion frequently replaces rationality and subjective power bases become more important than objective strategy. The answer is to *shape the political dynamics* – take positive steps to ensure that key power groups support the change rather than block it. This will involve gaining an understanding of who is likely to be affected by the change, and then work out a strategy to gain their support. The key support must be from the very top (i.e. the full board) – without it, the best you can hope for is a dilution of the results you are trying to achieve. It is also vital to ensure that leaders' behaviour is consistent with the change pursued. The use of symbols and rewards to communicate and recognise success will also help.

The third issue revolves around *control*. The transition should be seen as a separate state, and managed as such. The business should be managed separately from the change programme. This demands a high degree of control, as there is a real risk that if the change programme is not achieved, the wasted effort will adversely affect the business. To ensure control, you must *manage the transition*. A clear image of the future state must be developed and, more importantly, communicated. This communication will need to be planned and carried out with a high degree of quality. The technical techniques mentioned earlier, such as cross-functional project teams and a transition team based in a central projects coordination centre (PCC), will also help maintain control. And there must be a process for feedback and evaluation. It is to this latter point that we now turn.

6. MONITOR (TRACK IT)

> If you can't measure it, you can't hit it.
> *Anon*

Monitoring needs to concentrate on two things – monitoring the progress of action, and monitoring the results. This monitoring should be done in a 'project coordination centre' (PCC) set up specially for the process. The use of maps and planning boards can assist both in revealing what is going on, as well as in communicating to people in the organisation who come in for information. In effect it should resemble the operations room of a military campaign, and be open to all who wish to come and see how progress is being made. It should be staffed by a small full-time team, headed by a change management director. He should report direct to the top of the organisation (such as to the CEO or a nominated representative), and be a member of the Transition Team.

6.1 Monitoring progress of action

The PCC should monitor the progress of each project and report weekly to the Transition Team. The progress can be tracked via the project managers. Any problems should be solved by the small PCC team, and bought to the attention of the Transition Team or the senior management. The PCC team should, with time, get a full understanding of where the blockages to change are, and what is needed to remove them. The overall monitoring of the project budgets should also be undertaken, to ensure that the projects are not over-spending. Monitoring the action should also include monitoring how effective the process of change itself is, by seeing how well people feel informed, how committed the sponsorship for change is and how well the change teams are perceived within the broader organisation. This can be done by attitude surveys and discreet 'fireside' chats with those not initially directly involved with the change.

6.2 Monitoring results

The results should be directly linked to the individual projects' measures of success. These need to be quantifiable, and, as explained in more detail in Chapter 5, these should include more than just financial results. The monitoring should also include such measures as employee attitudes, customer perceptions, supplier responsiveness, etc. Although some of these variables are 'soft' (i.e. hard to get a handle on), as explained in Part 3, Appendix 1, section 3.6, almost anything can be quantified. The results should continue to be monitored after the project ends – after all, just because the action to introduce change stops, the pursuance of the derived benefits should not be forgotten!

But what happens if either progress is not made as fast or as well as planned, or if the results are not forthcoming? Does this mean failure? Is it time to shoot the involved, weary from effort, and reward the uninvolved? No, it does not. It means that the assumptions upon which the planning was based, using the best available information, were false – so revisit them!

7. CHANGING THE CHANGE, AND CONTINUAL CHANGE

Half the failure in life arises from pulling in one's horse as he is leaping.
Augustus Hare

When things go wrong during implementation – and wrong they will go – then there are three options facing you:

- Do nothing – accept the situation, or play the 80/20 game.
- Change what you do – pull one of the levers of cost, time or quality.
- Change what you want – major surgery, but only in dire emergency!

The reason why things will 'go wrong' is that it is rare for a plan to survive first contact with reality. And if that is so, I hear you say, then why bother with all the preceding analysing and planning? The simple reason is that the more thoughtful the plan, the easier to change it. And it is easier to change a plan than invent one. So when it all falls about your ears, at least the time spent in analysing and planning will put you in an ideal situation to choose the best of the three options, and get on and do something useful (instead of complaining, which most people do). Each of the three options is discussed below.

7.1 Do nothing

As the quotation at the start of this section intimated, most people are a bit too impatient and expect results sooner than it is ever possible to achieve them. Many 'problematic' change programmes I have seen seem to promise the riches of Shangri La in a flash of time. When the results don't flood in, there is a temptation to change everything again. The result is often increasing chaos. See if you can wait a while, like a patient fisherman. If not, play the 80/20 rule. Will you get 80 per cent of what you want? Does changing everything now, and risk having 100 per cent of nothing, make sense? How easy is it to change the change? If it's difficult, consider the down and up sides.

I suspect that many who read this are more Anglo-Saxon than oriental, and will no doubt rush to do something active. But before you do, don't forget that allowing events and fortune some leeway is always an option.

7.2 Change what you do

In many instances doing nothing is unacceptable – so the next option is to change what you do. This will involve replanning and going back a step (to 'Make a plan'). The three things you can change are time, cost (i.e. resources) or quality. These are the three fundamental trade-offs in any project. Pushing out the time scale is the easiest, if you can accept delay. Adding additional resources to achieve the project objective on time and to the quality you desire is another option, but this will have a cost implication as well as an organisational one. The final option is to change the quality of what you are trying to achieve – playing the 80/20 rule again, can you make do with 80 per cent of what the project is meant to deliver?

7.3 Change what you want

If doing nothing is unacceptable, and changing what you do in terms of time–cost–quality does not yield a solution, the only other option is to change what you want. This involves either scrapping the project (always an option), or changing the objectives.

This should only be done carefully, as the risk of increasing confusion and creating a degree of demotivation is high. It will involve going back two steps in the process, which will be frustrating for all concerned. Hence the importance of doing the first two steps right in the first place! Care must be taken to replan the project and understand what the impact on the assumptions regarding the results of the change programme will be – these assumptions may well have to be changed.

And when the re-engineering programme delivers, the organisation should continue to monitor, adapt (by re-evaluating the information gained from the 'Know what you want' stage) and improve (by seeing how the processes can be further enhanced). Re-engineering is as much a state of being as something you do as a discrete programme. All the companies and organisations in Part 2 will/should continue to improve and continually change even after they achieve the original goals of the re-engineering programmes they have put in place.

By moving the organisation into cross-functional teams, trained to be able to respond to change and quickly to form new teams, the changes will continue to be improved and adapted to meet changing external demands.

8. THE CHANGE PROCESS

He who refuses to change in his job is already dead ... and will soon be looking desperately for a change of job.

J. Bouvard

Underlying the four steps above must be a way of operating which may well be alien to the organisation. Cross-functional project teams, transition management systems, and the use of participative planning and action will, for many hierarchical organisations, be new and threatening. On top of that there will be the need for new skills such as competitor and market analysis, teamwork skills and project management techniques.

There are a variety of techniques which can be employed to facilitate the process of change. The first simple step is to give the change programme an overall name, and even a logo – this gives it an identity, facilitates understanding and allows for the vital separation of the change programme from the day-to-day running of the organisation. In addition there should be a variety of other elements employed, either all or some depending on the size of the programme:

- use of culture change programme;
- use of cross-functional project teams;
- workshops;
- use of facilitators;
- training seminars;
- establishing an academy;

- ■ ten commandments;
- ■ change programme newsheets.

These are dealt with in detail in Chapter 7, and are summarised below.

8.1 Use of culture change programme

Re-engineering an organisation from the traditional models of Adam Smith and Frederick Taylor is typically a massive undertaking. Much work is involved in analysing current processes, redesigning them and planning the migration. It can be worthwhile to run a culture change programme at the same time as all the planning and preparation, to position the organisation for the future changes. Sometimes organisations do this first, and only then introduce the more radical Business Re-engineering concepts. An example of this is Birmingham Midshires Building Society, with their 'FIRST Choice' programme (see Part 2 for details). Some others feel that the culture change should be carried out only after the trauma of change is implemented. Whether a culture change programme is run before, during or after the major reorganisation which process re-engineering typically brings, it should be borne in mind. Winning the hearts and minds of the people is vital for the success of Business Re-engineering.

8.2 Use of Cross-Functional Project Teams

The authority of the objective and the dynamic of an effective team is a far better way to get change than the authority of an individual with a driving idea that no one else really shares. We have touched on the use of project teams earlier on. In a change environment, traditional hierarchies and functional splits frequently fail to cope due to the level of ambiguity and diverse nature of skills needed to drive a change through. Cross-functional project teams help to overcome organisational inertia. The project team should have three components. The *project director* acts as a senior level sponsor to ensure that obstacles to the team can be removed quickly, and that the team can understand the broader strategic issues and environment within which it operates. The *project manager* is the champion who drives the project forward to completion. He or she not only achieves tasks but should also retain a fundamental concern for the project team members. He or she should be full-time on the project. The *project team members* are the individuals who achieve the detailed tasks to the times laid down by the project plan. All three of these components must work together on the plan and the project as a team, and be allowed the space, authority and budget to do so. They must also include people who will take the change, once implemented, into the day-to-day running of the organisation. Failure to do this will result in a change which will not be sustained.

8.3 Workshops

These are the engine of the first two steps, 'Know what you want' and 'Make a plan'. They are used to gain understanding, planning and commitment to focused action from the variety of persons involved. They can be run using internal resources, although those running the workshops should be experienced and trained in techniques such as facilitation (see below). Many organisations use outside consultants who have no axe to grind and can act as unbiased facilitators. Each workshop should have a specific aim, with concrete inputs prepared before hand and concrete outputs which should be used as the basic plans for the change programme. The workshops should use a series of plenary sessions (where everyone can gather to share information and views), as well as break-out groups (where small groups can work on particular problems and issues for presentation back to the plenary sessions). The participation should be kept to key managers (including top management), project managers and their teams. A suggested series of workshops to take you through the first two stages are detailed in Chapter 7, but obviously the programme can be flexible to suit the particular needs of the situation. Workshops should not be run for more than 2–3 days. In many cases they can last just a day.

8.4 Use of facilitators

The use of facilitators in workshops has already been briefly mentioned above. The use of neutral facilitators as a general resource can greatly assist the change process. Some of the cases in Part 2 found such resources very valuable. For example, Cigna International supported the newly formed cross-functional process teams with facilitators to help them adapt to the new culture of teams. Digital South Pacific used a facilitator to help the core re-engineering change team through some of its harder moments. Facilitation is a relatively new skill, but one which is vital for successful Business Re-engineering.

8.5 Training Seminars

These can be piggy-backed onto the workshops as an extra day (especially if the workshops are only a day long). For example, if the result of a workshop is for project managers to start on their particular plans, not only can the overall strategy be explained, but also some training can be given for project planning techniques. Further examples of useful training seminars to complement typical re-engineering programmes are discussed in Chapter 7.

8.6 Establishing an Academy

Most organisations have limited training room, and this is usually used for the day-to-day training needs. Thus organisations can find it hard to get space for extra workshops and seminars, and frequently resort to outside hotels (which is understandable as workshops in most organisations are not a frequent event). However, during a large Business Re-engineering programme the need for such facilities will be great. One possible option, therefore, is to establish an 'Academy' on a short lease with a training establishment (perhaps a school or university with spare space) for the duration of the change programme. This will give you the space for planning workshops and the training required to push the change projects through. It can be cheaper than using hotels. And it will give the Business Re-engineering programme itself a physical identity.

8.7 'Ten Commandments'

These are simple codes of practice that can be used to set down the basics of the culture and individual behaviours needed to support what the re-engineering programme is trying to achieve. They can be set down like the 'Ten Commandments' (which themselves act as the basic set of ground rules on which Christianity was built – surely the greatest culture change programme of them all). Examples of such are included in Chapter 7. They are a simple and effective way of communicating to all the behaviours necessary for what needs to be achieved. Similar ideas include 'service charters', which tend to be more complex but no less effective.

8.8 Change Programme Newsheets

One critical action for a successful change programme is 'communicate, communicate, communicate!' This should be done by meetings, feedback sessions, etc. In addition to such vital meetings and sessions, the use of a glossy one-page newsheet put out at regular intervals is also a good and complementary way to communicate across the organisation, especially to those not directly involved in the change programme itself. The project co-ordination centre (PCC) team can double up as a communication team to run it. The newsheet can include not only the aims and the objectives of the programme, as well as the personalities involved, but also can be used to promulgate early successes and 'quick wins'. It can also be used to give recognition to those who achieve successes in the programme, which itself can motivate others.

9. NEXT STEPS AND SUMMARY

So what now? The summary above gives you an overview of the book, which is explained in more detail in the coming chapters. The next step is to start the process of change itself, and successful implementation begins today. The first action is to gather your team in and, having agreed the need for change, discuss the establishment of the core team/s to complete the process which makes up the first step of the four, 'Know what you want'. Once these teams are briefed and motivated, the change programme will begin to work a life of its own. The secret then is to manage the process through the steps, ensuring each is completed to a high degree of quality. The process of change is never easy – using some of the tips and techniques in this book should, I hope, make it less painful. There is a simple form at the back of this book and we would appreciate your feedback for use in future editions.

SUMMARY ACTION POINTS

■ **Understand scope and key variables of Business Re-engineering**
  — Pain of the status quo.
  — Gain of the future change.
  — Need for change perceived by leadership.
  — Impact across the organisation.

■ **Understand rationale of four-step approach**
  — Know what you want:
    (a) clarify need for, and ability to, change;
    (b) understand needs of key stakeholders;
    (c) understand competitive environment;
    (d) clarify mission, goals, initiatives and objectives (the 'what');
    (e) clarify values statement and transition process (the 'how').
  — Make a plan:
    (a) prioritise SMART objectives – one bite at a time;
    (b) use project management techniques;
    (c) build effective change project teams.
  — Do it:
    (a) use 'hard' techniques: visible leadership and transition devices;
    (b) use 'soft' techniques: overcome resistance by motivating constructive behaviour; resolve issues of power by shaping the political dynamics; maintain control by managing the transition as a separate state.
  — Monitor:
    (a) monitor action: progress of change projects and effectiveness of change management;

  (b) monitor results: impact on customers, employees, suppliers and shareholders.

■ **Understand how to fine tune and achieve continuous change**
  — Change the change by either doing nothing, changing how you do it, or changing what you want.
  — Achieve continuous change by monitoring results and adding new change projects to maintain momentum, involving all levels of employees.

■ **Understand the dynamics of the change process itself**
  — Include culture change programme.
  — Empower cross-functional project teams throughout the stages.
  — Use workshops and trained facilitators.
  — Generate new training, and use an academy.
  — Use a variety of communication devices.

■ **Next steps**
  — Agree the need for change with the top team.
  — Agree the process for change.
  — Form cross-functional team to complete the first step: 'Know what you want'.
  — Demonstrate clear and unambiguous *leadership* throughout.

2

Know what you want

All the business of war, and indeed all the business of life, is to endeavour to find out what you don't know by what you do ...
Arthur Wellesley, Duke of Wellington

Knowing exactly what one wants can be difficult. In the fast-moving world we are in, previous reasonable assumptions change. To keep on top of it all, you need to understand the environment your organisation operates in. Working on the assumption that it is people, and not esoteric theories, that make things happen, the way to get on top of a situation is to *understand*, rather than judge, all the various people (and their needs) who have an interest in your organisation, and how they view the world. It is also worth knowing who, or what, you are competing against. To do this requires an amount of analysis, to ensure that objective decisions can be made. So who, what and how do you analyse?

The aim of this chapter is to help you decide what you want, based on objective analysis of facts rather than subjective emotional opinion and gut feel. There are three stages to getting to a position where the organisation can clearly state that it knows what it wants:

- Understanding the need and ability to change. Before any serious work is spent analysing the situation, the leadership needs to be aware of the need for change, and how well and capable the organisation is of changing.
- Analysis of key stakeholders and the environment. This effort includes pulling together a small team(s) (including external consultants if needs be) to do the analysis. This analysis will fully crystallise the need for Business Re-engineering, the extent to which the various areas of the organisation will be affected, and the diagnosed possible solutions.

- Constructing a 'Framework for Success'. This should follow the analysis, and is needed to aid communication (and includes devices like a mission statement and the supporting goals and objectives). The framework helps to start to build an implementation plan, as well as to prioritise the action.

Frequent reference is made below to Appendix 1 in Part 3 where, for ease of reference, a whole kitbag of analytical and process tools and techniques are laid out. Analysis requires a disciplined approach, but there are a few tools which can help (and even provide some interest!).

1. UNDERSTANDING THE NEED AND ABILITY TO CHANGE

1.1 Introduction

At the start of Chapter 1, four key variables were outlined as important for re-engineering: the pain of the status quo, the potential gain of re-engineering, the perceived need (for change) in the eyes of senior management, and the potential impact across the organisation. Before analysing too deeply, it is well worth while doing a quick 'fly by' to see what the likely scope and issues of a proposed re-engineering/change programme will be. This in effect is what Cigna International did, using a small team with internal managers and external consultants over a couple of weeks (see Part 2).

The analysis can look at two things:

- the pain/gain equation;
- the need/ability position.

1.2 The pain/gain equation

Using informal chats, and perhaps an attitude survey, one can quickly gauge how much the organisation feels it needs to change. You need to do this to understand the likely level of resistance and difficulty you may meet during implementation. In some cases the circumstances for change are so clear that doing a pain/gain analysis is a wasted exercise (i.e. if pain = death, and gain = survival!). For those organisations where the perceived need of change is not so obviously great, a quick analysis by speaking to and doing surveys of senior and middle management can yield useful results. Basically four options exist, as shown in Figure 2.1.

If both the pain of the status quo and gain of a change are seen as low, then question whether, *at this stage*, you need to enter a radical Business Re-engineering programme. Development of managerial perceptions, as well as smaller discrete changes, may be more advisable until the pain/gain equation can be developed more favourably to support change.

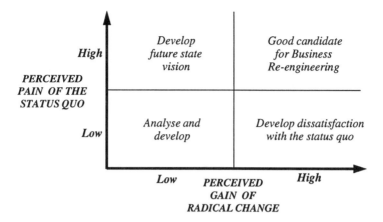

Figure 2.1 The pain/gain equation.

1.3 The need versus ability to change

If the pain/gain equation shows that there is a big need for change, then consider how able the organisation is to change. After reading this book, you will have a pretty good idea of what is involved and really the question is how much external help is needed. Getting such help on board earlier rather than later can help save time and expense later on. The best way to gauge the ability of how adept an organisation is at changing is to debrief those involved in suggesting and implementing change so far. Did the change go smoothly? Was it well executed? Again four options exist, as shown in Figure 2.2.

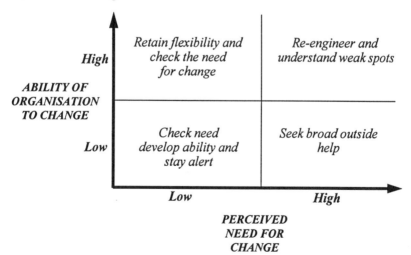

Figure 2.2 Both the need and ability to change should be understood.

2. ANALYSIS OF KEY STAKEHOLDERS AND THEIR NEEDS

2.1 Stakeholder analysis – First steps

The best place to start is by understanding the needs of the key stake-holders, and how those needs are currently being met. The four typical stakeholders are shown in Figure 2.3. The diagram also shows that, although these are distinct groups, they also have an interrelationship. This is key, and often missed. Many organisations stress objectives which only meet the needs of one stakeholder, and their plans often yield little result because they fail to balance the needs of others. After all, if we were really totally 'Customer focused' we would give away our products free – but we don't because we have costs to cover, employees to pay (and we all need to eat), creditor obligations to meet, and shareholders to give a return on capital to (or they would do better to put their money into a savings deposit!).

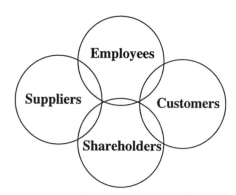

Figure 2.3 Key stakeholders of a typical business organisation.

The dynamic between the needs of the stakeholders is what holds the business system together. Customers pay an organisation which employs people and suppliers, and the resultant cash flow which ensues forms the basis of shareholder value.

Each industry, and often each company within each industry, has a unique business system. The secret is to understand how best to engineer the organisation in order to meet the needs of the stakeholders in a true value-creating way.

2.2 Customer analysis

This is the place to start! These are the people we serve, they pay for our salaries, they keep our suppliers in business and provide the cash from which the organisation generates the return for our shareholders. The first step is to gain an understanding of all customers – not only those belonging to you, but also the total market. Focus on needs, as well as numbers. Gain an understanding about why customers choose competitors rather than you. This understanding will give you the basis not only to segment the market into customer types, but also to gain insights into the true nature of competition. Sometimes this nature is not obvious. A story which well illustrates this concerns the two hikers crossing some African bush. Suddenly they come upon a lion, who is about to charge them. One of the hikers quickly drops his rucksack, and pulls on some running shoes. 'Don't be silly,' says the first. 'You'll never outrun a lion!'. The second replies, 'I don't have to. I have to outrun you!'

So how do you actually go about analysing customers? There are many ways, but it should include talking with and listening to them yourself! Too many organisations rely on third parties to get the data for them – while these should be used, it should never replace the need to do some research oneself. You'll be surprised how much the customers will appreciate being asked for some frank feedback – if nothing else it shows you care about their needs. Focus on *their needs* rather than their category (segmentation), or their 'product requirements'. For example, a watershed for Progressive Insurance was the move away from simply selling car insurance to focusing on reducing the human trauma and economic costs of their customers' car accidents (see Part 2). Or as the CEO of a power tool company, Black & Decker, was reputed once to say: 'We don't sell drills, we sell holes.'

The data gathered should allow you to do several types of analysis. The processes employed and techniques one can use to do this analysis are detailed in Part 3, Appendix 1, section 1. The SWOT analysis is quite a good general tool, as shown in Figure 2.4.

It is a good summary of research into how customers view you. The use of SWOT should be done with care, as it gives perceptions (which may not be facts). However, assuming that people's perceptions are their reality, it is a useful tool. It is worth using across a variety of groups so

S	Strengths
W	Weaknesses
O	Opportunities
T	Threats

Figure 2.4 SWOT analysis.

comparisons can be made – for example, comparing the senior management perceptions to those of customers in a SWOT format may show how 'in tune' the top of the organisation is with the customers! And further comparisons with staff perceptions may highlight internal issues as well.

Appendix 1 in Part 3 describes many other tools and techniques for customer analysis. The important thing to realise is that the analytical tools described there are not a panacea. They will not solve problems, but help you gain understanding. They are rather like a series of sunglasses with differing filters. Put one on, and you see the situation in one light, use a second and you see it in another light. The secret is to keep putting different ones on to gain a total view which will be invaluable when you start sorting out what you want to do. But use the tools selectively – if you use them all you may well achieve little more than paralysis through analysis!

Do not be blinded by the analytical tools that you find in Appendix 1, or by those you subsequently discover (or are introduced to by consultants). The most important things to understand are:

- What are your current and potential customers' *needs*?
- Who are your current and potential customers'?
- How are these needs currently served, and by whom?
- What are the key points of importance to your customers?
- How can you gain innovative and competitive advantage?
- What economic environmental factors play a part?

As far as the latter point is concerned, this book is not intended to turn people into budding economists, but any analysis of markets/competitors/customers etc. should never ignore the broader economic and political environment within which all these people live. Always ask yourself 'So what?' after completing such analysis. Economic analysis in itself will do little for you unless you understand what the *implications* are for your customers and your organisation, and what you can do to mitigate any problems.

The analysis so far is focused only on one side of the 'business system' – more analysis is needed further up the supply chain, specifically on suppliers.

2.3 Supplier analysis

Unless your organisation is fully integrated along the supply chain (and few are), then you need to understand the dynamic of the business system within which you operate. The best way to analyse suppliers is to talk to them. Arrange joint seminars and workshops where you can share an understanding of each others' strategies. Involve managers lower down, or else such get-togethers yield little more than a pleasant day in some hotel with fine restaurants and good golf (not to be sniffed at, but such meetings can yield so much more!).

A further quick and simple way to look at the supply chain can be achieved by doing a 'value chain' analysis. There are various ways of doing this, but I find the simplest is to take the price of a service charged to the end customer (i.e. the final one in the chain) and call it 100 percent – this can be done by taking the revenue figure of the company closest to the end customer. By analysing the costs of the company one can build backwards a picture showing where value is added (i.e. showing what the customer actually pays for). This will give you a picture of the value of your suppliers to the customer, and the value of their suppliers, etc.

The picture is useful for not only thinking about ways to enhance the value for the customer, but also ways of structuring the business system differently. Two examples of what a value chain might look like are shown in Figure 2.5. The first shows a chain where most of the value added is in production, which would indicate competition is about development of products (with investment in either production or product technology depending on the maturity of the market). The second shows the value is more at the retail end, which would suggest competition is more about marketing and service delivery, with a wider availability of suppliers.

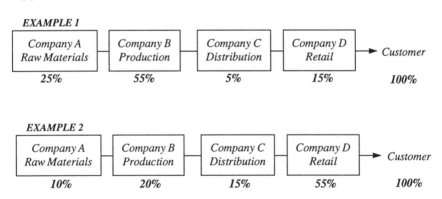

Each Company's % value added can be further broken down to show the value added of each company's activities – ie operations, marketing, administration etc

Figure 2.5 The 'business system' – value chain analysis.

The importance is to note your position in the business system, and how you can 'change the rules of the game'. IKEA did this in the furniture business, where they took the novel approach of moving the final production of furniture to the customer. Using large retail outlets, and working closely with selected suppliers, IKEA changed the rules and started to deliver furniture at a better quality and lower price than the traditional furniture manufacturers at that time.

Analysing the supply chain, and the suppliers in the market, can show areas for change which can create value. Although monetary values are used as a basis for value chain analysis, look too at the time the process takes. What do the black lines between the various components actually represent? What areas of opportunity exist if the use of information and communication technology is applied? Electronic data interchange (EDI) can help to improve quality and cut down lead times. Appendix 3 in Part 3 explains what is involved in EDI.

Talking to suppliers, and using the value chain business system, are just a couple of simple approaches to analysis. Many of the tools outlined above under 'Customer analysis' (and detailed in the appendix) can be used. There are some approaches which pull together customer and supplier analysis, such as the classic model of Michael Porter's which proposes an analysis of the five competitive forces in a company – suppliers, customers, competitors, new entrants and substitute products. This is a valuable approach and can help ensure that all the bases are covered.

Working in partnership with suppliers, and treating them as key stakeholders, is important. Some companies base their organisational strategy on this, such as many Japanese electronic manufacturers, who effectively subcontract many traditional in-house activities to smaller suppliers. However, there are many organisations who cannot do this, and for them the analysis of the 'internal suppliers' (i.e. the employees) plays an even more central role.

Before we turn to looking at some methods for analysing employee needs and opportunities for improvement, a final word on external suppliers. Do not focus your analysis solely on the obvious suppliers (i.e. those who provide the goods/raw materials which you add value to and sell on). One could argue that any external cost on an average profit and loss sheet goes to a supplier, be it power, cleaning or postage. Even tax goes to an important supplier for your organisation – the government (which, depending on the country, supplies economic stability, defence, education of future employees, health, roads to drive on, etc.). And interest payment is what you pay the banks for supplying you with the financial flexibility that your business needs (so keep them informed, as banks can deal with disasters but they hate surprises!). You need to bear these other, less obvious, suppliers in mind and ask yourself: 'What do I get for my customer's money?' (for it is they who pay for it in the end – the top line of a profit and loss account is revenue from them!). If you are not satisfied, then talk to the supplier concerned (either directly, or through pressure groups – after all your problem may not be unique)!

2.4 Employee analysis

It is people who get things done – a simple fact, but one frequently missed by those 'higher up'. And the 'lower' down one gets in organisations, the closer one normally gets to the customer. Very few organisations fully appreciate what this means – some of those who do even go to the extent of showing typical organisation charts upside down (i.e. with the customer at the top, and working through the layers, the CEO and main board at the bottom). To implement change you need to have a real understanding of the needs, desires, fears and feelings of those in the organisation which you are trying to change. Without this understanding, you seriously undermine the chances for success in a Business Re-engineering programme. Put simply, how can one change something which one does not understand? There are a variety of analytical tools one can use to get a feeling of both the 'hard' side of the organisation (such as structures, costs and processes) as well as the 'soft' side (such as culture, politics and values). Both are as important as each other. Too often I have seen organisational change fail as it concentrated on the 'hard' side and ignored the 'soft'.

To get a good understanding of the hard and soft side of an organisation you need to involve those within it in the analysis. At least you need to talk to those involved, either face to face or by using structured questionnaires (which can be filled in anonymously to encourage a higher degree of honesty). The use of outside consultants here is particularly effective, as people are often more willing to open up to an outsider than to someone from inside. As with customer and supplier analysis, the trick is to use a variety of tools and techniques to gain a broad understanding. The tools one can use are discussed in more detail in Part 3, Appendix 1, section 4.

As far as the 'hard' side is concerned, focus on *key processes* rather than just the reporting lines. The best Business Re-engineering tool to employ here is organisational design and process analysis. This looks at key processes using a variety of tools and techniques (such as process mapping, input/output analysis, effort/duration ratio, and value added versus non value added ratio). These are detailed in Part 3, Appendix 1, section 4.4. There are two basic ways to go about such process analysis (neither exclusive to each other):

■ **Brown fields process analysis**. This involves detailed process mapping of the current processes. Once this is done (and it takes some time), the processes are redesigned to reduce inputs, cut out non value added time, increase the effort to duration ratio, and reduce the overall duration. The work is typically done by a cross-functional team and involves much interviewing and observation. Its advantage over the green fields approach is that it yields a very thorough understanding of what the current processes are, and where the opportunities lie.

- **Green fields process analysis**. This ignores the current processes and just focuses on the end output desired by the customer. It then starts with a fresh piece of paper and designs the best possible way to deliver such an output. Its advantage over the brown fields approach is that it can often come up with more radical solutions, as the team involved are not constrained by what already exists. The downside is that it can produce a fine theoretical model which is nigh on impossible to implement without an unrealistic cost attached.

Each approach is not exclusive, and the best way to carry out process analysis is to include an element of both. The levels of hierarchy should also be looked at – how much are they designed to serve the customer better versus keep individuals' positions of power and influence intact? How much do they block initiative and delegation, rather than empowering and supporting the employees doing the work? Be wary of formulating a grand reorganisation plan out of such analysis – it is often better to get a current organisation working more efficiently across functional boundaries than to simply reshuffle reporting structures. After all, if the employees cannot deliver under one vertical and hierarchical organisation structure, what makes you think they can do better under another similar structure? I find the following quotation useful:

> We trained hard – but it seemed that every time we were beginning to form into teams, we would be reorganised. I was to learn later in life that we tend to meet any new situation by reorganising, and a wasteful method it can be for creating the illusion of progress while producing confusion, inefficiency and demoralisation.
>
> *Gaius Petronius (Arbiter) AD 60; committed suicide*
> *on orders of Emperor Nero AD 61*

Many may think that process re-engineering goes against the needs of employees, due to the often quoted level of redundancies which can occur. Such a view is negative and short term. A more positive and long-term view is that employees benefit from process re-engineering as much as the customers do for the following reasons:

- **Better job security**. An organisation which successfully re-engineers is going to be around a lot longer than one which does not.
- **Higher job satisfaction**. A re-engineered organisation is flatter with more empowered decision-making lower down. Employees feel more involved in the business. When linked to performance pay, the ability of employees to take sensible decisions and benefit from them leads to higher motivation.
- **Better teamwork**. Re-engineered organisations move employees from faceless bureaucratic functions into active cross-functional process

teams. The spirit of the team which has the power to take decisions, and to perform well, boosts morale.
■ **More development opportunities**. Re-engineering encourages employees to broaden their skills and become more flexible. If done well, this results in more training possibilities, and the opportunity to broaden one's career horizons. It also increases one's employability, which itself helps job security in the wider context.

As far as the 'soft' side of analysis is concerned, do not lose sight that the organisation is made up of emotional, sometimes irrational, human beings. Looking at the soft side is difficult and can often be subjective. However, there are a variety of objective analytical tools and techniques one can use, the details of which are in Part 3, Appendix 1, sections 4.6 to 4.15. The 'glue' between the soft and hard sides is the 'Three R's' – recruitment, retention and removal. Understanding how these currently affect employee motivation is vital.

The various analyses will no doubt give you a whole host of ideas about what you want to achieve with regard to changing the internal organisation and getting employees more motivated. You may also see ways of linking the various strategies to suit the ones you can see needed after the analysis of the customers and suppliers. And you will spot opportunities for process re-engineering. However, before you rush off and start planning an implementation programme, spare a thought for the shareholder, the people for whom the financial results of the company matter!

2.5 Shareholder analysis

No doubt the accountants who read this book will scorn the fact that no detailed mention as yet has been made regarding the money side of life, and actually making profit. That's because money is an effect, and people are the cause. However, if the business is not generating the returns which satisfy the shareholder, then some people may not be around for long – and in the extreme case that could include all the company! Financial analysis of the company will highlight areas to improve profitability and cash flow (and remember profit is not necessarily cash!). Both need to be managed – some companies have been profitable but due to poor control of the balance sheet have gone under due to a lack of cash.

There are many ways to analyse a company from a financial viewpoint. They all need a basic understanding of how a profit and loss statement (or income statement as it can be known as), a balance sheet and a funds flow (alias cash flow or sources and applications of funds) statement work. If you are one of those who do not fully understand the relationship between these, then the financial analytical techniques in Part 3, Appendix 1, section 5, will go some way to throw light on what can seem to be a thoroughly confusing matter. However, this book is about Business Re-engineering, not about financial analysis, and I would suggest you read a book called *Analysis for Financial Management* by Robert C. Higgins. It is a well presented book for anyone who lacks an accounting background.

Before any detailed financial analysis is undertaken, spend some time actually understanding who the shareholders are, and what their needs and expectations are in relation to their investment in the organisation. How loyal are the shareholders to the employees and management? Does the company just offer a financial return, or do shareholders get any 'perks'? How well do the shareholders actually know the company and their customers, or are the dealings with shareholders limited to a perfunctory AGM? How do the shareholder returns compare to those of other competitors? Once this understanding is gained (and opportunities highlighted to improve relationships with shareholders), then the financial analysis will have a backdrop to operate in.

The financial analytical tools in Part 3, Appendix 1, section 5, are not exhaustive, but they will certainly help clarify what is generating shareholder value, and what is not! The key tool is shareholder value analysis (SVA). Cash flow is more important than accounting ratios, and understanding the future cash flows of the business under varying scenarios is vital. Shareholder value analysis is a good way to cost out the future strategies and to evaluate the various options. By plotting out the future improved cash flows, discounting them back to the present, and comparing the figure with a 'do nothing' scenario, one can quickly evaluate the value that a Business Re-engineering programme can add to the overall shareholder value of the company. One can also use the technique to calculate the return on investment that a re-engineering programme can generate. This is a good objective way to evaluate the true benefit of such a programme, and such analysis can include sensitivity analysis to calculate the minimum a programme should generate to create shareholder value. Shareholder value analysis is a better way of looking at long-term benefits than just simply using a cash payback analysis. Although it is more sophisticated than payback, you do not exactly need a degree in finance to use the technique. The approach of SVA is explained in more detail in Part 3, Appendix 1, section 5.5.

The various financial analytical tools will give a good indication of where the opportunities lie to meet the needs of the shareholders more effectively. Coupled with the analysis of the customers, suppliers and employees it will give a sound financial understanding on which the action plans can be built.

2.6 Who does all this analysis?

As can be seen a lot of analysis and diagnosis should occur. The best way to carry it out is to form a joint team of internal managers (from across the main functions) and a few external consultants (to train up the insiders and lend experience). One can either use one team, or a few small teams (each conducting various aspects of the analysis):

■ **Single team.** This is certainly the simplest way, but has the disadvantage of slowing the process down due to the amount of work to be done.

■ **Teams split by stakeholder.** This can provide a focus for the re-engineering effort, but can lead to a functional bias. It can also lead to a certain repetition of effort. However, it can be easily dovetailed into the next phase of the 'Know what you want' step, which includes constructing a 'Framework for Success' (see below).

■ **Teams split by current and future state.** Another option is to have two teams running in parallel – one doing a current state assessment (with a 'do nothing' forecast), and another team formulating a future state vision. The former team articulates the pain of the status quo, and the latter team highlights the gain of the change.

If split teams are used, then have one or two people acting as a central hub to coordinate effort. After all, it would give a poor impression if two teams went to talk to the same customer without knowing that each were doing so.

By using small cross-functional teams from the outset of the Business Re-engineering effort, the organisation can begin to demonstrate and learn about the future needed behaviours of teamwork and group problem-solving.

2.7 When is the analysis done?

The timing of the analysis really depends on the unique situation of the organisation. It certainly needs to be done up front, but does not preclude simple and quick-win projects from going ahead. That was what Digital South Pacific did with their re-engineering project (see Part 2). The analysis does need to be planned as a project in its own right, at least with some key objectives, milestones and deliverables. The outputs of the analysis stage act as the inputs for the final stage of 'Know what you want', the construction of a Framework for Success, as shown in Figure 2.6.

Like all things, a fair amount of common sense is needed in the application of any of the suggested ways outlined above to carry out the analysis. However, if the analysis is done well, then the Business Re-engineering programme will have a solid and objective framework on which to be based. The data gathered can also be used as benchmarks against which later progress can be measured.

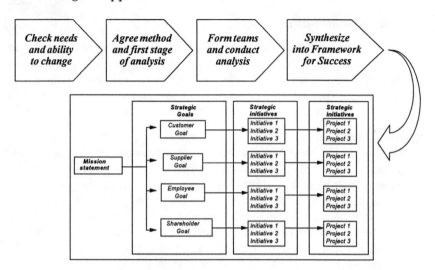

Figure 2.6 Synthesis of the analysis.

3. A FRAMEWORK FOR SUCCESS

3.1 Introduction

By now you are probably dizzy from the amount of analysis undertaken – and a whole host of change opportunities will be swimming before your eyes. Asking yourself 'So what?' will no doubt result in a long list of things to do in order to address problems and to seize opportunities. How does one go about actually making these things happen? The first thing to do is to step back and take a broad view of what it is the organisation is trying to achieve. This needs to be summarised into a clear succinct statement, known as a vision or mission statement. This is very useful for communication, which itself is vital for Business Re-engineering. It is from this statement that the goals and initiatives flow. These initiatives are themselves broken down into specific objectives which form the basis of the change projects and implementation plan. The goals which flow from the mission statement can reflect the four key stakeholder groups of the organisation – the customers, the suppliers, the employees and the shareholders. However, they can reflect other broad themes. An example outline framework is shown in diagram form in Figure 2.7.

The goals (which at this level can only be broad by nature) are broken up into distinct general initiatives. These are then broken down into the detailed objectives used for the change projects which are planned in more detail in the second step of the change process, 'Make a plan', using project management techniques.

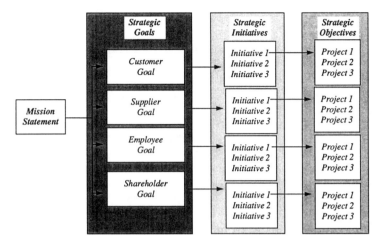

Figure 2.7 A Framework for Success.

3.2 Mission statement

This is a succinct statement which really answers the questions 'What business are we in?' or 'Where do I want the business to be?' It is used not only to build more detailed objectives, initiatives and projects, but also to remind all employees (who cannot be expected to remember the details of the strategy) what the organisation is trying to achieve. Examples of mission statements are given below:

> We are in the business of providing food and other regular consumable requirements to satisfy the needs of most types of households in the UK. Responsibility, integrity and fairness will characterise all our relationships, most importantly with our customers, suppliers and staff.
>
> *Leading UK supermarket group*

> To be the best community of our size in America, known to provide increasing employment opportunities and improving standards of living with the highest quality educational, cultural and recreational opportunities in a safe, caring and healthy environment.
>
> *County government*

> We aim to be a leading and flexible world manufacturer of audio acoustic products, meeting the needs of our customers, employees and shareholders.
>
> *Major Polish electronics manufacturer*

> We aim to be the friendliest Saudi bank which best anticipates and responds to the needs of our customers, employees and shareholders.
>
> *Leading Saudi Arabian Bank*

Other examples of mission statements can be found in some of the case studies in Part 2. Formulating a succinct mission statement for the organisation is not easy, but it can be fun. Obviously all the findings of the analysis will show what needs to be done. But you need a process to get the top team to agree to the wording. Here are a number of suggested ways to start to build a vision for the organisation, techniques which can best be used in a workshop environment:

- 'Back to the future' is a game in which the team(s) play act an imaginary interview ten years into the future with a 'journalist'. Senior executives describe how they have changed the company. The future state of the company is described in detail.
- Managers role play 'customers' of the future and explain why they changed from the competition.
- Draft vision/mission statements are used in a competition and voted on.
- Workshop participants cut out words and pictures from magazines which best describe the future organisation that they wish to achieve, and these are used to build up a statement.

The last technique was used by Mike Jackson, the CEO of Birmingham Midshires, to help his team formulate a mission statement (see below at end of chapter, and also in Part 2).

3.3 Strategic Goals

These summarise the broad goals the organisation needs to pursue in order to meet the needs of customers, suppliers, employees and shareholders. Many companies include them when they publish their mission statements – this gives a good summary of the overall strategy, service and direction which the company is pursuing. It is important to get the goals balanced as there are always conflicting needs. For example, while the customer wants the best value, the shareholder also wants the best return – meanwhile the employees want good compensation and the suppliers want a good price for their services! The goals can be linked to a profit and loss statement to show that not only do they have a horizontal relationship with the mission statement, they also have a vertical relationship with the profit and loss, as shown in Figure 2.8.

And don't forget the balance sheet! The assets therein not only serve the customers, they also show to what extent they themselves are part of them (debtors or accounts receivable). The suppliers provide some capital (creditors or accounts payable from banks), while the shareholders provide equity. And it is the employees who make the whole system work! So while the various goals can be defined as distinct in their own right, and be pursued along their own initiatives and detailed objectives, they not only share a link with the mission statement, they also share a financial link with each other. It is important to understand this link.

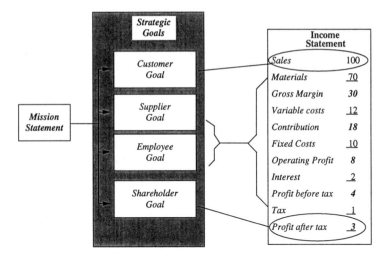

Figure 2.8 The link between the Framework and the income statement.

The analysis undertaken for each of the stakeholder groups will indicate the broad direction of action needed. This direction should be summarised into statements which form the goals. Examples are given below:

■ Customer goal: To increase and maintain leadership regarding quality and level of service and so provide the best value for money.
■ Supplier goal: To work closely with suppliers, employing Information Technology in order to increase speed and reduce lead times.
■ Employee goal: To provide a rewarding, challenging, efficient and enjoyable environment for our employees, and so be regarded as being the best employer in the industry.
■ Shareholder goal: To ensure true value is created by increasing positive cash flow, reducing our cost of capital whenever possible and supplying a superior return on all our investments.

Each goal should be benchmarked with clear measurements of success that can be used to monitor progress over the years to come. These should be backed by a clearly articulated and transparent process to measure and report progress. Such measurement processes are vital to ensure that the organisation can remain responsive. They often give rise to further change projects as more data and trends become available.

3.4 General Initiatives

So far the statement of what you want is summarised into a broad strategic mission statement, backed up by some strategic goals pertaining to the key stakeholders of the organisation. You now need to begin to think about *action* – what types of actions or initiatives need to be undertaken to meet the goals?

For example, the customer goal may refer to providing the right products at a competitive price with a high degree of service delivery. In this case the types of initiatives could be:

- provide the right product by understanding customer needs and having a process both for feedback and for re-action to customer ideas;
- understand competitor cost structures and exceed them;
- introduce customer care training to improve service delivery.

The employee goal in section 3.3 above could be split into a variety of broad initiatives:

- introduce IT enhanced cross-functional teams for key processes;
- redesign reward and appraisal systems in line with the new team–based processes;
- ensure each employee has a personal development plan with budgeted training.

3.5 Detailed Objectives

The general initiatives describe the types of actions that need to be pursued. These are broken down into detailed objectives. These objectives should be 'SMART', as described in Figure 2.9.

It is vital that these objectives are clarified as far as possible as they form the foundation for the next stage of the four-step change process, 'Make a plan'. If the objectives are too broad, then those planning the detailed projects to deliver the change will spend wasted time and effort clarifying what is needed. The tighter the objective, the more chance of a successful plan being drawn up. One needs to have a degree of flexibility as the objective may specify a time horizon which, when more detailed

S	Specific
M	Measurable
A	Achievable
R	Result orientated
T	Time specific

Figure 2.9 'SMART' objectives.

planning is done, is unrealistic. Examples of detailed objectives (linked to general initiatives) are suggested below:

■ 'To introduce new invoicing and payment collection procedures (including a training package for employees concerned) by the end of the financial year in order to reduce debtors by a minimum of 5 per cent by period 6 next financial year.'
■ 'To establish a product availability training programme using a mix of managers and training consultants in order to start training branch management teams by period 5, with all branch teams trained in initial modules by end period 13'.
■ 'To introduce five new retail products by period 2, with an established process to introduce three new products every quarter'.
■ 'To introduce a formal appraisal and staff development needs process by the end of the financial year, with a defined process for semi-annual update for managers and yearly update for staff'.

As can be seen by the examples, the detailed objectives are very action-oriented. One should not lose sight of the results (or benefits) which are trying to be achieved and these should be summarised within the overall project plan which is drawn up to support the implementation of the objective. We deal with the project planning activity in more detail in the next chapter.

It is best at this stage also to have a broad idea of the cost and benefit of any proposed objective. This will allow a degree of prioritisation and phasing – this is vital as any re-engineering and change will involve the time of managers and staff who are already committed to delivering current plans. So although it is vital to understand what you want, it is also important to understand what you do *not* want (i.e. what you need to stop doing). Any change programme will need to release resources, and you need to realise that the activities to which these resources are currently allocated will suffer. Too many strategic objectives are not implemented as the organisation fails to stop doing some current tasks in order to release people to start working on new objectives. To some extent this is also due to a failure of correct planning, which we deal with in the next chapter.

4. SUMMARY

In order to 'Know what you want' you need to understand fully the need for change, the organisational ability to change and the needs of the key stakeholders (which typically consist of customers, suppliers, employees and shareholders). Once these needs are fully understood a variety of re-engineering opportunities for improvement will become apparent. These opportunities invariably mean that you will need to introduce a number of changes. These changes need to be specified on a framework which ensures consistency. A framework based on an overall mission statement broken down into a succession of goals, initiatives and detailed objectives provides this consistency, and also assists in the overall communication of what the organisation is trying to achieve. A Scandinavian airline used this approach and below is highlighted one 'thread' from their framework:

Mission statement	To be the businessman's airline.
Goal	Running planes more on time than the competition.
Initiative	Reduce average delayed departures.
Objective	■ Buy more de-icing equipment for introduction by end of January. ■ Action: Airport Operations Manager to assess how many machines needed, solicit bids from 3 suppliers, prepare associated staff hiring/training plans and present for management approval on 6 January.

The strand above is a simple example. Another example, that of Birmingham Midshires Building Society, is as follows:

Mission statement	By being First Choice for our customers, our people and our business partners we will grow, profitably.
Goals	■ Be recognised by staff, the marketplace and business partners as First Choice. ■ Sustain improved value for members achieving top 3 returns on capital among the top 13 building societies. ■ Out-perform competitors in arrears and provision levels, be recognised as the industry's credit experts and gain competitive advantage through the Society's risk management processes. ■ Achieve superior growth performance among the top 13 societies. ■ Always exceed members' and customers' expectations by more than the competitors.

Each of Birmingham Midshire's goals are linked to defined measures which are regularly monitored and reported. They are also backed by a series of re-engineering projects. Part 2 has more details of their re-engineering programme.

A list of goals, initiatives and objectives is nothing more than a list. And it is not lists which get things done, it is motivated, well directed, knowledgeable people. There is a need to specify in detail who is going to do what and when, and what they are expected to deliver in doing it. These people need to be motivated and involved in the process to take ownership. This would suggest the need for cross-functional teams and detailed action plans. The tried and tested method of doing this in relation to re-engineering projects is by using project management techniques – it is to this we now turn.

SUMMARY ACTION POINTS

■ **Understand the need for, and ability to, change**
  — Resolve 'pain/gain' equation and agree need for change.
  — Clarify organisational ability to change.
  — Agree process of change.

■ **Form cross-functional project team to do initial analysis**

■ **Understand key stakeholder needs**
  — Customers: include SWOT and competitive environment.
  — Employees: include morale and efficiency of processes.
  — Suppliers: include value added, quality and speed.
  — Shareholders: include ratio and shareholder value analysis.

■ **Formulate a Framework for Success**
  — Mission.
  — Goals.
  — Initiatives.
  — SMART objectives (basis for change projects).

■ **Formulate values statement and agree transition management process.**

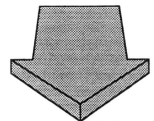

Go to next step: "Make a plan".

3

Make a plan

As the quotation in the executive summary states, 'If you fail to plan, you plan to fail.' And yet many do not plan the detail needed to ensure full success. There are a variety of reasons:

- **'I'm too busy to plan; I'm too involved in "fire fighting" to sit down at a desk'**. This is a classic – if the manager had planned properly in the first place, then the time spent 'fire fighting' would be a lot less, and he or she would be more effective. And if you think that planning just involves sitting at a desk then think again – it involves motivating a team to think ahead and agree the actions they are going to take!
- **'I haven't got the skills – and besides, no plan survives reality'**. The skills needed to plan complex projects are not so hard to come by. They are based on common sense even if they do appear to be a little technical at times. And whilst it is true that very few plans survive first contact with reality, it is easier to change a plan than invent one. The more time spent thinking through a plan in advance, the less time wasted when reality steps in and upsets things!
- **'Everyone seemed to have a good idea what to do – so why have a documented plan?'** While you may think that everyone understands, how do you know they really do? Many fail to speak up with doubts or queries for fear of appearing stupid or less than enthusiastic. A documented plan makes things clear and unambiguous. It also serves as a record over time.
- **'We haven't got the luxury of having time to do a detailed plan – it will take weeks, and we've got to get moving now!'** This is another classic excuse, and the resulting action, poorly defined and planned, will probably cost more and take longer to produce a worse result. Don't think that you save time by short-cutting the planning.

So much for the psychology. Documenting a detailed plan is often seen as a boring activity, but without it is the same as going into unknown territory without a map – it is very easy to get lost! The Framework for Success suggested in the last chapter is a good skeleton to hang some flesh on. Each objective should be assessed regarding complexity – if more than one or two functional disciplines are involved (and they frequently are) then using project management techniques ensures a high chance of achieving the objective. The planning will also verify the feasibility of the objectives set.

A key point to note is that it is vital to *include those responsible for delivering the objectives in the planning process.* Planning can be a fun and dynamic process. The use of workshops away from the work environment can be particularly effective – this is discussed in more detail in Chapter 7 'Change Process'.

1. SUGGESTED PLANNING OUTLINE

In this chapter we concentrate on some useful project management planning tools which can greatly assist in developing an effective project plan. A plan must be solid not only in the thinking behind it, but also it should be on paper with the relevant parts distributed to all those involved rather like the script for the actors in a play. To assist you, a suggested format is outlined below in order to show what a good and detailed project plan contains. The plan has a few distinct parts. Part 3, Appendix 2 has more detail, as well as examples of some pro-forma documents which can go towards making up a plan, and a fuller explanation of terms.

- **Project definition.** This is the first thing to get right. Although the objective will be stated (taken from the 'Framework for Success' described in Chapter 2), the project needs to be defined a little more clearly, including what the deliverables are, what desired benefits are trying to be achieved, and what the measures of success are. The definition should also include the names of the key players (i.e. project manager, project director, etc.).
- **Work breakdown structure (WBS).** Normally in a project there are a collection of tasks which need to get done. Using brainstorming techniques, and 'Post-it' notes, one can quickly identify all the tasks which need completion. Although not necessarily part of the documented plan, a WBS is a useful tool for the planning process.
- **PDM network (PERT chart), and the critical path.** Once all the tasks are on 'Post-it' notes in a work breakdown structure, the next step is to take the lowest level of tasks and order them into a logical sequence, having understood the inter-dependencies between them. This will also highlight the project's critical path (a term frequently used but rarely understood!).

- **Task summary sheet.** Once the tasks are ordered into a sequence based on logic the next step is to decide the effort for each task (i.e. how many person days needed) and then to allocate the *agreed* resources to each task. This will allow you to calculate the overall duration for each task (person day effort divided by persons allocated). These details are summarised onto a task sheet which lays the foundation of the timetable.
- **Milestone summary sheet.** This is a useful tool to help monitor progress. While it is sometime hard to assess an ongoing process, if there are clearly defined milestones throughout it, it is easy to gauge early on whether or not things are going well.
- **External dependencies.** There may be tasks within the project which depend on external dependencies. These could be tasks within another project, or events assumed to take place within the organisation, or even outside it. Many plans are built on assumptions about the external environment (either that new actions/situations will occur, or a status quo will ensue). The key assumptions need to be identified so as to ensure that they get checked at the critical times.
- **Resource summary.** It is also worth summarising which resources are to be used to see if there are any over-allocations, and also when these resources have downtime (useful to know when unforeseen problems occur).
- **Task programme (GANTT chart).** Once the start date for the project is decided, the PDM network and task summary sheet can be used to build up a task programme. This can be displayed in Gantt chart format.
- **Work-to list.** The Gantt chart can be used to draw up a work-to list (WTL). This details, week by week, the tasks which need to be done/started in that week. It also shows who is responsible for it being done. It is a useful 'hymn sheet' for every one to follow, and also helps in monitoring progress.
- **Cost summary and budget.** This is vital – too often costs are only given a cursory treatment, with the inevitable result of a project grinding to a halt due to lack of finance.
- **Amendment sheet.** Few plans survive contact with reality. Mostly we muddle through, but often we need to rethink the approach. If the plan is amended then document it – this serves as a useful record of what went on if nothing else.
- **Completion sheet.** When the project is over, then get it signed off and summarise any useful lessons learnt – this can be of use for future projects, and a documented record of the whole plan and lessons learnt can save people time later on.

Following a documented pro-forma helps to keep harmony. The work-to list is the most important to distribute. Like the score for a big orchestra, it keeps everyone in time. The process will help achieve a disciplined approach and will ensure that the quality thinking needed to deliver a complex change project is undertaken. Some 80 per cent of reasons why Business Re-engineering programmes fail can be directly linked to the failure of not having well thought-out, agreed and accepted quality project plans based on 'SMART' objectives.

During the planning process there are fundamentally three 'levers' you can plan to manipulate the project. These levers are essentially trade-offs:

- **Quality.** This is the quality of the desired result – it decides whether you want a first-class (and possibly expensive) outcome, or something slightly less (and possibly more pragmatic).
- **Time.** Every project has an end date. If it does not, it is not a project! And every project works in an environment which needs results, normally fast!
- **Cost.** A project not only needs money, but also resources. All this adds up to the cost. If the quality is set high, and the time is set short, then the project will need commensurate resources.

These three trade-offs should be borne in mind when planning. We deal with them more in Chapter 6, 'Changing the change and continual change'. Suffice it here to say that if a project is planned with a tight time scale and a lack of resources, do not expect the quality to be delivered!

2. THE PLANNING PROCESS

Once a 'SMART' objective is defined, with clear and tangible deliverables, the next step (if not already done) is to get a project manager and small core team on board to do the detailed action planning. It is important to try and involve as soon as possible the team which will be responsible for delivering the change project, and a good way to do this is to set them the initial goal of planning it. As project management techniques may be new to the team members, it is worthwhile to include a training course in project management planning which they can undertake concurrently as they plan the project. You should also include some team building and team dynamic training as well. That way you have a high chance of getting a motivated team with a quality plan. Such a course need not be more than 3–4 days, and is well worth the investment to safeguard against failure.

The reason why such project management planning training is a good idea is that some of the techniques are not exactly what one would call intuitive. Most people, when they plan, think along the lines 'First I'll do this, then I'll do that'. In other words they tie together tasks with time almost straight away. They often think of time first, and then look at tasks. While this approach is fine for the simplest of change projects, more complex re-engineering projects, which include resources and action from across the organisation, need a different approach. The logic for such planning should run in the following, iterative sequence: general tasks broken down into detailed tasks – detailed tasks' effort – detailed tasks' resource – detailed tasks' duration – inter-dependencies between detailed tasks and logic – total duration and project programme. As one can see, the element of time (i.e. what one does first and when) does not come into it until well into the process. The steps are not so much serial as iterative: as more detail is thought out, it will be necessary to go back and fine tune some of the earlier planning steps. And it may even be necessary to iterate back to the objective itself if it proves that the time scale is not possible, or if the costs outweigh the benefits.

To get such a logical process going the following steps are suggested as a minimum. More details can be found in Part 3, Appendix 2:

■ Start by **identifying all the detailed tasks** needed to be completed. Ignore time and resources at this stage. The best way to ensure that all the necessary tasks are identified is to use a technique called work breakdown structure (WBS). This starts at the top level (the project objective) and then, through a hierarchy of tasks, the overall objective is broken down into more and more detail, in order to arrive at the detailed tasks. So the levels might look like the following:
 — Level 1 would be the project objective.
 — Level 2 tasks = tasks by function such as finance, marketing.
 — Level 3 tasks = general tasks within function, such as 'Prepare marketing support plan', 'Arrange media', 'Communicate marketing plan', etc.
 — Level 4 tasks = detailed tasks supporting each task in level 3.
 The breakdown can go as far as one feels common sense dictates (i.e. well short of 'Marketing executive to get out of bed on Monday!'). The best way to get the WBS is to brainstorm in a group and use 'Post-it' notes.
■ Work out **how much effort** is needed for each of the lowest level of tasks (i.e. the most detailed ones). This is best expressed in person days.
■ Once the person days are identified, **work out the resources**, i.e. who is actually going to do the task. Make sure that whoever is nominated to do the task is aware, agrees in principle and has the backing of his or her boss before the plan is finalised!
■ With the resources allocated and the effort identified, the **task duration** can be worked out. So, for example, a ten person day task with two people available full time would result in a five day duration.

- Next **work out dependencies and logic flow** (i.e. some tasks cannot be started before other tasks are completed). The advantage of using 'post-it' notes is that they can be arranged into logical sequence.
- Once the tasks, duration and logic flow are worked out, one can **work out the programme**, with start and end dates. At this stage you find out you finish either far too late, or should have begun months ago, so some fine tuning can be done. You also start to get the feel for the trade-offs between time, resource and quality.
- Produce a **Gantt chart and work-to-list (WTL)**, showing who does what and when.

The final few steps can be done by computer project planning applications software. These are very useful for contingency planning and for helping the project manager to manage the critical path.

The suggested process above does look counter-intuitive. However, the more you use the approach, the better it gets. And it does produce a far better quality plan than the normal approach of 'First I'll do this, then I'll do that', especially for complex multi-functional projects.

There is much more detail in Part 3, Appendix 2. The approach above is the 'minimalist approach'. Remember, the quality and detail of the plan has a direct impact on the quality of implementation!

3. SUMMARY

The proposed project plan outline above is pretty exhaustive, and it is a task in itself to get completed! There are no panaceas and the use of the suggested format above should also rest on a degree of common sense. If an objective is easy to understand, and the delivery can be part of day-to-day operations in a single department, then you don't need to follow slavishly the detailed approach in Part 3, Appendix 2. Following the suggested process above, to produce a logical Gantt chart and work-to list, is sometimes enough. However, many re-engineering projects are complex and often involve a group of different people from across a variety of different functional groups. If this is the case, then following the format in Part 3, Appendix 2 will increase the chance of successful implementation.

A lot of these tools and techniques need a new way of thinking. Work breakdown structures and logic flows are not exactly something we all do intuitively. There are many opportunities to practise these skills. And if the project managers and teams you are putting together for a re-engineering programme do not know these skills, then remember to invest some time in getting them trained – if done wisely the training can also include them drawing up a first draft plan of their own actual projects which they can then fine tune.

The documented plan does not just serve as a road map. It also serves as a contract, between those who are contracted to design the changes, and those who receive them. If the plan is documented showing who is expected to deliver what, when and to what quality, then the expectations of all involved can be better managed.

So far we have focused on an objective, rational and sometimes technical approach in gaining an understanding of how to 'Know what you want' and how to 'Make a plan'. However, the world is as much driven more by subjective emotional opinion than objective rational facts. At this stage we may know what we want, and we might have a series of carefully planned and well thought-out projects to deliver what we want. The hardest part is yet to come – doing it!

SUMMARY ACTION POINTS

■ **Form cross-functional project teams, with project management and team building training.**

■ **Define project fully, including (as a minimum) SMART objective, clear deliverables, defined benefits and measures of success and definition of completion.**

■ **Identify detailed tasks via a work breakdown structure.**

■ **Assign resources, and work out effort and duration of each task.**

■ **Link tasks together using logic.**

■ **Work out overall timing and fine tune if necessary.**

■ **Produce Gantt chart and work-to list.**

■ **Ensure those delivering are fully involved in the planning.**

■ **Ensure communication and project management are fully understood.**

■ **Ensure technical and cultural techniques of next phase are planned for and in place where necessary.**

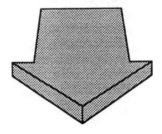

Go to next step: "Do it".

4

Do it!

If you have a good plan, based on a clear idea of what you want, with a high degree of ownership and consensus, it is nice to know that you have already avoided 80 per cent of the common pitfalls which cause failure. But what about the other 20 per cent? There is no formula which can guarantee success, but there are a few processes and techniques you can employ to shave down the remaining 20 per cent.

There are two broad types of technique you can use to assist in smooth implementation: technical and cultural.

- **Technical techniques**. These include using project teams to drive the change, the use of a central transition team (assuming a collection of projects linked to an overall Business Re-engineering programme), and the use of a 'project coordination centre' (PCC) to coordinate the activities and monitor the results.
- **Cultural techniques**. These include a range of activities to address issues regarding power and politics (present in any organisation of more than one person!), activities to overcome resistance to change (which occurs no matter what the change), and (assisted by the technical processes) activities to ensure control is maintained during a transitional period of uncertainty and flux.

The key point to bear in mind is that although the cultural techniques may seem 'soft', they are as important (if not more important) than the normal technical techniques.

1. TECHNICAL TECHNIQUES

1.1 Use of Cross-functional Project Teams

The way to achieve change is to get people to change their behaviour – and the best way to do that is to ensure they are involved. Business Re-engineering cuts across functional boundaries and traditional hierarchies, which is one reason why the change is so hard to achieve. Managers typically are tied to vertical and hierarchical structures. Rank and position often become more important than lateral, cross-functional, quality processes. The idea of internal customers and suppliers, and cross-functional teams working on day-to-day key operational processes, is often alien. One way to start to induce such a culture is through the formation of cross-functional project teams. And as change projects literally cut across traditional thinking, traditional behaviour and implicit traditional managerial values, the use of project teams is a key success factor for managing change. Indeed the project teams involved in changing a process could form the basis of the new cross-functional teams formed to take ownership of the re-designed processes. The use of cross-functional project teams will also serve as a foundation of the new culture needed to sustain Business Re-engineering.

We have already discussed the use of project teams during the planning stage, and in Chapter 7 we discuss in more detail the various team member roles, and their involvement in workshops and brainstorming sessions. Part of the success of implementation by members of a project team will be their involvement in planning their own action – this will increase motivation and commitment to getting things done. There are three ways of running such a project:

■ **Full-time project teams.** If the project is of the highest priority, and it needs to be done in the shortest possible time, then the best way to get it done is to form a full-time project team. The team will often need to be selected from various departments. It is important to realise that while the team is working on the project, the operation of the departments that they come from will be affected by their absence. One reason why change can cause so much conflict is due to department heads who do not wish to release people for fear of causing failure in the running of their own departments. It is important to understand these fears, and to make allowances. It is also vital to understand what will not be done (or halted temporarily) due to the change of focus of resources from day-to-day activities to a change project. It is worth re-emphasising again that many change projects fail as the concentration has been solely on what needs to be done, with no understanding about what needs *not* to be done! If the team is to work full-time together they will often need to have a project room (with PC and telephone support) to work and to hold meetings in. Using full-time teams without doubt is the best way to get results. However, there is a price to pay, and this must be borne in mind. Apart from the problem of pulling out quality people from the day-to-day running of the organisation, the team itself (by being full time) may lose touch with their home departments (and the 'political' temperature). When they return with a new process design or change, they could be rejected. So if full-time teams are used, make sure there is a process to manage the interface with the rest of the organisation. This is discussed in more detail in section 2.5.3 below.

- **Part-time project team**. The members of the project team will often already have day-to-day responsibilities. It may be impossible to release them full time. In this case the project team could be part time. This will inevitably extend the overall duration of the project. It will also detract from the focus of the team, and quality may suffer. It should be made clear when the team is working on the project, and when they are working on their day-to-day jobs. One way to do this is to allocate certain days of the week for the project team to work together. The monitoring of the progress will also have to be a lot tighter. Part-time teams, however, do have advantages, as the members stay in touch with what is going on in their home departments and can maintain a deeper sense of pragmatic reality when designing the changes. The re-engineering efforts of Oticon's head office used part-time teams. Ford also uses part-time teams for their process improvement projects (see Part 2).

- **Full-time core team/part-time support team**. This is a compromise of the first two options, and consists of a full-time core team for the main management of the project tasks, with part-time assistance from those less involved. It calls for full agreement between the core team, and the 'day-to-day' managers of the resources lend to the team on a part-time basis.

Of the three possibilities, the use of a full-time project team is often the preferred option, and the use of part-time or core teams should only be undertaken when the day-to-day operation of the organisation is seriously affected by the extraction of resources to work on the particular change project in hand.

The use of project teams should also include an element of recognition/reward. It should be made clear to those on the team that their work is valued and that they will benefit themselves, either from career enhancement, extra compensation and/or recognition. Too often project teams are cobbled together and fail to perform well as no thought was given to ensure that they get support, recognition and/or reward. **Things that get rewarded get done!**

In Chapter 3, we discussed the project management training that each team should receive. They should also receive team building training, and be trained to understand team skills and dynamics (discussed in more detail in Part 3, Appendix 1, section 5). Cigna International used such training to good effect with their core re-engineering team and new cross-functional process teams (see Part 2).

1.2 Use of Transition Team with top-level sponsorship

It is important to realise that a re-engineering programme will put an organisation into a period of transition from the current state into the future state. As shown in Figure 4.1, the transition state is a separate state. This period of transition will employ transitional devices which may not be needed in the future state.

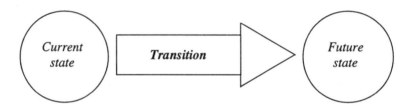

Figure 4.1 Three stages of organisational change.

It is useless to expect the status quo to change itself on its own. The managers of the organisation will be too involved in the running of day-to-day operations. The change can be greatly facilitated by establishing a transition team to manage the overall Business Re-engineering programme (which itself may be made up of more than a dozen or so distinct change projects and project teams).

The transition team should have the authority and clout to make trade-offs and take decisions. It should therefore be headed by a senior manager (the programme sponsor) reporting directly to the CEO. The role of programme sponsor is vital, and he or she must be a top level executive who has the delegated authority of the CEO to make things happen and remove blockages. The rest of the team should be made up of 2–3 top executives or senior managers who have a strategic view of the current circumstance of the organisation and a full understanding of the current state, transition programme and intended future state. They should be made responsible for the overall direction of the change programme, and also to resolve conflict between delivering the change programme, and the day-to-day running of the organisation. It should be made clear what issues should be resolved by the main board/top executive, and what issues can be resolved by the transition team. Once this is agreed, their level of responsibility should be clearly defined and communicated.

Be aware, however, of alienating the majority not at first included in the management of the change. It should be stressed that the transition team are as much to do with support and service as they are to do with leadership. Due to the seniority of the transition team, they will more often than not have other responsibilities in the organisation and so it is unlikely that they would be able to serve on the transition team as a full-time job. The day-to-day management and monitoring of the Business Re-engineering change projects can be achieved by a 'project coordination centre' (PCC).

1.3 Use of a 'Project Coordination Centre' (PCC)

If the re-engineering programme has a series of projects (and it is most likely that it will), then the establishment of a 'PCC' can assist in the over-all coordination, support and control of the projects. It can also act as a focal point of the programme and help in the communication of what is going on. The latter is particularly important, as change programmes inevitably give rise to uncertainty and rumour which can detract from the effectiveness of the action. The room acts as an operations centre, and can be run by a small full-time 3–4 person team, headed by a senior manager (who can report to or be a member of the transition team). These people will have to be carefully selected, and should include some systems qualified people who have project management experience. The roles of a PCC team can include:

- monitoring and reporting progress of change projects (by liaison closely with the project managers);
- providing support and advice either to those implementing the change, or to those affected by the wider implications of the change;
- producing reports for senior management;
- preparing and implementing an internal and external communication plan. This role can never be over-emphasised, and communications is dealt with in more detail in Chapter 7;
- providing project management techniques and systems support to project managers (who may be in such a role for the first time in their lives);
- keeping the project plans up to date. Although each project manager should be expected to do this, the storage of all the project plans using a project management system such as Microsoft Project or Open Plan will assist in centralising the plans. This will also help in checking if the project managers are encountering problems, and facilitate assistance and support to those who need it;

- acting as a referee in case of 'double booking' by project managers of cross-functional resources;
- keeping results boards and updating them for others to come in and see what is going on;
- keeping 'maps' of the action. These can include a geographic map (useful for an organisation with multi-site operations), as well as simple planning boards showing the plans and progress of action in hand;
- acting as a 'crisis resolution' team. Project managers will report blockages to change which will need to be resolved. The PCC team can act as a clearing house for such problems, and can either solve them themselves (through negotiation/facilitation), or bring such problems to the transition team to be resolved quickly.

The Cigna International core re-engineering team played many of the roles of the PCC described above, and this helped their re-engineering programme run a lot smoother (see Part 2). The establishment of a PCC and a team to run it will ensure that any problem is picked up early on and resolved. It will also show the more sceptical that the organisation is serious about seeing the change through.

As the programme unfolds, the PCC team will also be able to assist the transition team as they will acquire a detailed knowledge of the blockages in the change programme, and be able to offer advice on practical solutions.

1.4 Summary of technical techniques

The use of project, transition, and PCC teams ensures that when the action has been planned it is driven through with determination. The overall possible transitional structure is shown in Figure 4.2.

Backing up these three types of team with simple reporting processes assists communications (for example, weekly briefing and update meetings for senior management and staff). This is discussed more in Chapter 5.

The use of project management software can also assist in keeping on top of the need to produce reports, as well as helping project managers to keep their plans up to date.

It may seem a paradox that a Business Re-engineering programme which tries to eradicate hierarchy seems to need one to manage itself. One should remember that the structure above is transitional, and that the emphasis is on cross-functional teams (rather than functional hierarchies) with support and help from PCC/transition teams as well. This cultural transition is vital, and a number of 'soft' cultural techniques can be used to help. It is to these which we now turn.

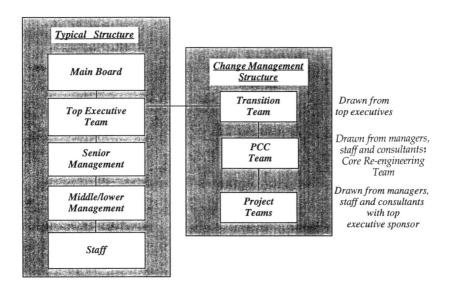

Figure 4.2 Possible transition management structure.

2. CULTURAL TECHNIQUES

2.1. Introduction

The key 'technique' is one of *active* leadership. The CEO and his team must not only 'talk the talk', but also 'walk the walk'. They must act and communicate in such a way that people *want* to change rather than feel they *have* to. Any Business Re-engineering programme will be met by a variety of reactions within an organisation, depending on the level of support or opposition. Typically five groupings will emerge, as shown in Figure 4.3.

The aim of cultural techniques is to isolate those who are actively anti (and either convert them or move them), get commitment from those who are indecisive, and preach to and convert those who are indifferent by using 'missionaries' from those who are supportive.

The cultural techniques are designed to get over the issues of resistance, power and control and thus avoid the frequent pitfalls of change usually hidden in the quagmire of organisational politics.

2.2 The first step – change yourself and provide a firm lead!

I will assume here that the reader of this book is at the top of a chimney organisation, looking to re-engineer it. Before we get into the issues of power, resistance and control, the first question to ask yourself is 'How

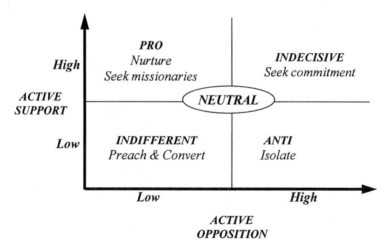

Figure 4.3 Opposition/support map.

will I change?' *Changing oneself is the first step to changing an organisation.* Too frequently change in an organisation is driven by the perception of how *others* should change, rather than oneself. If everyone follows this route, nothing gets done! There is a real need to lead by example.

If it is efficiency you are after, look to your own time management – the CEO who suddenly meets all his time obligations punctually, instead of being late and keeping others waiting, can send out a powerful message. If you are looking to reduce costs, then how about reducing your own – too often one sees company directors trying to drive cost saving programmes through but they still cling on to their own expensive company cars and expense accounts. Putting a wage freeze or redundancy programme through is always difficult, but leadership is helped if you take a wage cut yourself first!

If it is service you wish to improve, then see how you personally can improve the service to customers, employees, suppliers and shareholders before expecting everyone else to. If you want things to become less bureaucratic, then spend less time behind your desk and cut down on the paper inputs you ask for. If you want managers to be more action oriented, then get out of your office and spend time at the 'sharp end' supporting, praising, motivating and showing middle managers how you would like *them* to act. Team work is key for Business Re-engineering: when the top executive team of Birmingham Midshires went on a team building course, a powerful message was sent to the organisation.

If you feel that communications are poor then increase your own (not only by talking, but more importantly by listening!). If you feel that the quality of the management needs improving through training, then go

on a training course yourself – the person who does not need any t
ing to help in his or her own development is either foolish or dead! ...y
Business Re-engineering programme will need a high degree of training,
not just for new skills but also for new attitudes. Senior management
standing up saying they support training is not enough – they must
undergo training, and be seen to do so, themselves.

And remember that leaders can best lead by serving those who they
lead. It is not for nothing that the motto of the Royal Military Academy
Sandhurst is 'Serve to lead'. You want to get to the situation where people say: 'Your actions are so loud, I can't hear what you are saying!'

The leaders of successful organisations spend their time using three
key skills in four crucial activities, as shown in Figure 4.4.

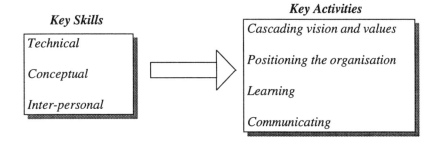

Figure 4.4 Leadership time.

The higher up one is in an organisation, the more important inter-personal skills become. Once the vision and values are set, leaders spend
time ensuring that these are cascaded to all levels of the organisation and
are upheld. They ensure that the organisation is positioned to deliver the
required results, and they empower all levels to take the initiative in
achieving results. They also spend time learning how to improve the
organisation and spotting opportunities. And they spend a lot of time
communicating, both by speech and also by actively listening to what the
organisation is saying. These activities are important for forming a cultural environment which supports Business Re-engineering.

The type of leadership needed in a organisation to sustain Business
Re-engineering is different from the typically conventional model. Re-
engineered organisations need leaders, not bosses. The difference
between the two is outlined in Figure 4.5.

The boss behaviour in Figure 4.5 is very typical of 'chimney' organisations. The leader behaviour is appropriate for 'grid' organisations, and
vital for 'bubble' organisations.

The boss...   *The leader...*

Drives people	*Inspires people*
Directs and bullies	*Coaches and encourages*
Does things right	*Does the right things*
Tells his ideas	*Generates others' ideas*
Is quick to judge	*Is quick to understand*
Talks first	*Listens first*
Tells people the deadline	*Helps people to plan*
Depends on rank and authority	*Depends on personality and good will*
Evokes fear	*Radiates support*
Tells what's needed	*Asks what's needed*
Says 'I'	*Says 'We'*
Shows who is wrong	*Shows what is wrong*
Tells how it should be done	*Shows what needs to be achieved*
Demands respect	*Commands respect*

Figure 4.5 Be a leader, not a boss.

When things happen in a bubble organisation, the words of the Chinese philosopher Lau Tsu are enacted:

> A Leader is best when people hardly know he exists, not so good when they obey and acclaim him, worse when they despise him. But of a good leader who talks little, when his work is done and his aim fulfilled, they will say 'We did it ourselves'.

The real life examples of how Lars Kolind re-engineered Oticon's head office, and how Peter Lewis leads Progressive Insurance, demonstrates some of the themes highlighted above (see Part 2).

The importance of the involvement of top leadership cannot be stressed enough. Business Re-engineering is like running a presidential campaign – the top leadership must spend a lot of time helping to shape it, and communicate it. You will have a lot of new ideas to sell, and if you cannot sell them and change the attitudes of the individuals in the organisation, the re-engineering programme will more likely fail. The CEO and his team will need to spend a large amount of time personally involved (sometimes more than 50 per cent of time). From the first step of 'Know what you want' through to 'Monitor' the leadership need to act like candidates running for office – inspire the people and win the campaign!

2.3 Overcoming the issues of Resistance – Motivate change!

2.3.1 Introduction

People naturally resist change. They have a need for stability, and change can cause anxiety and uncertainty and reduces the sense of self-control. Change not only upsets formal structures, but also informal structures. There are two broad reactions to change, especially to the type of radical change which a Business Re-engineering programme heralds. The two types can be classified as the negative curve and the positive curve. Both reactions give rise to resistance, both are natural and both need to be managed in an active (rather than reactive) way.

The negative curve is normally the reaction of those who are targeted for the change (as opposed to the change agent teams which are designing and planning the change). This is summarised in Figure 4.6.

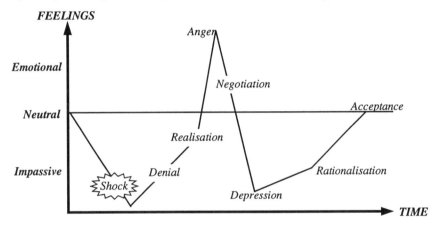

Figure 4.6 The negative curve to major change.

After shock, the first reaction is to deny the change ('Oh no – you must be joking!'). When realisation sets in ('You mean you're *not* joking?!'), anger follows. Then a stage of negotiation begins ('Maybe I can dodge the changes'), with depression following. Acceptance follows only after rationalisation.

This curve will occur more often than not. For some it will be very fast, while others may remain angry (and resistant), or depressed (and so not supportive). The secret is to recognise the various stages in people, and help them get through the curve as fast as possible.

It is often assumed that those who are involved in designing and planning the changes do not go through such a reaction, and this is broadly correct. However, these teams (and even the top management which originally instigates the changes) can go through the positive curve, which has its own dangers as shown in Figure 4.7.

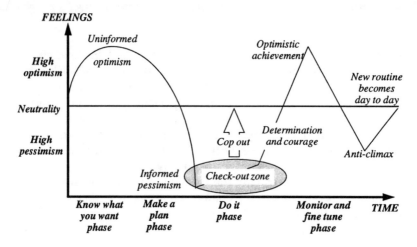

Figure 4.7 The positive curve to major change.

Once the initial optimism occurs, and the details of what is involved dawn, change teams can quickly move to the stage of 'informed pessimism'. This pessimism can be reinforced by the resistance of others not involved (but aware) of the re-engineering programme. This resistance can even manifest itself by open threats to the change team members. What can happen is that the members 'cop out', either publicly (by distancing themselves from the programme), or privately (by staying on the programme, but not enthusiastically so). Those who pull the re-engineering teams together need to be aware of this dynamic, and continue to inspire, motivate and support the members of the teams who are doing the work.

So resistance is a natural occurrence. To overcome it, one must *motivate changes* in people's behaviour. There are several techniques that can be used to do this:

- Bring resistance to the surface and continually gauge readiness for change.
- Create and maintain dissatisfaction of the status quo.
- Generate new training for new skills.
- Allow participation in planning and implementing change.
- Reward needed behaviour and results in the transition and future states.
- Provide time for people to disengage from the current state.
- Use pilots and reposition the remainder.
- Burn bridges and build ambassadors.
- Actively manage in/out-placement in a firm, clear and sympathetic way.

2.3.2 Bring resistance to the surface and continually gauge readiness for change

Once it is realised that resistance will occur, active steps can be taken to bring it to the surface as soon as possible. A degree of analysis concerning resistance will have been made during the first stages of 'Know what you want', by gauging the extent to which people see the need for change, and how able they feel the organisation can change (see Chapter 2). Once the future state vision is known, and the mission statement and broad approach of the re-engineering programme is clarified, communicate it in a series of communication meetings. The attendees can then be asked to fill in (anonymously) a questionnaire to gauge their reactions and level of support. The technique one can use for this is detailed in Part 3, Appendix 1, section 4.6. The technique is similar to a market research quantitative approach. One can supplement this exercise with another technique, which is more qualitative, with small focus group discussions using an outside independent facilitator. This approach was used by Siemens Nixdorf Service in Germany when they ran a series of 'fireside chats' during the implementation of the re-engineering project (see Part 2). Once the fears and concerns of individuals have been brought to the surface, the leadership can take positive steps to address those fears and concerns. The use of quantitative and qualitative techniques should be employed at all stages of the programme in order to be continually aware of the level of resistance and of support.

2.3.3 Create and maintain dissatisfaction of the status quo

If people are comfortable and happy with the status quo, resistance will be high and the change will be harder to achieve. The level of dissatisfaction with the status quo will have been clarified in the first stage of 'Know what you want' by the pain/gain analysis (see Chapter 2). You must continue to create dissatisfaction within the organisation. There are many ways of doing this. One can use the data gathered from the first stage of the change process ('Know what you want') to communicate the need for change. Don't forget that at the end of the day the change will be driven through by people at all levels, and they need to understand *why* the need for change exists. You need to create a 'burning platform' to encourage people to jump. If the organisation is happy sunning itself on the lilo of life, floating on a contented sea, then you need to point out the imminent danger from the sharks to get people paddling. Comparing the organisation with more successful ones, demonstrating customer dissatisfaction and resultant terminal decline is a common way to do this. Using internal data such as employee attitude surveys can also help convince the more sceptical. These facts should be communicated within an overall communication plan, the start of which should aim to convince people that the status quo is not good *for them*. This invariably involves a projection of the status quo, showing the potential problems the organisation will face and what it will mean for *individuals*.

2.3.4 Generate new training for new skills

Typically, training concentrates on work skills to train employees to deliver day–to–day tasks. It frequently concentrates on the 'what' of action rather than the 'how'. Change management and Business Re-engineering programmes need a whole new set of skills, concentrating mainly on the 'how'. Such training is vital – without it, the risk of failure increases. The importance of project management training has already been mentioned. There are other important new training courses that should be run.

These new training courses should concentrate on giving people the inter-personal skills and attributes to manage in a change environment. Most of them include an element of psychology, outdoor tasks from which behavioural lessons can be learnt, and a degree of team building activities. The lessons learnt from psychometric tests (such as Myers Briggs, FIRO F/B, Belbin's team types, etc.) will help project managers and their teams enhance their individual personal skills. This will enable them to work more effectively in a change environment. The use of outdoor activities which push people outside of their personal comfort zones will help them deal with the difficult situations which they will face back in the organisation when change occurs. There are four basic types of activities around which training experiences can be structured, as shown in Figure 4.8 (redesigned Figure 1.4 from Chapter 1).

Such training is often viewed with a high degree of scepticism – normally by those who have never received it in the past. But it greatly enhances the chances of success. There are many niche consultancies which offer such courses. Make sure the one you choose uses as much

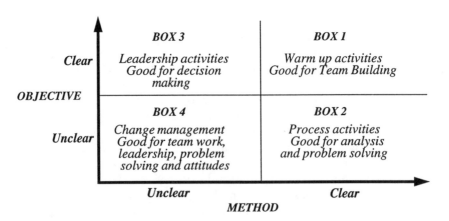

Figure 4.8 Training activities for change.

review sessions as activities, so that participants can learn as much as they have fun. Ensure they have qualified staff to run outdoor sessions in a safe and controlled way, and skilled facilitators to run review sessions. The review sessions are key, and are used to draw out from participants the observed behaviours and emotions felt by individuals and teams during a particular exercise. Lessons can then be learnt for application back in the new re-engineered work environment.

This type of 'new' training can be structured to be of use in a variety of ways. It can help to form the change teams and give them the skills to work through the 'check out zone' of the positive curve. It can be used by senior management to help evolve their leadership skills. It can help introduce IT into a conservative organisation which may feel that PCs are for secretaries not for managers (two bad attitudes to overcome regarding hierarchy/status and IT). The training can also be used to help form the new cross-functional process teams, assisting them to normalise their team dynamics and move quickly to be a good performing team. This type of experiential training was used by Progressive Insurance, and continues to be used by Birmingham Midshires, where the top leadership consider that it was (and still is) vital to the re-engineering effort (see Part 2).

2.3.5 Provide for participation in planning and implementation

A Business Re-engineering programme which is totally formulated external to the people who will be directly affected will carry a strong risk of failure. The increasing involvement of people in the organisation should mirror the increasing level of detail in the planning and implementation, as shown in Figure 4.9.

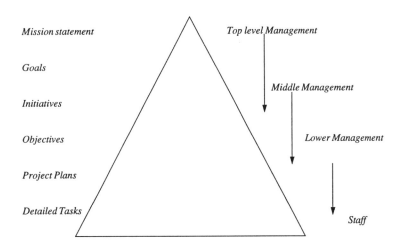

Figure 4.9 Increasing detail = increasing involvement.

In Chapter 3 the importance of involving all levels in planning and implementation has already been discussed, and the comments earlier in this chapter on the use of teams reiterates the point. This involvement needs to be managed to minimise wasted or duplicated effort, and guard against unnecessary frustration.

If you find that top level managers are heavily involved in formulating the project plans, then the degree of delegation is amiss! Similarly, you do not need to have people lower down in the organisation spending time on formulating a mission statement to guide the organisation through to the required future state! It must be borne in mind that even when the right balance of involvement is struck, more time will be spent on planning and preparation than one might want. This is more than made up by the speed and effectiveness of the implementation that ensues.

2.3.6 Reward needed behaviour and results

It is vital during a change programme to emphasise quick wins and early successes. This is even more important at the start of a programme, when cynicism is usually highest. Any success should be communicated rapidly. Those who achieve results, no matter how small they may seem, should be elevated to 'hero' status. Recognition by an organisation of an individual in itself is a powerful way not only of motivating but also showing what behaviour is now required. Similarly, those who consistently block and prevent change must be dealt with – either by counselling to change the person's attitude or, in the extreme, by removal (sideways, down or out). The creation of legends and folklore incidents to highlight the simple but effective actions of those lower down in driving change forward can assist in creating the action-oriented and initiative-seeking culture needed for change.

2.3.7 Provide time for people to disengage

One can often be less than sensitive when enthused by change. Remember that at a senior level, you may be involved for some time in drawing up the initial parts of the change programme. You need to be sensitive to those lower down, and give them time to disengage from the current state. After all some may be very happy with the way things are, and may have spent a lot of emotional currency in getting things organised the way they are. Involvement in data gathering to assist the first stage, as well as involvement in the planning, will help. One can use a variety of techniques to help the organisation disengage from the current state. One possible technique for a large Business Re-engineering programme is to organise a 'launch' event – perhaps a convention with some social activity. Another technique was exemplified by Oticon, which held a furniture auction where the old opulent furniture (which differed depending on the level of manager) was sold off to the staff (see Part 2).

For many the changes may spell death for hard felt beliefs and assumptions – give them time and space to get over it! And then focus them in a positive way forward.

2.3.8 Use Pilots and reposition the remainder

Business Re-engineering gives rise to new and radical ways of doing things. Often the designers of such change will feel in the dark, and thus try to plan every last possible detail before rolling out the concept across the organisation. Many will be sceptical about the feasibility. There sometimes exists the opportunity to pilot the new designs prior to rolling them out. Pilots have advantages as well as disadvantages:

- **Advantages**:
  - the new processes can be confirmed and fine tuned by the pilots;
  - the global roll-out will hit less resistance if the pilots can be seen to be working well;
  - the projected benefits of the programme will be clearer as the pilots are measured;
  - the re-engineering programme will be easier to manage in chunk-sized bits.
- **Disadvantages**:
  - the re-engineering programme will take longer to roll out;
  - the pain of the change and the pain of the status quo will last longer;
  - the 'check out zone' will last longer;
  - the re-engineering programme will, for some not in the pilots, loose momentum;
  - the rest of the organisation may be more complex to manage.

To minimise the disadvantages, if pilots are used you should run a parallel programme for the rest of the organisation. This could include a culture change programme, which can focus on needed future state behaviours rather than the new processes themselves (see Chapter 7 for more details). Leadership roadshows and training for managers can be undertaken for the rest of the organisation to ensure they do not loose sight of what is happening. The training should focus on getting managers to demonstrate future state behaviour within the current functional and hierarchical structures. This parallel programme will also assist the roll-out after the pilots are successfully completed, as the organisation will be in a better position and state of mind to embrace the changes.

If the pain of the status quo is very acute, there may not be enough time for the Business Re-engineering programme to deliver the results urgently needed. It should be remembered that Business Re-engineering is not a quick fix, and takes some time to be done well. If pilots are used, the organisation may be sunk before the roll-out begins. One option is to run a parallel programme to gain short-term improvements in the current processes, before they are eventually subsumed into the newly designed and managed cross-functional processes. This is what Digital South Pacific in Australia did in the initial phases of their re-engineering programme (see Part 2).

2.3.9 Burn bridges and build ambassadors

The more one communicates what is going to happen, the more one burns one's bridges. The communication should be both external and internal, and be such that it will be difficult, not to say impossible, for people to turn back to the current state. While the bridges are being burnt, seek out ambassadors. There may be many requests for further information, and the best ambassadors are those who have been converted from a resistant state to a supportive one. They should be the opinion leaders of the organisation, and be encouraged to talk to others about the change. This effectively is what happened to Oticon, whose re-engineering programme was so radical, it gained a lot of media attention. Employees were invited by their personal associations (old schools, previous colleges and unions) to come and talk about the changes. This helped to make resistance disappear (see Part 2).

2.3.10 Actively manage in/out-placement in a firm, clear and sympathetic way

A prime reason for resistance to change is due to the fear about what the change may mean. Redundancies are a common outcome of Business Re-engineering, so it is not unnatural for people to resist such programmes. There are two reasons for out-placement as a result of Business Re-engineering. Firstly the re-engineering can result in a surplus of manpower, and secondly those who continue to resist must be dealt with. The way the organisation manages this is key. If out-placement is managed in an unsympathetic way, morale will suffer and those left behind may become more negative. The 'survivors' could end up envying the 'dead'. On the other hand, if the situation is managed in a firm, clear and sympathetic way then the negative effect that redundancies have on morale will be lessened. So be firm, clear and sympathetic:

■ **Firm**. Once the scale of redundancy is known (probably during the 'Make a plan' stage), it needs to be communicated. No matter what one does, one will always get an angry reaction, but the aim is to move the people through the negative curve. Explain how the redundancies will be handled, rather than what they are (which may not be known then). Also explain that the changes will demand a new type of behaviour, and those that find it difficult to adapt will be given every support, but if they wish to leave they also will be helped. Support the resisters, but if they continue to refuse to support the change, then take firm action.

- **Clear**. Form a project team (by selection, or ask for volunteers) to manage the in/out-placement. Their role will be to see what opportunities and vacancies exist elsewhere in the organisation (in-placement) and outside the organisation (out-placement). Their aim is to manage a well planned project (using techniques in 'Make a plan'), the objective of which is to ensure that all those made redundant are given every help to find a new job, and are supported through their own period of personal change.
- **Positively sympathetic**. Being firm and clear does not mean being 'tough'. Do not talk about 'getting rid' of people. Instead talk about giving everybody the 'opportunity to succeed'. Explain that the organisation has to change, and the opportunity to succeed has also changed. The number of opportunities in the organisation may be more restricted (due to less roles), even though the quality of opportunity may improve (due to broader personal development). Explain that a team is being set up to actively help those who, due to circumstance, cannot be offered an opportunity in the organisation. This support will need to include:
  — personal counselling to help people set new personal objectives;
  — training for people to improve their CVs and interview skills;
  — use of external agencies to find jobs;
  — adverts in local press of availability of skilled people;
  — in-house 'job centre' with news of job vacancies trawled from outside;
  — in-house training information with details of external courses for people to broaden their skills and employability.

These out-placement activities need to be set up as quickly as possible so that the team is in place and ready to support people as soon as they know if they are personally affected. The team should be suitably motivated and rewarded, and ideally include those who are themselves affected. The techniques above will not prevent the anger at redundancy, but it will positively help people through their own personal change, supporting them to identify what they want, and making a plan.

2.4 Overcoming the issues of Power – shape the political dynamics!

2.4.1 Introduction
In any organisation of human beings with more than a couple of people (and even in those with two!), political behaviour will occur. It is a natural and expected feature. During a state of transition, however, this political activity intensifies. Change can threaten some people's power and position, and issues of 'turf' become more important than the strategic issues facing the company. Action can become based on people's perceptions of how the change affects their power, and what they think

their position will be in the future state. This can be compounded if the change is inconsistent with their current values and belief. Dysfunctional behaviour will occur, and this can jeopardise the re-engineering programme.

There will be the need, therefore, to *shape the political dynamics* and take active steps to ensure that the organisational politics work for the change, and not against it:

- Get the support and active involvement of key power groups.
- Use leadership behaviour to support change.
- Use symbols.
- Build stability.
- Give the re-engineering programme an identity with power.

2.4.2 Get the support of key power groups
If the leaders at the top of an organisation are against change, then change will not happen without serious disruption. A Business Re-engineering programme that does not have the support of the top of the organisation will fail (or else those at the top will need to be replaced if they continue to refuse support). It is vital to get full agreement – too often change programmes launch with only partial agreement in the hope that the agreement at the top will evolve with the programme. Leadership needs to 'walk the walk', not just 'talk the talk'. Time spent in individual and group meetings to thrash out differences and gain consensus and contracted agreement is seldom wasted. One must also remember that 'power' does not necessarily concentrate at the top. Functional specialists, worker representatives, etc., can all torpedo change programmes. Before the programme is launched it is essential to spend some time convincing those groups that change is needed. If nothing else you will clarify who is for and who is against. And make sure that clarification is gained. Silent foot-draggers are often the worst danger to success because they lie low, play safe and remain undetected for a long time. When they are detected it is often too late, and the re-engineering will be failing to the extent that they have ammunition to say 'I never believed it would work in the first place!' – a real self-fulfilling prophecy.

2.4.3 Use symbols
The use of symbols is a cheap and effective way of assisting communication, and gravitating the power of politics to within the change programme. For example, giving the programme its own name and logo gives the programme an identity and provides a banner to rally around (see section 2.4.5 below). Forming project teams and calling the project managers 'champions' shows that the organisation is delegating power to those actively involved in driving the change programme through.

If the project team has a trickle of people moving though it, then returning those people with clear recognition and even promoted status is also a symbolic gesture. Other techniques also exist. The use of 'service charters' and value statements ('Ten Commandments') are discussed more in Chapter 7. These are powerful symbols which can summarise and clarify in simple form the overall direction which the change programme is pursuing. Issuing all employees with a plastic card with the mission and goals statement, as well as perhaps the values statement, can reinforce the messages that are needed throughout the organisation. Rewarding successes visibly, and making 'heroes', are also symbolic and important gestures which can help solidify the cultural foundation needed for change. Some symbols have no material value in themselves, but what they represent are valued. Medals for soldiers is one example. Service stars for employees in a fast-food change is another. Birmingham Midshires makes use of a First Choice lapel badge (see Part 2). A more bizarre example is the CEO who, when faced with an executive who had out-performed expectation, gave him the first thing that came to hand – a banana! Banana badges began to spring up in the organisation taking on the significance of a medal for over-performance! Although the example may seem 'tacky' and trite, the underlying lesson is that we all like to have recognition. Good leaders recognise this human trait, and use symbols to make positive advantage of it.

2.4.4 Build stability

Business Re-engineering creates short-term instability. Therefore active steps are needed to build in some stability within the change process. The use of a transition team reporting direct to the highest levels, as well as an operational 'project coordination centre' accessible to all, will help. However, one must not forget that (especially early on) most people in the organisation will be involved in the current day-to-day operations of the organisation. For these people it is important to link the change to what they are doing to show where the consistencies are. They need to be told what role they are expected to play in the change process. Many re-engineering projects are simply attempts to introduce new processes to allow people to do what they do, but do it better. This should be highlighted to allow people to see that there remains an underlying stability.

One should not forget the impact that a change programme will have on the day-to-day operations, and some management time must be directed to this issue. See if some current operations can either be simplified, or stopped, to release resources for the change teams, but also to ensure that the day-to-day stability of the operations can be maintained during the period of transition. The role of the CEO is key – he or she needs to communicate the vision and values and demonstrate the behaviours which are required. The CEO must be consistent, and in so being can play a great part in providing people with the stability they seek.

2.4.5 Give the re-engineering programme an identity with power

Giving the re-engineering programme a name will establish its identity. For example, the programme in Kingston Hospital is called 'Patient Focused Care', while in Digital South Pacific it is called 'Quantum' (see Part 2). As stated in section 1.2 above, the programme will need to have a named top-level sponsor, either the CEO or one of his or her top team, who can act to remove blockages which the team itself may not be able to do. The organisation must recognise that a new and capable power base has been established to give the re-engineering programme the clout it needs to get things done.

2.5 Overcoming the issues of control – manage the transition!

2.5.1 Introduction

Change disrupts the normal flow of activities within an organisation, and can lead to the organisation becoming out of control. In many situations the current management systems are inappropriate for managing the transition. This means that formal systems and structures must either be enhanced or re-designed to ensure that control is not lost. They should be designed specifically for the transition period. In order to assist maintaining control, the following activities can be undertaken:

- Develop and communicate a clear image of the future state.
- Address all organisational components and manage the interfaces between re-engineering projects and daily routines.
- Use transition management structures and systems.
- Build in feedback and evaluation systems.

2.5.2 Develop and communicate a clear image of the future state

The use of mission and goals statements can serve as a useful method to help people understand overall what it is the organisation is trying to achieve. These should be widely communicated to all staff who, sooner or later, will be affected by the changes. Other devices can be used to communicate the future state, including frequent staff briefings to update progress but also to remind people of the mission, videos to show at briefing sessions lower down (which can be sponsored by suppliers), and regular newsheets (which are discussed in more detail in Chapter 7).

2.5.3 Address all components and manage the interfaces

A Business Re-engineering programme will be run concurrently with the daily routine of the organisation. While the management of the change projects should be separate, the interface between the two must be managed. There are three key interfaces which need to be managed, as shown in Figure 4.10.

- **Formulating the need for change and establishing the change projects.** This passes the problem identified to the newly formed change

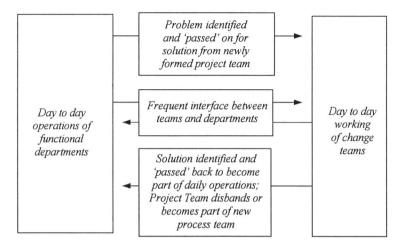

Figure 4.10 Key interfaces.

project team to come up with a solution. The team must include someone from the department who will be most affected by output from the project, to ensure that not only is the transition of the problem to the project team a smooth one, but is also a help when the solution is passed back to become part of day-to-day operations.

■ **Frequent interface.** There will be conflict between the needs of the project team to solve a problem, and the needs of the functional departments to get on with the day-to-day running of the organisation. These conflicts can vary, but it is vital to manage them. Clear and frequent communication between the two groups will go a long way to help reduce the conflict.

■ **Passing the solution back for daily implementation.** At this stage the project team is wound down, having delivered their project objective. It can either disband or form the core of a newly designed cross-functional process team. It is vital to ensure that those responsible for onward implementation have full ownership and understanding of the proposed solution. This is achieved not only by including department members in the project team from the start, and by frequent communication between the two groups, but also by use of workshops and seminars to 'sell' and if necessary refine the end product. Again active and visible leadership will be vital.

While the link between the re-engineering project and the department it will directly influence is obvious, it is also important to ensure that all parts of the organisation are kept informed about the change, and that the implications for change are understood. This will ensure consistent leverage, and add significantly to ensuring the change culture is developed.

2.5.4 Use transition management structures
The use of project teams, a transition team and a PCC team have been discussed in the section above dealing with technical processes. From a cultural point of view it is vital that these structures are used to control and coordinate the change, and thus must be given real authority and power to get things done and to remove blockages. If they are not given power, then the chances are that a lot of work will be done, but no real change will ensue. The credibility of the changes themselves will be compromised.

2.5.5 Build in feedback and evaluation systems for the transition
This forms the cornerstone of monitoring the change and is discussed in fuller detail in the next chapter. The systems for monitoring must be in-built at all levels, from the project teams through the transition team to company-wide indicators. From a cultural point of view, those doing the monitoring (best placed in the PCC) must be given voice to express not only fact but also opinion and further recommendations. Remember a plan rarely survives first contact with reality – if changes must be made then those monitoring the situation will have valuable thoughts as to how best to adapt the plan to reality in order to meet the objective. Those involved in the team will need to be given frequent encouragement and support by top management.

2.6 Summary of Cultural Techniques

It is mainly the behaviour of those at the top which sets the culture of an organisation. While the above techniques help to establish a cultural environment within which the change programme can flourish, if leadership behaviour is inconsistent with these techniques, then the programme will only achieve a fraction of what it could. Once these processes are put in place they must be respected and used, not ignored and abused. There is therefore the need to get the full agreement for these techniques amongst the top leadership.

3. SUMMARY

Successful implementation depends on knowing what you want, and making a coherent plan to get it. However, getting things done is also about MC³, explained in Figure 4.11.

By giving the re-engineering programme an identity and management structure, and creating the cultural environment for it to operate in, you

$$E = MC^3$$

Figure 4.11 Excellence equation.

will give it life and the people directly involved a sense of real purpose. This must be backed by consistent leadership behaviour to support the change and the processes put in place to manage the transition.

One aspect which has an impact on driving through change is dealing with those who are having difficulty adapting to the new roles and objectives ascribed to them. They should be set clear, mutually agreed objectives and monitored closely, with frank and honest feedback. Again, everyone should be given the *opportunity to succeed*. If they are not succeeding within the changes, then they should be counselled and either moved sideways elsewhere in the organisation or out to another organisation where they can succeed. Dealing with consistent failure in a positive and courageous manner is also vital for success in any change programme.

While the processes are put in place to implement plans, it is also important to have a process in place to monitor progress – if you can't measure it, you can't hit it. It is to this we now turn.

SUMMARY ACTION POINTS

■ **Use technical techniques**
— Cross functional project teams to design and implement change.
— Transition team to manage the re-engineering programme.
— Project coordination centre (PCC) team to coordinate activities and manage communications.

■ **Use cultural techniques**
— Clear, inspirational, supportive, sympathetic leadership – lead by example!
— Overcome resistance by motivating constructive behaviour.
  (a) understand the negative and positive curves to change;
  (b) bring resistance to the surface and continually gauge readiness for change;
  (c) create and maintain dissatisfaction of the status quo;
  (d) generate new training for new skills;
  (e) allow participation in planning and implementation;
  (f) reward needed behaviour and results;
  (g) provide time for people to disengage from the current state;
  (h) use pilots and reposition the remainder;
  (i) burn bridges and build ambassadors;
  (j) manage in/out-placement in a firm, clear and sympathetic way.
— Overcome the issues of power by managing the political dynamics.
  (a) get the support and active involvement of key power groups;
  (b) use leadership behaviour to support change;
  (c) use symbols;
  (d) build stability;
  (e) give the re-engineering programme an identity with power.
— Overcome the issues of control by managing the transition.
  (a) develop and communicate a clear image of the future state;
  (b) address all organisational components and manage the interfaces;
  (c) use transition management structures and systems;
  (d) build in feedback and evaluation systems.

■ **Give everybody the opportunity to succeed!**

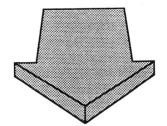

Go to next step: "Monitor".

5

Monitor

It is vital to put into place a process to monitor closely the re-engineering programme and the results it achieves. As has been discussed in previous chapters, the best team to do this is the project coordination centre (PCC) team, into which should report the project managers regarding their progress with the plan. Departments responsible for other aspects of monitoring (such as finance and marketing) should also report in data regarding the progress towards the measures of success as soon as it is available. As these departments fade, and the new cross-functional teams take ownership of the redesigned processes, these teams too should also report in. The PCC team will be able to brief the transition team at their weekly update meetings, and bring to their attention any problems which need resolution, together with options and recommendations. The PCC should also be in a position to produce status reports and reports on results for senior management as part of the daily reporting process in place.

Both action and results need monitoring:

- **Action**. Monitoring the action will mainly be against the project plans. The four areas which need monitoring are: time ('Will we meet the deadlines planned?'), cost ('Are we on budget and are resources sufficient?'), quality ('Will we meet the objectives and are we doing a quality job?') and effectiveness ('Are we implementing the changes in a way which gets full support?').
- **Results**. The key areas which need monitoring here can be lifted from the measures of success which each project plan should be striving to achieve. Bearing in mind that the whole change process is focused on key stakeholder needs, these results should be based on the benchmarks used to monitor how well such needs are currently met. Shareholder results will primarily be focused on financial and market

benchmarks; customer results will be based on market data and customer feedback; employee results will be based on operational benchmarks as well as employee attitude surveys; and supplier results will be based on cost benchmarks, as well as quality and speed of delivery. These benchmarks should have been established during the first phase of the re-engineering process 'Know what you want', with each goal having clearly defined measures of success as targets to be achieved.

Too often re-engineering programmes focus on monitoring the action, without linking these actions closely to expected results. This in itself gives birth to change projects which have as much effect on the organisation as a rain dance on the weather: lots of people tearing around but with little outcome. Call it the 'busy fools' syndrome – it's easy to fool ourselves, when the whole organisation is galvanised into action, that we are all achieving something!

Although action and results are the main areas for monitoring, they are not the only ones. Another key area (often forgotten until it is too late) are the key assumptions on which the re-engineering programme is based. These should be listed (there should not be many) and monitored – if they change, then the fundamentals on which a change project is based could be at risk. Even if it means frustration and a short delay, it is better to call a halt, regroup and replan than go charging on regardless. Operation Market Garden in the Second World War (made famous in the film *A Bridge Too Far*) assumed the enemy opposition to be light, but by coincidence a strong Panzer force was posted to the Arnhem area for rest and recuperation just before the Allied offensive – the rest is history. If the assumptions for a plan are changed, stop, check and, if necessary, fine tune. Although it is better to act and be 80 per cent correct than do nothing by trying to get 100 per cent, a change in basic assumptions is so fundamental that it warrants some thought!

There may be other areas which you may wish to monitor. If the change programme calls for a radical culture change, then it is worth keeping an eye on the political temperature. The occasional questionnaire for anonymous completion, asking people how they feel, will not only allow senior management to gauge progress and organisational temperature, but will also allow the organisation to let off some steam.

1. MONITORING ACTION

1.1 Introduction

The projects represent the detailed action of the re-engineering programme and they need to be monitored with regard to time, cost and quality. Most of the monitoring can be done by a simple pro-forma, an example of which is shown in Figure 5.1.

Project name :				Ref:	
Project manager:			Date:		
Status (please tick):	Red..		Amber..		Green..
1. Will the next milestone be reached?	Very early 1	Early 2	On time 3	Late 4	Very late 5
2. Will the project be completed on time?	Very early 1	Early 2	On time 3	Late 4	Very late 5
3. Will the project be completed to budget?	Way under 1	Under 2	On budget 3	Over 4	Way over 5
4. Will we meet the project objectives?	Very easily 1	Easily 2	OK 3	Difficult 4	Very Difficult 5
5. Have you sufficient resource?	Too much 1	Enough 2	OK 3	Tight 4	Not enough 5
6. Do you have sufficient support from senior management?	Very high 1	High 2	OK 3	Low 4	Very low 5
7. Do you have sufficient co-operation from organisational departments?	Very high 1	High 2	OK 3	Low 4	Very low 5

Figure 5.1 Project status form.

The pro-forma can be completed weekly by the project managers and sent to the project coordination centre on a regular (probably weekly) basis. These reports can be aggregated for simple reporting to the transition team. They can also be used to spot potential problems early on, to be resolved by either the PCC team, the transition team or by higher authorities if need be. By allocating numeric scores to each question, reports can be generated showing progress in graphical form, and an aggregated score can be monitored at a high level to indicate the general trend. The higher the score the better the progress, with the median score of 3 indicating that all is going according to plan (see Part 3, Appendix 1, section 4.6 for more details of this technique).

Be careful how you communicate the use of this form. It is *not* about checking up on people. It is about making sure that the project teams are getting the full support they need to achieve their objectives. It is also a simple reporting process to keep senior management informed and off the backs of the project managers, allowing them to get on with the job in hand. The pro-forma above covers time, resource and quality, which are considered in detail below.

1.2 Monitoring Time

Most projects work to a time constraint. Three areas can be used to assist monitoring this constraint:

■ **Colour code reporting.** Each project can report at a high level using three colour codes: **green** indicates that all is well with the project and deadlines will be met; **amber** indicates that the project is suffering problems, but the final deadline will be met; **red** indicates that the project is suffering major problems and cannot meet its final deadline – re-planning is necessary (using the amendment form of the project plan to document any major changes – see Part 3, Appendix 2). The difference between red and amber is whether the delayed task is on or off the critical path (see Part 3, Appendix 2 for a detailed consideration of critical path analysis).

■ **Interim milestone monitoring**. The project should be broken up into milestones. These should be monitored closely to ensure that the overall programme can be met. Although some interim milestones may suffer delay, this does not mean that overall the project will be completed late, as the milestone may not be on the critical path. However, such delays can change where the critical path itself runs, and this needs to be monitored.

■ **Critical path monitoring**. Activities on the critical path should be monitored to ensure that the end date of the project can be met. If delay occurs, then one of three things also needs to occur: the deadlines need to be moved; or more resources (and more costs) should be allocated to future tasks to shorten their duration; or the quality of the end deliverable needs to be downgraded to allow some activities to be done faster.

Monitoring time on its own is not enough. It is all very well to learn a project is suffering delay, but it is more important to understand *why* the delay occurred in the first place. This is either due to insufficient resources and budget, or due to quality aspects (either the task was harder to achieve than envisaged, or the quality of work has suffered due to human failure).

1.3 Monitoring resources

Each project manager should have a resource plan within his or her own project. The questionnaire in Figure 5.1 above looks at two main resources: people and budget.

■ **People**. Asking project managers if they have sufficient people will give an indication of how well planned the project was and the assumptions made for what was needed to get things done. If project managers say they are beginning to suffer from lack of resources, this will also give an early indication of possible delays and quality problems.

■ **Budget**. Each project should have a budget. Any overspends which occur should be highlighted as soon as possible to allow management action to either increase the budget, or reduce the quality of the work done to meet the final budget. Another option would be to change the method of delivering the project, but this needs time to work out and will probably have an impact on meeting the deadlines.

1.4 Monitoring quality

Quality is worth a whole book in itself (and several are available!). In terms of monitoring a change project you need to focus on three areas: objectives, management support and inter-departmental cooperation.

- **Project objectives.** Each project plan should have a clearly defined objective. You should ask the project managers (using a form like the one in Figure 5.1 above) to what extent this will be met. It is also worth checking the effectiveness of delivery by asking those at the receiving end how well the objectives are being met (for example, if a project is designed to deliver some new training, have a process to elicit feedback from the trainees).
- **Management support.** Project teams typically work outside normal management structures. However, they may well have day-to-day contact with senior management. If senior management support is not forthcoming, this will have a serious impact on the project delivery. Asking project managers if they have enough support and cooperation from senior managers will help identify any 'political' problems.
- **Departmental cooperation.** Following on from management support is the cooperation needed from daily operational departments. Again this needs to be monitored for the project's sake. It will also highlight any areas of conflict between the change programme and the daily operations. These conflicts, if not resolved, can sink a change project as fast as any other organisational torpedo you may care to mention!

The quality of implementation will depend on an effective, well thought-out plan with committed resources. If there are major problems with the delivery in quality terms then look at the plans and look at the people delivering. If failures are inherent in the people, then ensure they understand (and agree to) clear deliverables and objectives. In the worst case, remove those who cannot succeed in the project environment (to give a chance to someone who can, and to enable the person who fails on the project to succeed elsewhere).

1.5 Monitoring effectiveness

This aspect focuses on the organisational aspects of change management effectiveness (i.e. the 'how'), rather than on the effectiveness of a project against a time scale (i.e. the 'what'). It is not therefore included in the project manager's report form shown in Figure 5.1 above, as the monitoring needs to be done across the organisation, especially among those not directly involved in the change projects. This was considered in the previous chapter in the section dealing with the management of resistance (Chapter 4, section 2). The monitoring should cover how much support is there for the changes, how constant the support is from sponsors, how well the changes are being communicated, etc. The use of questionnaires or discussion groups run by an outside facilitator can be used to do this monitoring. It should be carried out at regular intervals throughout the running of the programme. The process can also include short half-day sessions with project teams to talk about how the programme is being run (and lessons learnt), rather than what the teams are doing. Regular monitoring of this kind can help a re-engineering programme keep on the rails, and avoid being thrown by political behaviour or poorly managed resistance.

1.6 Summary on monitoring action

Once the key areas of time, resources and quality are identified and monitored there should not be too much trouble. Using standard pro-formas should help the process. These pro-formas should not be viewed by project managers as 'check ups', but as a process whereby they can bring to the attention of senior management any additional support they need to drive their project through an organisation which may be resistant to change. One should also encourage project managers to monitor the quality of the work done by their project teams, and to hold regular meetings with them to see how quality of the project implementation can be improved. Concurrent monitoring on change management effectiveness will help steer the programme clear of the traditional risks associated with complex change in a proactive, rather than reactive, way.

2. MONITORING RESULTS

2.1 Introduction

The big problem with monitoring results is understanding the full relationship between cause and effect. For example, if a project is designed to have the benefit of improving sales, then if sales go down that does not necessarily mean that the project failed. Sales can be influenced by many other factors, and the truth could be that without the project the decline would have been a lot worse. So although results should be monitored, don't forget that these results can also be affected by factors other than the change project! If it is vital to understand the detail of cause and effect, then research will need to be undertaken – this could be a project in itself!

There are a variety of results which should be monitored, grouped for convenience under the categories of the key stakeholders – remember that the projects link back from the objectives, through the initiatives and goals, to these stakeholders. The benchmarks below should have all been studied during the first stage of the change process 'Know what you want' – the results will provide a starting point to measure against. Processes will need to be put in place to update the position regularly and so provide indications of how successful the change projects are.

2.2 Monitoring Customer results

The list below is not exhaustive, but does indicate the kind of results which the projects may be trying to achieve. Some indicators of results should be easy to get, others will need some research. Don't be put off by using outside data, even though it is harder to get than that readily available inside the organisation. One good way of seeing if the customers like the result of a project (or if they even noticed it) is to ask them!

- **Sales**. This is a key figure – after all, the customers are paying for what you are providing. Sales are a result of *product mix* times *volume* times *price*. You need to understand the detailed interrelationship of those three variables.
- **Market share**. Customers have a choice – some of your projects may be designed to give you a 'USP' – a unique selling proposition. The jury on this is the customer, and the measurement is market share. If you have a defined customer segment, with a focused offer, and you understand the competition, then market share trends will tell you how successful you are.
- **Perceived value**. Asking customers direct (either through your own resources, or via a commissioned market research study) about the perceived value of your offer (versus the competition) will give an indication of how price competitive you are.
- **Perceived level of service**. Any product sold has the opportunity to include a high level of service. This ranges from taking the order, to speed of delivery and after-sales service. Although it is the product which the customer primarily needs, never forget that there will be a human interface between the customer and the organisation. If this interface does not leave the customer feeling valued and warm inside, then there are opportunities for improvement. The best way to measure this is to ask – either by research using internal resources, or by using commissioned external resources. Many see this as too difficult – it need not be. Simple and regular questionnaires (using questions based on 1–5 scored replies) for anonymous completion by a sample group can quickly be entered onto a spreadsheet to give an indicative trend. This is one of the key measures monitored by Birmingham Midshires using internal resources, and by Siemens Nixdorf Service (ITS) using external resources (see Part 2).

The above are some examples of results which you may monitor. The key point is to focus onto what results (as opposed to actions – don't confuse the two!) the change projects are trying to achieve. These results should be driven by the analysis in the first stage of the change process 'Know what you want', and then monitored by a designed process in the last stage 'Monitor'. This monitoring process needs to be designed, planned, budgeted and resourced before the 'Do it!' phase of implementation begins. If a PCC is used, this is the best place to base the coordination of the monitoring process.

2.3 Monitoring Supplier results

Three key areas for improvement with suppliers are cost, time and quality. Again the list below is not exhaustive, but shows a few measures which can be monitored. The benchmarks you look at very much depend on what the specific projects are trying to achieve:

■ **Costs: Profit and loss impact.** The cost of supplies, which directly drives your gross margin, can be affected by a variety of actions from negotiating more favourable terms to widening the supply base. If the change project is focused on suppliers, these costs should be monitored closely on a regular basis.

■ **Costs: Balance sheet impact.** Payment terms and inventory have a balance sheet impact. Your suppliers to some extent finance your working capital assets. Cutting down on inventory, redesigning the supply chain process and negotiating more favourable payment terms can have a favourable impact on cash flow and the balance sheet.

■ **Speed of delivery.** The idea of using time as a competitive weapon is not new. Time-based competitive advantage will, to some extent, rely on the speed of reaction and delivery of suppliers. Working closer with suppliers, and helping them to move to Just In Time (JIT) operational methods, is one of many ways to get faster delivery. The use of computer systems and Electronic Data Interchange (EDI) will also help (see Part 3, Appendix 3 for more details on EDI). The point here is that time needs to be measured and monitored to assist improvement. This can be done using techniques such as work flow process analysis (see Part 3, Appendix 1 for an example).

■ **Quality.** The quality of goods received can be measured by the amounts of rejects on goods inward manifests. One can also measure the level of service (remember you are a customer of the supplier!). The measures used will depend on the goods and services provided, but these must be clarified and, working closely with your suppliers, improved.

Suppliers play a key role in the service/products which you provide to your customers. Measuring results, and sharing the findings with your suppliers, can in itself help improve relationships and effectiveness.

2.4 Monitoring Employee results

The employees (including management) are the engine of the organisation – without them you have an empty shell of buildings and equipment. There are two sides of employees to measure: the 'hard' operational side (such as productivity) and the 'soft' psychological side (such as morale). Concentrating on one alone will lead to poorer results than can be gained by keeping both aspects in mind. The 'Ghengis Khan School of Management Thought' would state 'grab 'em by the processes, and their hearts and minds will follow'. While this might be true in the short term, in the medium term it leads to a lot less than could be achieved. Such a top-down dictatorial approach is more suited to a functional hierarchical organisation, and does not serve well in a re-engineered 'bubble' organisation. It is not for nothing that 'morale' crops up as a key fundamental principle of warfare in several military academies. Ignore it at your peril!

- **Operational results.** There are a variety of ways to measure operational results. The most common is to look at staff costs as percentage of sales to spot productivity trends. The same can be applied as a cost per unit of volume. Time can also be measured in terms of speed of operation achieved by employees, as well as by effort to duration ratios. Another measurement which can be used is 'value added', using the same type of analysis used to assess the 'value chain' discussed in Chapter 2.
- **Morale.** There are many ways to monitor morale. Staff turnover and days sickness are measures which are readily available in organisations, and which can give an indication of trends in employee satisfaction. For some reason employee attitude surveys are not regularly used, but they do give a very good indication of how employees feel. Questionnaires using 1–5 scored responses completed anonymously can enable management to see graphically the organisational temperature (see Part 3, Appendix 1, section 4.6). The responses can be put into a spreadsheet to see their distribution, which is as important as the average. For example, the average score of responses to the question 'How supportive is management in enabling you to complete your job?' could be 3 (based on a score of 1 being completely non-supportive to 5 being very supportive). However, if the distribution is split between 50 per cent scoring 1 and 50 per cent scoring 5, this

would show a very different picture to everyone scoring 3! So once you have decided what the change projects in this area are trying to achieve, have regular questionnaires to seek feedback, which can be expressed in numerical (and hence graphical) form. These questions can range over a variety of 'soft' issues from trust, loyalty and commitment, through to compensation and recognition. And the process of asking for the feedback and sharing the results will itself improve morale by showing that the management of the organisation is serious about the change projects, and values the feedback from employees.

Measuring employee effectiveness and morale should not be done in isolation – after all it is pointless having a happy, motivated and productive workforce while the strategy means that the customers switch their custom to other competitors and the shareholders witness a radical decline in value! Seigfried Sassoon wrote a poem in the First World War, where happy soldiers were slaughtered due to a bad plan of attack. Adapted for business the poem might read:

> 'Good Morning! Good Morning!' the CEO smiled,
> As he toured round departments, the factory and tools.
> Now the workers he joked with are most of them fired,
> And curse him and his staff for incompetent fools.
> 'He's a really great guy,' said Harry to Sam,
> Happy in work and the way it all ran.
> But they all lost their jobs to a bad business plan!

2.5 Monitoring Shareholder results

If you have achieved the results regarding customers, suppliers and employees, the results for the shareholders should look after themselves. However, there are a few benchmarks which you need to monitor as a safety check that all these changes are generating shareholder value.

- **Profit and loss benchmarks**. Revenue growth and operating margin are key value drivers on the profit and loss statement. Without these, the earnings (profit after tax) per share potential is seriously compromised. Looking at tax is also worthwhile, especially if there is an international aspect to the organisation.
- **Balance sheet benchmarks**. The capital side of the balance sheet (liabilities and equity) determines your cost of capital. This cost should be monitored and optimised. On the asset side, the working capital and fixed assets needed to sustain and increase revenue should be monitored. These will have an impact on cash flow.
- **Cash flow**. Concentrating on the profit and loss statement and Balance sheet in isolation ignores the dynamic between the two. The

cash flow implications of the changes to the way an organisation works can be very large. Thus it is also important to monitor the amount of cash generated by the organisation.

■ **External results.** The share price is perhaps the final arbiter of changes which an organisation undertakes. Monitoring this by simply reading the city pages is not enough – you need to monitor the feelings of the market analysts by understanding their perceptions (and helping to clarify them if necessary). This will involve not only reading their reports, but inviting them down to discuss their perceptions with you. If there are large blocks of shareholders not represented on the board, it is also worthwhile monitoring their perceptions as well – if nothing else this will help you sort out an effective communication plan to clarify misunderstandings.

3. SUMMARY

Monitoring both action and results is vital to the success of a re-engineering programme. Bear in mind that there will be a lag between the two. Most people see action and expect results overnight. This can lead to unnecessary changes of direction and implementation, with an overall worst outcome as a result.

Actions should be monitored against the constraints of time, cost, quality and change management effectiveness. The monitoring process should not only be passive, but also be active in terms of helping projects which are getting into trouble. The use of the PCC team as a 'crisis resolution' team can be particularly effective in helping to remove obstacles.

As far as results are concerned, most people try to measure everything using financial criteria – this is nigh on impossible. How can one measure the effectiveness of management training using financial criteria? The costs can be measured, but the specific financial results are sometimes hard to quantify. This is why other criteria (such as motivation and commitment) should also be included. The great failing of typical Western organisations (as opposed to Japanese ones for example) is that because they cannot measure financial benefits, they do not invest in necessary programmes. So use a wide range of criteria, and balance these against financial ones!

What does one do when the monitoring shows that the project(s) is not achieving its objectives, either in terms of time/cost/quality against the plan, or in terms of results? This is the time when one can either change how one acts, or change what one wants, as shown in Figure 5.2.

'Changing the change', and moving to continual change, is what you do – the next chapter!

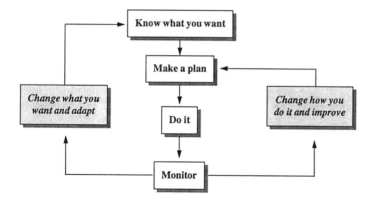

Figure 5.2 Four steps to Business Re-engineering.

SUMMARY ACTION POINTS

■ **Ensure monitoring process is in place managed by central PCC team**

■ **Monitor action**
— Monitor time using red, amber, green summary for each re-engineering project.
— Use interim milestones.
— Understand where the critical path runs (when changes occur).
— Monitor resource levels and budget.
— Monitor quality:
  (a) likelihood of achieving objectives;
  (b) support from management;
  (c) cross-functional cooperation.
— Monitor change management effectiveness: morale of change teams, support for change in organisation, effectiveness of communication.

■ **Monitor results**
— Customer results: customer satisfaction, share of market, sales, 'best of breed' competitor benchmarks.
— Employee results: morale, satisfaction, productivity, willingness to continue change and improvement.
— Shareholder results: cash flow, P&L/balance sheet ratios, share price and market ratios, level of shareholder loyalty/satisfaction.
— Supplier results: quality of delivery, speed, P&L costs, balance sheet impact.

■ **Ensure progress on action and results are communicated widely.**

6

Changing the change and continual change

This chapter looks at two aspects of re-engineering:

- changing the change when the projects do not yield results;
- moving the organisation to achieve continual change.

1. CHANGING THE CHANGE

1.1 Introduction

As the quotation in Chapter 1, p.29 suggests, a lot of failure in life is due to pulling in the reins before the horse has leapt. Once the plans have been finalised, the organisation must let the project teams get on with it. This will call on senior management to delegate effectively, and not interfere (hard though this may be). However, things do go wrong, and the reasons for this are due to a variety of causes.

Most of the reasons for failure shown in Figure 6.1 are due to failure in the first two stages of the change process, 'Knowing what you want' and 'making a plan'. If the initial analysis is not done well, if the investment in new training has not been made and the subsequent planning is weak, then implementation will be poor. This reiterates the importance of getting those first two steps right before you charge off and implement.

Even with sound planning, and with the best will in the world, plans sometimes fail the test of reality. Sound plans can easily be refined – poor ones fall apart. There are three options open to you when the results you want do not ensue from the actions undertaken:

Roles and support:

> Lack of consistent support
> Lack of definition and understanding of roles and responsibilities
> Lack of accountability

Definition:

> Lack of agreed acceptance criteria
> Poor specification of requirements

Planning and control:

> Inadequate early planning
> Poor communication
> Poor control of changes

Individual:

> Inadequate involvement and understanding
> Lack of skills and attributes training
> Poor inter-personal skills
> Poor teamwork

Circumstance:

> Failure to recognise change in underlying assumptions

Figure 6.1 Common reasons for business failure.

- do nothing;
- change how you do it;
- change what you want.

Of the three options the most common (and advised) is the middle option – the first one can lead to inaction, and the last one can lead to indecision. However, there are occasions when each option is best, and each therefore needs particular consideration. Before any option is taken you need to understand why the planned action did not yield the required result. This could be due to a variety of reasons, ranging from unsound assumptions on which the plan was based, to human failure. Whatever the reason, a little time spent in analysing the situation will be invaluable. Seek to understand rather than judge!

1.2 Do Nothing

If the results from a project are not forthcoming to the original time scale, consider if the time scale was realistic in the first place – and then consider if waiting a while longer is an option. This is like the classic fly fisherman's dilemma – will changing the fly make a difference, or will the original fly selected yield a result? This can be a dangerous option as it can lead to prevarication. If you do decide to 'do nothing', then also decide a date when, if the results are still not coming through, you will take action (and have an idea of what that action will be).

This option should be done in an active way, rather than a passive way. Making a contingency plan, with a date for implementation, will clarify how long this option is pursued before definite action is taken!

1.3 Change how you do it

In many instances, taking definite action is the preferred route. However one should be weary of too much change in a well communicated plan: 'Order – counter-order – disorder' is a common path of events. You must understand what it is you are changing, why, and what the implications of the change are. Any change will need to be well thought-out and communicated to prevent a chaotic state of affairs from ensuing. If the objective is still relevant then there are three levers you can pull: time, cost and quality:

■ **Time.** If a delay occurs on the critical path, then stretching the time frame is a common approach. This will mean that some downstream details will need to be rescheduled. This will call for an element of replanning and communication to those involved. The implications and costs of delay will also need to be calculated.

■ **Costs.** If delay is unacceptable, another option is to invest more money into the project. This can either be in terms of raw cash (to buy, for example, some outside help) or it can be in terms of putting more people onto the project. If extra investment is decided, then the amount needs to be well thought-out and compared to the original benefits which the project is striving to achieve. It is also worth understanding why the project budget was not accurate, and what assumptions were false. These assumptions could have a bearing on other projects.

■ **Quality.** Quality is the last thing you want to change. However, pragmatic experience suggests that when time cannot be stretched, and the budget cannot be increased, then quality will suffer. If it must suffer, then make sure you understand how it will suffer! There are four areas where quality can be manipulated (either up or down) to help a project in trouble: quality of action or quality of resources could be improved, while quality of end product or quality of life could be lessened.

— *Quality of action.* The action undertaken to achieve the individual tasks within the project could be viewed to see if they could be done smarter. For example, by looking at the project plan again, one could see a way where some tasks could start earlier than they were originally planned. Or maybe two tasks could be doubled up. There are a variety of ways of looking at this, but they all take some thinking time, sometimes laterally!

— *Quality of resources.* It may just be that the people who are working hard on the project do not have the skills to deliver. Some tough decisions will need to be taken, but in a positive way. Explain that the project no longer gives the person who needs to be replaced the opportunity to succeed, and for their own good they are being replaced by one who has better skills. The resources may not just be people – they could be consumables or outside contractors. Whatever the resources, there may be the opportunity to improve their quality to get the project back on the road.

— *Quality of end product.* The quality of the end deliverable can be compromised. For example, instead of having two windows, a garage can be built with one. Instead of a process delivering 80 per cent faster, it can be changed to deliver 50 per cent faster. Or an ambitious training programme could be targeted at fewer people. *Think very, very carefully before manipulating this aspect.* For example, Exxon decided to have some tankers built with one hull instead of a double hull – that cost millions for the *Exxon Valdez* disaster in Alaska! Compromising on the quality of an end product is very dangerous – especially if it is targeted at a final consumer market. You can make money quickly, but it takes years to regain lost credibility! And in the long run it is that credibility which keeps your relationship with customers. Once quality in an organisation can be seen to be compromised, the attitude can spread like fire.

— *Quality of life.* What frequently happens more by default than by planning is that people see a deadline coming and know that if they continue to work at the planned level of activity they will not hit it – so they simply work harder and longer. This is either due to the team not working hard enough in the first place, or because the plan is not sound and the other trade-offs of quality/time/costs cannot be manipulated. Weekends are given up, people get home very late, holidays are sometimes cancelled, family life of those involved suffers – all part of the joys of project management. But it need not be thus, and if this does occur then the very least one can do is be aware of it, and give recognition to the people whose quality of life suffered for the sake of delivering a project! The second thing to realise is that there is probably a deeper problem in the project which needs to be looked at – people don't normally cancel holidays unless something is very wrong! So instead of just patting people on the back for working late, try to change things so that they can get a balance in their lives and devote time to their families! Good time management leads to efficient results and good quality of life. Any fool can work hard – it takes good management to work smart.

Changing how you do it could involve more than fine-tuning the project plan with regard to time/cost/quality. If the objective still stands, then a more radical option would be to completely replan the project from scratch. This would need to occur if there was a radical change to one of the basic assumptions on which the original plan was conceived. This will mean that the project team will need to go to a 'retreat', away from phones and day-to-day distractions, and come up with another plan, i.e. go back to the start of the 'Make a plan' stage.

1.4 Change what you want

The project plan is based on the 'Framework of Success' – a series of objectives, built from a mission statement and supporting goals and initiatives as described in Chapter 2. Unless something very wrong occurred in the 'Know what you want' phase, or some basic assumptions changed radically, the 'strategic' mission statement, goals and initiatives should not be changed. They should be reviewed at yearly or so intervals, and the initiatives refined/ improved if necessary. If you have communicated the mission and goals then you should pursue them. An organisation which changes strategic direction every few months or so becomes disorientated and uncertain. In the long term, it will fail. The worst case is a 'weathercock' CEO who changes direction as often as the wind. This can drive an organisation to distraction and ruin. It is symptomatic of a lack of discipline (and sometimes intelligence) by ignoring, or paying lip service to, the first two steps of change management ('Know what you want' and 'Make a plan').

On the other hand, the supporting 'tactical' objectives might well change. It could be that these objectives were not defined well enough, or that they were the wrong objectives to support the broader initiatives and goals. An example of this is a project in a supermarket to improve the availability of trolleys. This was to support an initiative to improve general customer perceptions. Although trolley availability improved, customer perceptions did not – in the end trolley availability was not a key issue. Frequently, part of the problem is that cause and effect are never fully understood. So in the first stage of the change process ('Know what you want') a lot of assumptions are made in the 'Framework of Success' about the objectives which support the strategic initiatives and their goals. It is assumed that the achievement of the objectives will lead to the achievement of the initiatives. The quality of results will reflect the quality of research – if the initial analysis was too shallow, then it may well be that the project objectives are achieved, but the results don't follow through.

This can be frustrating – a project team would have worked hard to meet its deadlines, and succeeded in the project, only to meet failure in the results. You need to change what you want in detail. Review the initial data on which the assumptions of cause and effect were based. If necessary go back and start the research in the particular area again. Refine the objectives, make a plan and then do it!

The point to note is that once the mission, goals and initiatives are set, they should be pursued with tenacity. If the supporting objectives don't yield the required results, then define new objectives and go for them. And if you find that the objectives which are achieved continue to fail to get the results pursued, then something pretty serious is wrong. Either the outside world has changed beyond belief, or the 'Framework for Success' is based on such loose analysis that the mission, goals and initiatives were too far out to be possible in the first place. A management team which changes its long-term strategic goals every year is one which normally gets changed itself. So be doubly sure when you build your 'Framework for Success' that it is based on sound, analytical and objective research.

1.5 Summary

Any change programme must be flexible. This is because it will start in a situation where objectives and methods are unknown. Once the objectives are clarified, the method of achieving them can be planned, but until the action starts it is not known for sure that the achievement of the objectives will gain the results required. So you need to be patient first, then flexible in action, and if that does not work, flexible in objectives. The aim is always to move from box 4 to box 1, via box 2 or 3 as necessary, as shown in Figure 6.2 (adapted from Figure 1.4 in Chapter 1).

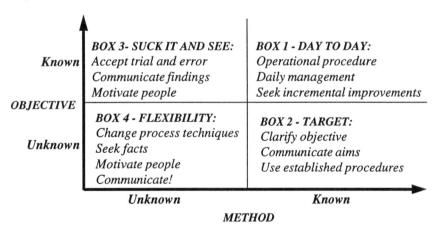

Figure 6.2 Change dynamics.

Changing the change is always difficult to do, as much emotional energy and enthusiasm will be spent in setting up the change programme in the first place. It also extends the 'check out zone' (see Chapter 4, section 2,

Figure 4.7). Communication is therefore vital in keeping people informed and empowering them to understand the need for flexibility in pursuance of the results required.

2. CONTINUAL CHANGE

For some, continual change sounds like a nightmare of chaos and uncertainty. That is because we are used to having roles and functions defined, with clear divisions of labour. I believe that functional and hierarchical organisations – chimney organisations – cannot by their very nature achieve continual change. However, in our fast-moving world, continual change will be vital to stay ahead. Outside circumstances change, competitors change their tactics, and customers are becoming more demanding as their needs change. To stay with it, organisations will need to be able to achieve continual change.

Continual change is about an organisation keeping in touch with its customers and its competitive environment, rather than that being achieved by a functional department (like marketing) or part of a hierarchy (like a main board). Continual change is about every individual being empowered to act in a 'controlled' way, to instigate and make the changes the organisation needs to make to delight customers. Continual change is not about chaos, it is about *continually improving* to delight customers, to develop and motivate employees, to achieve synchronicity with suppliers and create real value for shareholders with superior returns.

Sounds like a dream? It shouldn't. Some of the companies in Part 2 are well on the way, with perhaps Oticon showing best what a state of continual change means (for their head office at least). If a re-engineering programme is done well, and the organisation is moved from chimneys to grid and on to bubbles, then it will achieve the skills and learning to enable it to achieve continual change. Having gone through the four stages of Business Re-engineering well ('Know what you want' – 'Make a plan' – 'Do it!' – 'Monitor'), and having learnt the two steps of how to change the change ('Change how you do it and improve', and 'Change what you want and adapt'), the organisation will be able to move forwards to a state where it achieves continual change.

The continual change cycle is summarised in Figure 6.3, really an adapted version of the 'Four steps to business re-engineering' shown in Figure 1.3 in Chapter 1.

The following three reasons highlight, at a micro level, why it is that an organisation that goes through Business Re-engineering well can enable continuous change:

■ **Enhanced individual skills and attributes**. The training in skills and attributes for the employees now operating in cross-functional process teams will enable them to be more flexible and responsive to

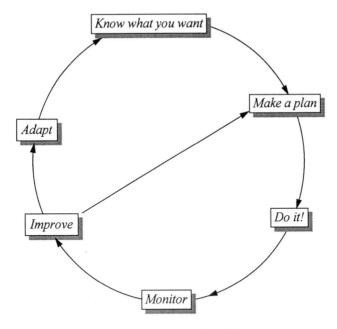

Figure 6.3 Achieving continual change.

change. They will be better able to deal with ambiguity, the kind of positive ambiguity which functional organisations kill. They will be used to forming teams to solve problems and introduce improvements. They will share a common vocabulary of change, what it means, and what it needs to get done well.

■ **Lack of hierarchy.** A successful Business Re-engineering programme should remove the hierarchy, and so remove the organisational blockages to continual change. Hierarchy makes continual change difficult for three reasons. Firstly, those at the top find it difficult to push change through the various levels of hierarchy – middle management are often resistant. Secondly, when change bubbles up from below, top management are resistant! Finally, hierarchical organisations typically have a culture where rank and position are more important than serving customer needs.

■ **Monitoring.** As has been stated previously, a successful Business Re-engineering programme includes establishing a sound monitoring process. If well designed, this process will pick up the need for change automatically. It will alert the teams inside that something needs to be improved, and given the new culture and structures that re-engineering can achieve, the organisation will respond.

It would be naive to say, however, that an organisation just has to carry out re-engineering once and continuous change will just flourish and stay intact. It will need leading, inspiring and cultivating. Leadership will remain as important as ever, only it will need to be manifested in a different way than typical functional and hierarchical organisations experience (see Chapter 4, section 2.2, Figure 4.5).

SUMMARY ACTION POINTS

- **Understand the common reasons for project failure**
- **Decide appropriate action**
  - Do nothing.
  - Change how you do it: use lever of time, cost/resource, quality.
  - Change what you want.

- **Move to continual change**
  - Provide responsive, active, inspirational, firm but supportive *leadership*.
  - Enhance individual skills, attributes and flexibility.
  - Reduce hierarchy and continually empower.
  - Move from the authority of the boss to the authority of the objective.
  - Ensure monitoring process acts as a catalyst for further change and improvement.

- **Learn from the experiences of the initial Business Re-engineering programme, change the culture and apply the lessons**

7

The change process

So far we have looked at some tools and techniques you can employ to guide you through the four basic steps of Business Re-engineering:

- **know what you want**, by understanding the need for change and the key stakeholders' needs;
- **make a plan**, by forming cross-functional teams and using project management techniques;
- **do it**, by employing some simple but effective technical and cultural techniques;
- **monitor**, both actions and results by using a project coordination centre (PCC) team;
- **change the change and continual change**, when the results you want don't come through, and if they do how to continually improve and adapt.

Behind this approach are additional process techniques which you can employ to help some or all the various stages. They work. They also typically need a change of attitude in senior management to make them work well:

- **culture change programme**, to position the organisation;
- **project teams**, to drive the re-engineering through;
- **workshops**, to gain quality, understanding and commitment;
- **facilitators**, to assist the smooth process of change management;
- **training seminars**, to develop the skills needed to drive the change;
- **an academy**, to act as a focal point for the Business Re-engineering programme;
- **ten commandments**, to summarise the values needed for the change to succeed;
- **change programme communication**, to keep everyone informed of the process, successes and further opportunities.

1. CULTURE CHANGE PROGRAMME

One of the failings of some Business Re-engineering programmes, especially those focused on business process re-engineering (BPR), is that they concentrate on the 'hard' processes, and pay little attention to the 'soft' issues. These issues are very hard to quantify. While it is easy to analyse and understand cycle times, throughput, volume per employee, customer complaints and other metrics commonly associated with process re-engineering, it is hard to get a handle on soft things like attitudes, values, feelings and world view. However, it is as vital (one could argue more vital) to change attitudes as it is to change processes and organisational structures. Successful re-engineering programmes normally include a culture change programme. It is too risky, and wrong, to assume that one can 'grab 'em by the processes, and their hearts and minds will follow'.

A culture change programme will need to focus on the organisation as a whole, rather than just the initial pilots or processes being re-engineered. Business Re-engineering often takes years to implement redesigned processes across an organisation, but that does not mean that you cannot start to work on changing the attitudes of those who are not initially affected.

The content of culture change programmes will differ from organisation to organisation. They will typically have elements already discussed in earlier chapters such as the communication of vision, leadership roadshows, the use of a values statement and, most importantly, 'new' training aimed at attitudes and inter-personal attributes rather than technical skills. There is much debate about whether one should or should not run a culture change programme before any detailed approach at re-engineering processes. The main advantage of changing the culture first is that by the time the detailed processes are re-engineered, many of the old attitudes will have been changed. This approach is the one which Birmingham Midshires Building Society has followed. After a few years of changing the culture of the society (and some of the processes), the organisation has now turned its attention to a more detailed process re-engineering exercise (see Part 2). Others argue that if a process redesign is going to result in a lot of redundancy (and the commensurate negative impact of morale), then it is better to re-engineer the processes first, reorganise those who remain into the new cross-functional process teams, and then run a culture change programme. The right answer is that it depends on the organisation, the level of anticipated redundancy, and whether or not the organisation has the luxury of time to choose. The timing also depends on the extent of the change of attitude needed versus the change of processes needed, as shown in Figure 7.1.

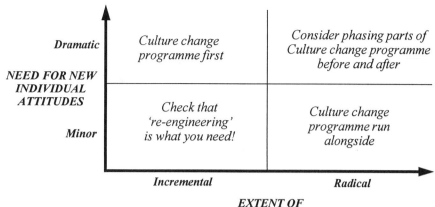

Figure 7.1 Culture change programme timing.

Like many aspects of Business Re-engineering, there is no single right way to do it. The timing and content will depend on the unique circumstance of each organisation. The main thing is to recognise that certain things need to be done, and achieving culture change is one of them.

2. THE USE OF PROJECT TEAMS

The use of project teams has been discussed in broad detail in previous chapters. They should be used at all stages of the four steps. They will lay the foundation for, and even themselves grow into, the cross-functional process teams (the bubbles) which are needed for a re-engineered organisation. Let's look at their use in detail. Business Re-engineering needs a different management approach to the type of approach used in day-to-day operations. This is because the change environment is unique. Unlike day-to-day operations, change does not operate in an environment of 'smooth corners' – the objectives are new and the method to achieve them is not fully clear. There are a lot of 'sharp corners' as shown in Figure 7.2.

Another reason for using project teams is that change projects often cut across traditional hierarchies and lines of reporting. There will often be the need to bring together people with differing functional skills to achieve a common short-term objective. So the key technique for achieving effective change is obtained by establishing project teams.

A change team must be made up of quality people, and be recognised as such. Business Re-engineering is a serious undertaking, and one should put one's best people forward to drive it. Even the act of doing so will be beneficial, as it will send a powerful message to the rest of the organisation.

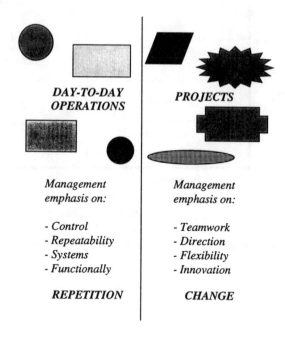

DAY-TO-DAY OPERATIONS | **PROJECTS**

Management emphasis on:

- Control
- Repeatability
- Systems
- Functionally

REPETITION

Management emphasis on:

- Teamwork
- Direction
- Flexibility
- Innovation

CHANGE

Figure 7.2 Approach to business activities.

Once formed the team must be quite clear who the 'client' of the project's deliverables is. They will also need support from the top, and a consistent level of sponsorship. A project team is made up of three types of players:

■ **Project director sponsor.** These are senior management 'mentors', and the key sponsors for change. They ensure that the project manager gets the support he or she needs, and also ensures that the constraints within which the project team are operating are understood. The project sponsor is the 'client' of the project, and keeps the lines of communication open between the project team and the senior management. This can also be facilitated by the transition and PCC teams. The project sponsor's involvement therefore should be at a high level. He or she ensures that the project gets off to a good start and intervenes only if problems occur. He or she should also ensure that the project manager's personal development continues, and that the project manager gets recognition for any achievements. This should include a fair personal and mutual appraisal of the project manager at the end of the project for feedback and input for personal development. Being a project sponsor is a different role to being a senior executive in a functional organisation, and so sponsors too will need some training. Ford Motor Company has a process improvement methodology which not only includes a four-day course for project managers, but also a one-day course for project sponsors (see Part 2).

■ **Project manager.** The project manager acts as the 'champion' of the project. Normally as a full-time job, he or she plans the detail (with input from the team players), and controls the resources and the players to ensure the project delivers to plan. He or she should not only take an interest in the tasks which are performed within the project, but should also maintain a fundamental concern for the well-being of the team players, ensuring that those assigned to the project can develop themselves from the experience, and that they get recognition for their achievements. The project manager should also provide an appraisal for the team players before they go back to their respective departments to carry on their normal day-to-day tasks. If important change projects are viewed by people in the organisation as a sidestep for career progression, then the motivation of those involved will suffer. It will also become increasingly harder to get people to want to be involved in such projects!

■ **Project team players.** These are the individuals who complete the tasks which make up the project. They will either be full time, part time or (more commonly) a mixture of both. For them, being part of a project team will be viewed as a risk. They will be taken out of a work environment that they are used to, and be expected to achieve tasks in a flexible environment with risks of failure. They will need support, guidance and recognition from the organisation which they serve.

If the deliverable from the project team is a designed new process to be employed within the day-to-day operations of the organisation, then the project team organisation must include individuals from those departments which will be affected. Failure to do so will probably result in the 'NIH' – Not Invented Here – syndrome where the departments affected fail to pick up the change implemented by the project team. A common and classic case is one of systems analysts putting in a new IT system with no end user involvement in the planning and implementation stage. The hardware and software which results from such projects often end up as expensive paper weights.

The 'life cycle' of a project team typically follows the process shown in Figure 7.3.

The psychological team dynamics of a successful project team should be borne in mind. Successful teams go through a typical cycle of 'Forming – Storming – Norming – Performing'. There will be times when team members have stormy relations – these should be expected, and not avoided. With some storming, as long as relationships are then normalised, the team will fully perform. Don't just expect to throw together a whole load of strangers from different departments and expect them to become a team. They will not. Many organisations say they use teams, few actually have them. You need to invest training time into the team to

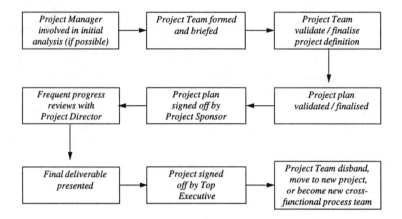

Figure 7.3 Typical life cycle of a project team.

include not only the skills they need, but also to develop personal attributes and an understanding of team dynamics, group psychology and individual character types. If you do that you will get a 'true' team, rather than a 'false' team – see Part 3, Appendix 1, section 6, for more details about team dynamics.

The 'adjourning' or breaking up of the project team should be marked by an event. A night on the town at the organisation's expense, with a 'thank you' presentation from a respected top-level executive, is a cheap but effective way of giving recognition to the team. The team's successes should be widely reported – peer recognition is often more important than recognition from above.

3. THE USE OF WORKSHOPS

'Workshop' is a term which has crept more and more into the management vernacular. It is a term more widely used than applied! Many gatherings call themselves workshops, but are little more than seminars or presentations, where most of the talking is done by the guy standing in front!

A true workshop is where the participants actually do most of the work – typically through debate and break-out groups' presentations for discussion in plenary session. It should have a result, normally firm agreement and commitment to specified action. Workshops are very useful to get clarification, understanding and commitment (through involvement of those present). For workshops to be successful, they need a few ground rules:

- **Location**. Ideally the workshop should be located off-site, away from phones, distractions and interruptions. You'll need a large room for plenary sessions, ideally laid out in a 'U' format as opposed to long tables in a line which can restrict communication. You'll need flip-charts and large pens, Blu Tack (to put up completed flip-chart pages on the wall), an overhead projector (with spare bulbs!) with blank transparencies and lumnocolour pens, and possibly a video player and slide projector. Each person should have a pad and pencils, glass with water/juice and mints (keeps the mouth fresh!). They should also have a name card for all to read (remember not everyone will know each other). Depending on the numbers involved, you'll also need 3–4 syndicate rooms for break-out groups to work in. These will also need flip-charts etc. Most decent hotels now run a conference service which can provide for all your needs.
- **Duration.** A workshop should not last more than three days or less than one day. A day-long workshop will need a very tight objective. A possible series of workshop objectives is detailed in Figure 7.4 below. If the workshop needs more than three days, then it is probably trying to achieve too much – it might be possible to break it into two separate workshops with a delay between.
- **Facilitator.** A good workshop will need a facilitator, preferably someone who has no axe to grind in the ensuing discussion. His or her role is to help (or facilitate) the group in meeting their workshop objectives. The facilitator ensures that everyone can get a word in and that participants respect each other's 'air time'. He or she acts as a process manager, ensuring the group sticks to the agreed timetable, keeps to the subject, achieves the stated workshop objectives and avoids waffle. He or she should be trained (yes, facilitation courses do exist!). The broader role of using facilitators is considered below.
- **Starting the workshop.** A reception with coffee should be available at least 30 minutes before the start to allow people to get themselves oriented. Administration (such as hotel check-in etc.) can also be covered. When the workshop starts in the plenary room, each individual, including the facilitator out front, should introduce themselves to the group. The objectives of the workshop (as published by the warning letter sent to all in advanced) should be agreed. People should also be given the opportunity to share any 'hidden agenda' which they might want to achieve in the workshop. The timetable should then be discussed, and administration points covered (such as meal times, phone calls, etc.). The facilitator should also establish the ground rules for discussion (such as being brief, respecting each other's air times and views, and treating the workshop as a 'protected' environment which will allow frank discussion without recrimination back at work!). Once this is covered, the workshop can properly begin.

- **Presentations in plenary session.** These should be short, concise and to the point. They should be used to engender discussion and agreement rather than simply inform. *If participants need to assimilate information, this should be sent out prior to the workshop, together with an agenda and workshop objectives.* Discussion should be managed by the facilitator, noting down salient points/views and agreements on the flip-chart. Plenary sessions should not last longer than one to one and a half hours each, as people's concentration will erode. Use natural/coffee breaks to allow people to recharge their 'batteries'!

- **Use of break-out groups.** When certain areas need much discussion to clarify a proposed solution, and to get the best from all involved, one should use break-out groups of 5–6 people working in syndicate rooms. They can then come back and present the group solution in plenary session. Ideally a facilitator should be made available for each group. Break-out groups should be given a specific objective (like brainstorm possible solutions to problems posed by data presented in plenary session), and should have a physical deliverable (such as handwritten flip-chart or transparencies for presentation back to plenary). The break-out sessions should not last much longer than one and a half hours, otherwise the law of diminishing returns soon applies itself!

- **Ending the workshop.** The last hour of the workshop should be used to agree the next steps. If action does not ensue from a workshop, then it is not a workshop! Summarise the tasks to do on a flip-chart, list the names alongside each (drawn by someone in the room!) and indicate a deadline for achievement. Someone in the workshop should be tasked with taking minutes of key points agreed, and key tasks for action. These should be distributed quickly after the workshop to show who is doing what by when. The objectives and hidden agendas which were noted at the beginning of the day should be reviewed to check that all are happy that the objectives were met. If they were not met, then another workshop should be scheduled with any additional preparatory work agreed.

So much for a detailed consideration of how to run a workshop! The facilitator is key – if the facilitator is good, then results will ensue. If he or she is not, then the workshop can quickly disintegrate. The workshops come into their own during the first stage of the change process, 'Know what you want'. They can also be used by the project teams during the second stage, 'Make a plan'. Because so much analysis is needed during the first stage, and there will be the need for discussion and action, it is best to break the workshops up over a period of time. As they will involve senior/middle managers, one should not forget there is still an organisation to run. A suggested workshop schedule (showing inputs and outputs) is summarised in Figure 7.4.

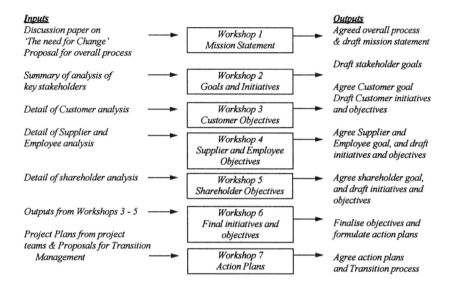

Figure 7.4 Possible workshop sequence for business re-engineering programme.

The summary above assumes a major Business Re-engineering programme for an organisation. Let's look briefly at each workshop. Overall you're looking at a minimum of 10–12 days spent in workshops, with many more days in between doing the analysis and preparation. The overall output for the workshops are the 'Framework for Success' and the detailed project plans. Leave good gaps between the workshops to accommodate the time needed for analysis and subsequent preparation of workshop inputs and outputs. Possible details of each workshop is as follows:

■ **Workshop 1 – 1 day**. Participants need to have received a paper on the need for change, and a paper on the proposed process for change. The aim of this workshop is to create dissatisfaction with the status quo, and create the desire for change. It is also aimed at gaining agreement on *how* the change will occur (what the process will be), rather than talking in too much detail about what needs to occur (which will be covered by future workshops). The teams to do the analysis on the stakeholders will be agreed, as well as the timetable for the first stage of the change process, 'Know what you want'. The output from this workshop should be a document stating the agreed need for change, the process of change and the draft mission statement. A draft values statement can also be drawn up. These statements can be refined during subsequent workshops. Building a 'Framework for Success' is an iterative process.

- **Workshop 2 – 2 days**. The outline analysis of the stakeholders, with key issues, should be distributed to participants beforehand, with summary presentations used to spark debate in the workshop. The mission statement can be validated in light of the analysis done after the first workshop, and the broad stakeholder goals can be agreed. The analysis needed to further clarify the goals and their supporting initiatives and objectives should also be agreed, as well as who will carry it out and by when (normally in time to prepare the inputs for the next three workshops). The output of this workshop should be the validated mission statement and the supporting draft goal statements.
- **Workshop 3 – 1–2 Days**. The participants of this workshop should have the detailed analysis needed to validate the draft customer goal agreed in the previous workshop, as well to develop the more detailed initiatives and objectives. The workshop should then discuss and agree the initiatives and objectives, as well as identify in outline the resources (i.e. warm bodies!) and the project managers needed to deliver the supporting projects. The output from this workshop should be the validated goal, initiatives and draft objectives for use by the project teams to plan the detail.
- **Workshop 4 – 2 days**. This should follow the same detail for workshop 3, but instead cover the supplier and employee goals, initiatives and objectives.
- **Workshop 5 – 1 day**. Again this should follow the detail of workshop 3, covering the shareholder goal, initiatives and objectives. At the end of this workshop, all the goals, initiatives and objectives should be checked to ensure that there is consistency between them.
- **Workshop 6 – 1–2 days**. Project planning. This will probably consist of a series of separate workshops run with the project managers and their project teams to finalise the project plans, which should be used for the input for the final workshop. They can be run concurrently with project management training.
- **Workshop 7 – 1–2 days**. The project plans should be agreed and a timetable for their implementation finalised. It may be necessary to phase the implementation of the projects if there are too many of them. The details of transition management structure should also be finalised, with the establishment of the transition management team and the PCC team.

At the end of the series of these workshops, the change programme will be ready to launch. If it is a large programme which will affect many people, then arrange a launch event (a mixture of communication and social interaction) for all the managers who will be involved and affected. This will ensure that the programme gets off to a solid start, and also acts as a venue to demonstrate through presentations the commitment and quality of thinking behind the programme.

4. THE USE OF FACILITATORS

Facilitators are trained and skilled individuals who can work, with a team to help them, with process skills get to an agreed output. The use of facilitators in workshops was discussed above. However, they have a lot of other uses. In Cigna they were used to help newly formed cross-functional process teams perform, and in Digital South Pacific the core re-engineering team found an external facilitator useful to help them get through the 'checkout zone' (see Part 2). Facilitation is a skill, and people with the right basic attributes can be trained. You can also use external facilitators (sometimes vital due to the political sensitivity of what is being discussed by the group which is being facilitated). Facilitators help a group/team by fulfilling four key roles, summarised in Figure 7.5.

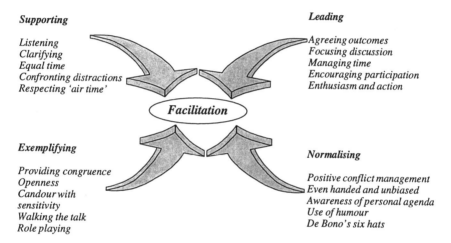

Figure 7.5 The art of facilitation.

A more detailed description of facilitator skills and roles can be found in Part 3, Appendix 1, section 6.

5. THE USE OF TRAINING SEMINARS

You can see that the majority of activity during the first two stages of the change process is spent researching, preparing data and drawing conclusions, discussing the findings in workshops and making detailed action plans using project management techniques. Much of this activity will involve a variety of people who will be involved in this sort of work for the first time in their lives. Although much can be gained from enthusiasm, it is unfair to expect people to produce good results if they do not have the necessary technical skills. Short 1–2 day training seminars can be used to supplement the process. For example, analysis using the techniques outlined in Part 3, Appendix 1 will need some training to ensure that those using the techniques do not waste time. These seminars can be linked directly to the research undertaken, and one can normally arrange short-term contracts with consultants or a business school to assist in the research process and deliver the training. The project managers should be trained in project management techniques either before or while they draw up their action plans. The importance of quality planning has already been stressed – giving people the skills to develop quality plans reduces the risk of failure.

The training seminars can be held as events in their own right, or they can be linked to run concurrently with the workshops. If this is done, the time allocated to the workhops will have to be lengthened accordingly. However, it can save time to link the two – for example, the project management workshops used to draw up the plans can be carried out at the same time as the training, giving participants the chance to use their new skills straight away, and saving the time and expense of running two separate events.

The training itself should focus on the skills that are needed to drive the change process. These can range from analytical and general business skills, planning and project management skills through to 'softer' skills such as team building, inter-personal skills, facilitation and group psychology. These 'new' skills were considered in Chapter 4.

6. THE USE OF AN 'ACADEMY'

With the amount of workshops, training courses and seminars which are sometimes needed to implement Business Re-engineering, it may be worth looking at establishing an academy. Although hotels can provide the venues, the costs are high and so, if the volume is great, using one's own venue can save money. An academy can be especially cost-effective if the change programme will include a large training effort. There are benefits other than just the financial – an academy gives the change programme a physical identity.

The academy can be established using the assets of training organisations which have unused space, or a lease on a suitable building could be taken. The academy will need its own facilitators, which should be a mix of trained facilitators/trainers and managers from within the organisation. They can be assisted by outside resources. These managers must be trained to facilitate and deliver training, which will be good for their own development.

The academy should be seen as a stepping stone for fast-track managers, and not as a sideline to a career. It can also act as a focal point for the whole change programme and further on it can be used not only to deliver training, but also to act as a venue for continuous change. After all, the objectives and initiatives will need to be reviewed with new objectives to improve continually the organisation's capabilities.

7. THE USE OF 'TEN COMMANDMENTS'

It is not for nothing that there is an implied religious context to using 'Ten Commandments'. The original Ten were used to describe simply the behaviour needed to get change, and bring the tribes of Israel closer to God. Any organisation can employ the same method to communicate to all employees the basic simple behaviours and philosophy which under-pin the principles of the direction which the organisation is trying to follow. An example of those used by a large multi-site retailer is shown in Figure 7.6.

The company in question established a large culture change programme aimed at managers to help them increase their managerial and leadership ability and to respond better to customer needs (both internal and external). The company had a history of ill-advised and ill-managed mergers, and the resultant culture of distrust and disharmony was damaging the organisation's abilities to respond to an increasingly changing and competitive market environment.

An example of another company's Ten Commandments, shown in Figure 7.7, belonged to a small computer company working in the same market as giants such as IBM. They could not compete head on, but

---

1. Tell me the truth.

2. Explain what we are doing so that I understand.

3. Tell me what you expect me to do.

4. Pay me to do it.

5. Let me do it.

6. Help me do it.

7. Tell me how I'm doing.

8. Listen to me so that you understand.

9. Reward me if I do it well.

10. Sack me if I fail to try.

Figure 7.6 'Ten Commandments' for managerial effectiveness.

could supplement the giants (hence the significance of Commandment No. 5!).

> 1. Sell before you buy.
>
> 2. We know markets we serve.
>
> 3. You get one earthquake.
>
> 4. A .45 beats 4 aces.
>
> 5. Sharks don't eat pilot fish.
>
> 6. A handshake is a contract.
>
> 7. The boss is busy, so be the boss.
>
> 8. Fixed costs are nixed costs.
>
> 9. Share profits, don't hoard perks.
>
> 10. Use the network, don't hold cards.

Figure 7.7 A computer company's 'Ten Commandments'.

And just to give you some more, in Figure 7.8 are a couple of others.

A major conglomerate	*An equipment manufacturer*
1. We can do anything we really want to.	1. We lead in technology.
2. We're no. 1 or no. 2 in our served markets.	2. We're proud of our products and charge accordingly.
3. We are better than the best in the eyes of our customers.	3. We own 100% of served markets.
4. We seek quantum changes, not incremental ones.	4. Everyone sells, at all times.
5. We always seek the low cost solution.	5. 20% of what we sell will be new products, or we die.
6. Every decision makes financial sense.	6. Suppliers, customers and employees define our ethics and our business.
7. We reward performance, not tenure.	7. Expect respect and give respect.
8. We are lean, agile, and entrepreneurial.	8. Bring me solutions, not problems.
9. Make it worth the try.	9. Bad outcomes may not mean bad decisions.
10. Attack problems, don't analyse them.	10. Indecision is worse than a poor decision.

Figure 7.8 Further examples of 'Ten Commandments'.

While you may not agree with some of the sentiments expressed in the above examples, the symbolic significance of such statements is simply that they can help to drive the culture and individual behaviour in an

organisation. It is worth developing your own, preferably in the first workshop which defines the organisation's mission statement. A few good individual commandments I've seen include: 'Kids don't fail school, schools fail kids' (for a school), 'If you wouldn't buy it, don't sell it' (for a retailer), and (for a distribution company) 'Shoot the guy who shoots the messenger!'

8. THE USE OF CHANGE PROGRAMME COMMUNICATION

If change brings uncertainty, communication removes it. Without good communications, Business Re-engineering will fail. Communication is the oil of change – without it things tend to grind to a halt. Communication becomes paramount to guard against confusion, inefficiency and demoralisation. There are a variety of ways to communicate what is going on:

- **Cascade sessions**. While the managers at the top may know what is going on, those below will frequently not. One way around this is to organise cascade sessions – top managers present the change programme and direction to their managers, and they do the same. The process is repeated all the way down. It is important for the messages to be consistent or, as the old Chinese Whispers game can prove, 'Send reinforcements, the General's going to advance' can turn into 'Send three or four cents, the Generals are going to a dance'! So if cascade sessions are going to be done, they've got to be done well. A central team can produce all the communication aids such as slides, transparencies and hand-outs and each manager should be provided with a pack to use. If managers are not good at public speaking, use the occasion to give them a bit of training and practise beforehand!
- **Roadshows**. Cascade sessions should not obviate the need for top leadership to get on the road and canvas. Remember what was said in Chapter 4 – running a Business Re-engineering programme is like running for presidency. And no president gets elected without going out to meet the people and share with them his vision.
- **Videos**. Almost everyone has access to a video these days. Videos can be very effective in a multi-site organisation. They can be used to show graphic details of what is happening and what the end result could look like. They can also help leaders in large organisations to project their personality and leadership.
- **Newsheets**. Establishing a glossy four-sided newsheet for the change programme can be used to give the programme more identity. It can also be used to communicate the what, why and the how of the change programme, tell everyone of early successes, and have stories of people demonstrating needed behaviour to not only recognise those people's contribution, but also to show others an example to

copy. The newsheet should be frequent (say twice a month) to ensure that the change programme does not drop out of sight amongst those not immediately involved.

The three simple ideas above are not exhaustive or exclusive – they could all be used. If the organisation is large, then you should have a project team which plans and delivers the change programme communication. They can be based in the PCC. Communication should be frequent, consistent and relevant. If you stop communicating, then don't expect the organisation's motivation for change to remain high! Some of the case studies in Part 2 show how re-engineering programmes have used a communication strategy to good effect, with Birmingham Midshires being perhaps the best example.

9. SUMMARY

The Business Re-engineering process can be helped by using a culture change programme, project teams, workshops, facilitators, training seminars, an academy and communications. If your programme has none of these, then do not expect too much! They are not simple to achieve or organise, and they do cost money. However, the effort put behind the *how* of change should help the *what* deliver the results needed.

Process is as important as substance; implementation is as important as strategy.

SUMMARY ACTION POINTS

- Incorporate a culture change programme in the process, and understand the best timing for the various component parts

- Use cross-functional project teams throughout the process

- Use workshops to build consensus, awareness, commitment and feedback

- Use facilitators widely to assist smooth implementation

- Employ training seminars to develop new skills and attributes

- Establish an academy to act as a focal point of change and learning

- Use a values statement ('Ten Commandments') to summarise needed behaviours

- Communicate, communicate, communicate! Use a wide range of media, manage the communications process and remember: actions speak louder than words, so lead by example!

8

Next Steps

So now you know that effective Business Re-engineering depends on completing four defined, iterative steps. Each step has a series of technical and cultural techniques that you must put in place to help them succeed. Re-engineering also depends on leadership and empowered teams. You also now know the things you can do to fine tune the change you are trying to get if the actions fail to produce the required results. It is important to note that the techniques in this book will suit some or all of your needs. Although the four basic steps will always remain for a successful change (no matter what) the extent to which you employ the techniques will depend on the size of your organisation, and the size of the required change. After all you hardly need to establish an academy for a small four man team which needs to change a simple work process!

So what do you do now? How do you get this process up and running? The five things to realise are:

- It's up to you!
- Get your team involved!
- You are not alone!
- Set a realistic time table!
- Strive for continual improvement!

1. IT'S UP TO YOU!

If you want change in an organisation to happen, you need to gain the high moral ground and see how you should change yourself! Only you know what this means, but at its simplest it means that you have to act, rather than think and discuss.

So on an individual level complete the first two steps:

- **Know what you want**. You need to decide what organisational benefits you want to gain out of the change you are considering, and what you personally want to get out of it. You'll need to set yourself some clear objectives, which should include how you are going to change yourself to provide an example and a lead. It could be in the way you treat subordinates, in how you manage your time, in the car you drive or the salary you pull. There are a whole variety of things that you can do.
- **Make a plan**. Once you've done that, you have to sit down and make a plan of action. It does not need to be one like that in Chapter 4! That type of planning is for multi-functional task teams on a complex project. Your plan should simply say what you are going to try and achieve by when, and how you'll measure your success. It must include a plan of action showing how you are slowly going to get more and more people involved. This leads us to the next phase of attack.

2. GET YOUR TEAM INVOLVED!

Changing an organisation needs teamwork, both at the top and within the project teams working on the objectives. The first step then is to get your team together and gain an agreement on the need for change, and the process to be employed. This first meeting is crucial, and will be difficult to manage. People will want to move straight to the possible solutions before agreeing the extent of the need and, more importantly, the process which needs to be put in place. If you get the 'how' sorted out, the process should deliver the 'what'. One reason why so many change programmes fail is because top management concentrate solely on the 'what' and ignore, until too late, the 'how'.

It may seem counter-intuitive to focus on the need for change and the process, while not discussing solutions. However, if you get the top team to accept the need and the process, then the solutions (based on sound research and planning) will formulate themselves under the guidance of the top team. The top team *must* work as a team – the road ahead will be difficult and there will be a need for real leadership. A split team will result in a confused organisation. So resolve your differences now, and get the team in place to work together to drive the change. And if this means loud debate, and some 'storming', then instead of avoiding such conflict, get the team to work through it. Without some storming, it is rare for a team to achieve its peak.

3. YOU ARE NOT ALONE!

Teamwork can be very powerful. Once a team accepts and respects each other's strengths and weaknesses, and has the skills and knowledge to drive change, there is not much which that team cannot accomplish. It may be that the team does not have the skills or knowledge – however, there is nothing that you cannot learn! And there are plenty of people who are willing to teach – so get an outside consultancy to work with your team and, more importantly, pass on their knowledge to you and the organisation so that you can get them out again quickly!

A word on using consultants. Always be quite sure what you need, and what you are buying. They are expensive, and too often large consultancy projects fail to result in successful implementation. It is vital that if you use consultants, they work *with* the people in the organisation, and not alone. This means that the time of managers needs to be made available.

4. SET A REALISTIC TIMETABLE!

You also need to have a good idea of how long the first two steps of the change process takes. A typical time frame is shown in Figure 8.1.

It may surprise you to see that it takes around five months just to get to the start! Believe me, if you want to get the consensus in place, and the

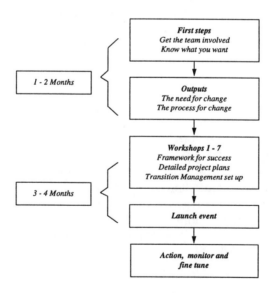

Figure 8.1 Possible time frame for a large change programme.

quality thinking and decision-making behind the action, then that's the minimum you're looking at! The time will depend on the size of the organisation. Many of the case studies in Part 2 took longer. But a five-month period should give you enough time to get 'critical mass' in the top of the organisation to want change, as well as time for deciding the process, forming the teams and bringing consultants on board – if you need them. It also leaves a good few weeks for work to be done between the crucial workshops, as well as setting up the transition management, a communication plan and a launch event. And it also leaves time for the day-to-day management of the organisation. Be patient – 'Revolutionary in design, evolutionary in implementation!'

5. STRIVE FOR CONTINUAL IMPROVEMENT!

Business Re-engineering is not a quick fix, or a one-time change programme. It is not an undertaking for the faint hearted, and demands dogged determination, patience and constancy of purpose. It is not an event, but a journey. Business Re-engineering is as much about moving an organisation to achieve effective continual change as it is about re-engineering processes and changing structures and culture. The main benefit is the progression to continual change, a source of sustainable competitive advantage. In the 1980s, competitive advantage concentrated on *what* you did to outpace competitors. In the 1990s and beyond, competitive advantage will be gained by *how* you act and behave. Do not lose sight of that, and strive for continual improvement.

6. SUMMARY

I said at the start of the book, change can be a fearful thing. If you double the difficulty that you think lies ahead, then you're about half way there in understanding the reality of implementing Business Re-engineering. The techniques in this book are not a panacea – but they can provide a map and some techniques to help you through the state of transition.

Part 2 which follows contains eleven case studies of organisations from around the world which have embarked on Business Re-engineering, and now continue to improve.

Part 3, Appendix 1 contains a variety of analytical and process tools and techniques to clarify and shape reality, an understanding of which is vital for the first stage. Appendix 2 details some project planning techniques which can be employed to help turn your visions into reality. Both these appendixes support the first two steps to get successful change: 'Know what you want' and 'Make a plan'.

Appendix 3 then gives a brief 'Business Re-engineers' introduction to information and communication technology.

Never forget, however, that logical and sometimes fancy change management techniques do little without honest, clear, committed, sympathetic, intelligent and courageous leadership. *Without such leadership, as far as Business Re-engineering is concerned, the techniques in this book are like a lighthouse in a desert – seemingly bright, but of little use.*

SUMMARY ACTION POINTS

- Realise that change starts with you: on an individual basis know what you want and make a plan

- Get your team involved, and focus initially on 'why' and 'how' rather than 'what'

- Remember that you are not alone: form teams and, if necessary, use consultants

- Set a realistic timetable, and remember Business Re-engineering is a journey rather than an event and is not a 'quick fix'

- Strive for continual improvement – Business Re-engineering is only the first step

- Ensure appropriate leadership is in place

Part 2

Case Studies

Introduction

The eleven case studies which follow are intended to show, at a high level, how a variety of organisations across the world have implemented, and continue to implement, Business Re-engineering. All of the organisations continue to evolve, demonstrating that Business Re-engineering is not a simple exercise you do just once. It is an exercise which leads you towards a state of being able to manage and implement continual change. The cases differ by industry and approach. They are presented in alphabetical order, and an outline of each case is below:

- **AT&T Global Business Communications Systems (USA)**. The case study shows how a process re-engineering project rolled into a wider culture change programme following the merger of two business units.
- **Banca d'America et d'Italia (BAI), Italy**. The case study shows how the CEO's vision of a 'paperless' bank was implemented in the retail operations of this Italian bank.
- **Birmingham Midshires Building Society, UK**. The re-engineering efforts of a new CEO and team are described. Having concentrated initially on culture change, their programme continues, and so far has resulted in dramatic improvements.
- **Cigna International, UK**. The case study shows how the company reorganised into cross-functional teams backed by enhanced IT systems.
- **Digital South Pacific, Australia**. This case study describes how the Australian operations of the Digital Corporation took on the re-engineering initiative started in the US, and started to implement successful change.
- **Ford Motor Company, US/Europe**. This case study tracks the evolution of Ford into re-engineering, through a series of initiatives, and shows how a major worldwide company is ensuring that it has the skills and methodologies in place to assist the various operating subsidiaries across the world achieve effective change.

- **Kingston Hospital, UK**. The case shows how a hospital is implementing a health care re-engineering approach called 'Patient Focused Care' to achieve improvement in the quality and value of care provided.
- **National Vulcan, UK**. The fast implementation of the re-engineering of customer-facing processes is described, which included the rapid introduction of new structures and enhanced IT systems to achieve dramatic improvements.
- **Oticon, Denmark**. This case study describes how the company changed its traditional and conservative head office from a typical functional and hierarchical organisation into a flat, team-based 'bubble' organisation.
- **Progressive Insurance, USA**. The evolution of Progressive into re-engineering is described, and the case demonstrates that Business Re-engineering does not necessarily have to be implemented in a single revolutionary programme.
- **Siemens Nixdorf Service (ITS), Europe**. This case study describes a re-engineering programme of the computer service arm of Siemens Nixdorf, and how the company changed its customer-facing processes to achieve value-added service improvements.

As can be seen, the organisations above have approached Business Re-engineering in different ways, employing a variety of different techniques. The best value a reader can get from this Part is to read the cases, understand *how* the changes were achieved, and 'cherry pick' ideas and techniques to suit their own individual circumstances. Together with a knowledge of the other tools and techniques described elsewhere in this book, the reader will be able to understand how to undertake Practical Business Re-engineering to achieve effective change.

1

AT&T Global Business Communications Systems

INTRODUCTION

AT&T needs little introduction. The company can trace its roots back to the invention of the telephone by Alexander Graham Bell, and was incorporated in 1885. Before the divestment of Bell Telephone Companies at the end of 1983, the company had grown to more than 1 million employees. In 1989, AT&T reorganised into some 20 business units, and currently employs over 300,000 people with operations in more than 50 countries. This case study is about one of AT&T's business units.

Global Business Communications Systems (GBCS) is the business unit of AT&T which specialises in selling, installing and servicing PBX telephone switching systems as well as other communications systems, such as voice processing, to businesses worldwide. The organisation currently has sales in excess of $3 billion, and a total staff of nearly 25,000. If the unit was an independent business, it would rank as a Fortune 140 company. The GBCS of today was formed by merging two previous business units, Business Communication Systems (BCS) and General Business Systems (GBS), in 1992. BCS served clients with large systems needs and GBS served clients with smaller systems needs. The re-engineering effort described in the case study was primarily started in BCS, with the culture change programme being initiated in the newly formed GBCS.

The case study is interesting as it shows how a primarily process re-engineering project became a wider Business Re-engineering effort with the introduction, well after the initial project had started, of a massive culture change programme. The Business Re-engineering of GBCS is thus really the story of two change programmes. The case also highlights how long it can take to fully re-engineer a business. Like many other cases in this book, the process of improvements continues, and many of the lessons learnt in the re-engineering of GBCS are being applied to other re-engineering programmes within AT&T.

BACKGROUND AND THE IMPERATIVE FOR CHANGE

BCS was first founded in 1980. During the 1980s, although market share performance was good, the company never really made money for the wider AT&T corporation, and despite a series of initiatives, the performance of the business unit remained unsatisfactory. Towards the late 1980s, sales performance began to decline significantly. Options were even discussed within AT&T to divest the business, but the fact of the matter remained that with performance so low, a suitable price would probably not have been realised. The company was unprofitable, its sales were declining, its customer satisfaction (measured by willingness to repurchase) was low at 53 per cent, and its employee satisfaction was even lower at 38 per cent.

Some initiatives had already been started. For example, plans were being executed to have customer calls for service to be answered at one location, where specialists could take advantage of remote diagnostic capabilities to solve systems problems. However, it became clear that unless BCS was changed more radically, the company would continue to lose money and the divestment or break-up would become an increasingly attractive option for AT&T.

INITIAL STEPS – FORMING THE TEAM: JUNE 1989

In June 1989, the President of BCS at that time, Jack Bucter, decided to pull together a joint team of external consultants and internal managers from across the functions in BCS. The functions represented included sales, services, product management, product marketing, research and development, manufacturing, materials management and federal systems (who served governmental clients). The total team numbered some 25 people. Initially the team was to be formed for six months, and was headed up by Carol Knauff. It was made clear to the team that the business unit was suffering, and would not survive if it did not change. The brief was simple: examine current processes, and define a more profitable way to operate that well satisfies customers and employees.

DATA GATHERING, ANALYSIS AND DIAGNOSIS:
JULY 1989 – FEBRUARY 1991

After the initial team briefings, the team quickly got to work. The team intended that the scope of their effort should be broad and cover the whole process from an initial customer contact through selling, contracting, manufacturing, installation, billing and the collection of funds. It was soon realised that the team would need to split into two. One group looked at 24 historic (or about to be completed) orders, and the other group did a detailed time and motion study of those involved in the process. There were two main reasons why the team work was split. Firstly, the order cycle time could take many months (even years) and so to track actual orders from start to finish (some of which might not come to fruition) was not really feasible. Some historic work had to be done to understand the process. The second reason for the teamwork split was to ensure that current practice was fully analysed. This would confirm the historic case study work, and also acted as a safeguard against the possibility of the historic analysis concentrating on a process which had subsequently changed.

The 24 actual case studies looked at the full process to fulfil orders for a variety of different customers. They tracked every single action which had occurred to meet the order of a customer. This included interviewing every single BCS employee who was involved in the order process. Once the internal process was understood, detailed interviews of the customers showed where they saw the areas for improvement lay, and what the expectations of the customers were. It took some three months to map out in detail the processes across the functions which supported each of the 24 case studies.

Some of the diagnostic work was politically sensitive as the manufacturing and sales organisation did not in fact report through to BCS – they were part of the wider AT&T organisation. The exercise also provided benchmark figures against which future progress could be measured. These figures included customer satisfaction and employee satisfaction, as well as the cycle times, profitability and efficiency of current processes.

The time and motion study involved team members joining those involved in the process, and studied in detail how they actually spent their time in their respective work centres. This activity based analysis included sitting with account executives, travelling with installation engineers and looking at the manufacturing processes. Some 300 person days of observation were used to confirm the data from the case studies.

Although split into two, the two sub-teams remained in touch as they were co-located for most of the time. This co-location physically moved a few times over the six months, and the team worked from a variety of sites in New Jersey, Boston, Denver and Seattle.

Three main problems of the current process surfaced:

- **Rework.** Each order resulted in a large amount of rework, and the whole process was thus manifestly inefficient. This was due to a variety of reasons. Because so many people and different departments were involved in the process, no one took ownership. This was especially frustrating for customers as there was no clear, knowledgeable, single point of contact. Actions by individuals upstream often resulted in unnecessary work downstream. In addition to the lack of clear control, the manufacturing delivery cycle was too long and the in-house distribution was not efficient. On top of all of this, the product was fully specified when the customer and account executive agreed on a deal. Since months (up to a year) passed between the specification and delivery, customer needs often changed dramatically, resulting in a large amount of rework. And when installations occurred, they generally did not fully meet the customer needs, which resulted in a large amount of customer dissatisfaction.
- **Profitability.** Although those involved believed the cases were profitable, in fact only a few of the 24 actually were. Front-line employees were insensitive to profitability. It was only at President level that full profit accountability was held. The systems were not geared up for reporting profitability. This was symptomatic of an organisation whose roots were based in a public utility. The situation was compounded by sales teams who were rewarded when they satisfied customers, whatever the cost.
- **Indirect expenses.** The lack of clear profit accountability was not helped by the degree of excessive indirect expenses. The team discovered that headquarters and centralised support services were used to sell and install the systems, and so even if direct sales and provisioning expenses were under control, overheads contributed to the level of unprofitability.

The team identified a series of recommendations, at a high level. These included orders being shipped direct, contract value to equal invoice value, a clear project management process across the functions, more technical orientation in account executives, and a focus only on profitable business (which would mean sharing financial information a lot wider than under current practice). Manufacturing was recommended to move towards Just In Time (JIT) operation, and distribution was to become outsourced. In addition to the recommendations by the process analysis team, Jack Bucter was convinced that the company should have its own dedicated PBX sales team.

Between November 1989 and February 1990, the team made several presentations to various groups of management to share their findings and initial conclusions. In early 1990 it was decided to take the recommendations, design the detail and try the new process in a pilot site.

PROCESS RE-ENGINEERING DESIGN:
MARCH–SEPTEMBER 1990

The core team was changed, to release people back to the business and also to have an injection of fresh new blood. New skills were going to be needed for the detailed re-design, and in addition many of the team members had been working stringent hours away from families for long periods time. Glenn Hazard took over the lead of the team, and some 50 per cent of the original 25 were changed. The cross-functionality of the team was maintained, with representatives from information systems and training added. Many new members brought in were from different levels. The team thus included many of the 'doers' rather than just the managers. The consultants were retained. Those who left the team found themselves to be a rare breed back in the day-to-day running of the company. Their time away had turned them from functional specialists into generalists having a sound understanding of how the whole process worked. They saw that not many had that knowledge, and they found it frustrating to have to wait for the process changes.

The team relocated again, this time to San Francisco, where it had been decided to run the first pilot. The San Francisco office also covered Sacramento and San José, but the first pilot was focused on San Francisco. The team redesigned the process, working closely with the San Francisco location. They split up responsibilities within their team for various parts of the redesign, and worked for the next few months to come up with a faster, cheaper and better quality process. They were helped by the news that the company was to get its own sales team, and an AT&T veteran, Pat Russo, was given the task to build this up. She worked closely with Glenn Hazard and the redesign team.

The re-engineering team realised that one of the major tasks was to shorten the lapsed time between customer commitment and final installation. Manufacturing processes were redesigned to encompass a JIT approach. Distribution was outsourced. A new role – project manager – was created to estimate costs for each job and manage it to completion. Hand-offs were minimised, and reduced from twelve to three. The redesign included customer action, with more training up front to ensure that the customer fully appreciated his or her needs earlier on in the process. In addition, the installation process was simplified: instead of ordering phones which were set up differently for each employee of the customer, PC-based software was used to allow individual phone feature selection to occur when the customer's employees understood the phone system better and could fine tune their own phones to meet their own individual needs. It was anticipated that the changes would reduce typical cycle times from three months to three weeks.

PILOTING THE NEW DESIGN:
SEPTEMBER 1990 – APRIL 1991

By August 1990 the new design was complete. The pilot started in September 1990, and its aim was to determine if the newly designed process had the impact expected, as well as to fine tune and eradicate any bugs. People who had worked in the process in different functions in isolation were brought together. Job responsibilities and skills requirements changed dramatically, and substantial effort was spent developing training programmes and job aids to help people understand and be more effective at their jobs. This included, for example, professional project management training, and also giving account executives who made the sales more technical understanding of their products. Existing IT systems were augmented and redesigned to simplify configuration and order entry, estimate and track profit, and support the new project management discipline.

The team then concentrated on fine tuning and preparing for roll-out. As far as fine tuning was concerned there were opportunities for improvement. The team was visited by one of the managers from the headquarters quality organisation, who pointed out that the team had been so focused on their own individual part of the redesign that they had not pulled the whole process together in a very coherent way. Using quality improvement techniques from the corporate quality department, the team was able to tighten up the new processes even more. New sub-teams, organised around sub-processes, developed end-to-end process training and embedded continuous improvement steps into the final process design.

PREPARING AND IMPLEMENTING THE ROLL-OUT:
APRIL 1991 – APRIL 1992

Apart from the fine tuning in late 1990 and early 1991, the team planned the roll-out of the new PBX sales and installation process. The roll-out process would take five months per region to be repeated across seven regions, covering two regions at a time. A total of 20 offices would be covered, each with 100 people. Each regional roll-out would be supported by a specialist IT team and a process team (each numbering 3–4 people). Three such process teams were formed, drawn from the redesign team. An overall core team provided coordination.

Management commitment, conviction and courage were critical to roll-out. This commitment started with the President. In addition, the new head of sales and service, Pat Russo, ensured that her managers were clear that roll-out would occur, and she made successful implementation a key measure for her field managers. To allow resources to be released (at a possible cost to current operations) budget dispensation was granted. In the end this dispensation was not needed as, although suffering a slight dip during the implementation, the improvements gained by the new process quickly ensured yearly budgets were not adversely affected.

The roll-out plan was tested on the two remaining offices which reported into San Francisco, namely Sacramento and San José, in April 1991. The teams then rolled out the new design into the other regions in 1991 and early 1992. The implementation was assisted by a variety of techniques. Communications were helped by a video, where the new sales and services VP, Pat Russo, talked through the new processes. That a new functional head could display so much detailed knowledge of the whole process itself sent strong messages to all employees. In addition to Pat Russo, employees working the new process in the pilots also gave testament to the advantages of the changes. Everyone was kept informed through cascade sessions, and the company in-house magazine. Communication was key, and Glenn Hazard had full-time resources dedicated to communication alone.

Within each region a small transition management team was set up, headed by a regional transition manager. The regional teams included 'branch experts' trained up in detail by the process team and able to give their branches support to follow up the branch training programme. To minimise disruption, the training within the branches was conducted targeting groups of employees at a time, rather than training everyone at once. Although there was a degree of resistance, the success of the pilots and the support from the top overcame any blockages. IT systems played an increasingly important role in supporting the new processes. The mainframe systems became more open and user-friendly by using UNIX systems, enabling access by field-based people across functions. After initial roll-out, the systems were enhanced further towards client/server networks and laptops for those with customer interface responsibilities.

The pilot was beginning to show good results. The average cycle time was cut from three months to three weeks. The costs of the process were reduced by 30 per cent. Customers were very pleased with the new approach to project management, and employees felt better with their new value-added roles. These successes helped overcome some cynicism in the regions which had yet to be transferred. The transition was not easy, and had to include a transition design to allow those parts of the company which had been process re-engineered to operate with those which had yet to be changed. This transitional design was done by the core design team, who had to implement it as the new process was rolling out.

During 1991, the president Jack Bucter moved onto another business unit in AT&T, and was replaced by Jerre Stead. Jerre Stead came from outside AT&T, having been recruited by the AT&T Chairman, Robert Allen. Losing their main sponsor could have been a disaster for Glenn Hazard and his team, but Jerre Stead was impressed with what he saw of the process re-engineering project, and gave it his full support. At that time AT&T was planning the merger of BCS and GBS. It was clear that with the birth of a new business unit, and the effective business process re-engineering of BCS, the opportunity to Business Re-engineer the new GBCS would be a natural evolution. Jerre Stead kicked up the change programme efforts a few notches. He realised that not only the processes of the company had to be re-engineered – so too did the attitudes and minds of the staff.

THE COMMON BOND – 1991/2

While Glenn Hazard and his process re-engineering team rolled out their newly designed PBX sales and installation process, Jerre Stead worked with the top executive team to formulate a vision, mission, values and objectives statement for GBCS. The team formulated these during a series of workshops. The vision statement represents the organisation's purpose: 'To be your partner of choice: dedicated to quality, committed to your success.' The mission statement was formulated as follows: 'To be the world leader in providing the highest quality business communications products, services and solutions.'

The values statement stressed seven key principles, each with their own supporting statements:

- *Respect for individual*: 'We treat each other with respect and dignity ... listening to each other regardless of level or position';
- *Dedication to helping customers*: 'We truly care for each customer ... by understanding and anticipating our customers' needs and by serving them better each time';
- *Highest standards of integrity*: 'We are honest and ethical ... we keep our promises and admit our mistakes. Our personal conduct ensures AT&T's name is always worthy of trust';
- *Innovation*: 'We believe innovation is the engine that will keep us vital ... our culture embraces creativity ... and risks pursuing new opportunity';
- *Teamwork*: 'We encourage and reward both individual and team achievements ... We freely join with colleagues across organisational boundaries ...';
- *Accountability*: 'Each of us takes ownership for the success of GBCS';
- *Excellence*: 'We will be satisfied with nothing less than being the best in everything we do'.

The statements were accompanied by a new language. Employees were renamed 'associates', managers renamed 'coaches'. The objectives revolve around the 'value equation' which, simply put, states that objectives which increase associates' satisfaction will increase customer satisfaction and this will lead to profitable growth and increase of shareholder value.

Jerre Stead recognised that simply re-engineering the processes and formulating a series of vision, mission, values and objectives statements was not enough. The organisation needed a series of cultural processes that would complete the Business Re-engineering and ensure that the vision and mission statements would become reality. He selected Fred Lane to head up the HR organisation in late 1991, and gave him the task to create an environment which 'supports our people as our only sustainable competitive advantage'.

CULTURE CHANGE PROGRAMME – 1992/3

Fred Lane and his team got to work and during 1992 and 1993, working closely with functional managers, put in place a whole series of changes which, when added up, resulted in an effective culture change of GBCS. The top leadership team of GBCS became known as the Quality Council, and they played an active role in the changes introduced. These changes were aimed at linking the strategy and processes to the individuals of the organisation, and they included:

- flattening of hierarchy and empowerment of staff;
- Performance Excellence Partnership (PEP);
- new compensation schemes;
- GBCS recognition schemes;
- new communication programmes;
- HR organisation reorganised into process teams.

Flattening of hierarchy and empowerment of staff

The 14 previous levels within BCS, and similar amount of levels within GBS, were reduced to five. Managers were trained and encouraged to become 'coaches' and employees were trained in new attitudes to enable them to become 'associates'. Managers were given every support to change their behaviour, and few had to be moved. The approach to help these managers change was 'Coach, Coach, Coach, Change.' The vision, mission, values and objectives were cascaded to all staff, and the broad details of what the new culture would be like were widely communicated.

Performance Excellence Partnerships (PEP)

This is a series of techniques and processes which moved the traditional appraisal systems away from ranking and grading people to helping them develop their full potential. Full training was rolled out to assist people to learn and change their traditional attitudes. PEP include:

- a process for each person to set and monitor his or her own SMART (Specific, Measurable, Achievable, Relevant and Timely) objectives, monitored three times a year with performance feedback;
- a formal annual performance review that equally considers the achievement of objectives and demonstration of behaviours which reflect the values statement;
- upward and 360° feedback where associates give anonymous feedback to their coaches and peers about their leadership and behaviour;
- development, where individuals plan their training to enhance their own and their team's performance.

New compensation schemes

These include two bonus schemes: the Progress Sharing Plan (PSP) and the Special Long-Term Plan (SLTP). The PSP provides associates with the opportunity to share in profit improvements based on achieving customer satisfaction and financial objectives. SLTP mirrors PSP, but is aimed at senior management and is not only based on customer satisfaction and financial objectives, but is also based on improvement of associate satisfaction. SLTP includes multiple leverage with a ratchet formula over the years to ensure that long-term improvement and action is not sacrificed for the sake of short-term gain.

GBCS recognition schemes

A variety of recognition schemes were introduced which give associates and coaches recognition for significant performance. These include:

- *Achievers Club* – aimed at all associates in sales and services who meet high performance criteria;
- *Partner of Choice (POC)* – awarded to those who demonstrate a dedication to quality, nominations by associates, selection by team of six associate;
- *President's Council* – awarded to associates for outstanding contribution, coaches nominate, Quality Council select;
- *Bureaucracy Busters* – awarded to associates who suggest changes to reduce bureaucracy;
- *Touch Award* – awarded to associates for outstanding contributions to the wider community.

New communication programme

The company had an internal magazine, but that was about it. The culture change programme introduced many more means of communication. In itself this helped to change the culture by acting as a conduit for the vision, mission, values and objectives statements. The communications programme includes:

- *Ask the President* – associates can write or call with their questions, which are answered within 48 hours;
- *Answer Line* – associates can call an 800 number with a question or request for information, and they will receive a reply from the relevant subject expert;
- *Chats* – GBCS president holds informal and regular chats with small groups of associates;
- *All Associate Broadcasts* – quarterly inter-active video broadcast which can be watched live with call-in questions, as well as audio recording with information available on an 800 number.

HR reorganised into teams

The HR department team were the ones who managed the culture change programme. However, in so doing they realised that they too would have to change to meet the new demands of the organisation. To this end they have organised into six teams to lend support to all GBCS associates. These teams include:

- *Associate Communications Team* – who manage the communications programme and ensure multiple lines of communication remain open;
- *Education and Training Team* – who focus on delivering leadership training, as well as technical training;
- *Diversity Planning Team* – which provides seminars, counselling and advice to all associates to achieve awareness, understanding and acceptance of all types of diversity;
- *HR Business Strategy and Planning Team* – which ensures that HR policies fully support the strategy of the business;
- *Labour Planning Team* – which ensures good partnerships with the unions and also works on preparing associates for future changes such as self-managed teams and new technology;
- *Associate Services Team* – which administers associates' salaries, recognition schemes, associate surveys, and provides expertise and advice in other HR related matters.

MONITORING AND RESULTS ACHIEVED

The project teams kept the top executive team regularly in touch with what was going on, and in this way progress was measured. The results were measured by three main criteria:

- *associate satisfaction* – which is measured by a regular Associate Opinion Survey completed by all associates semi-annually;

- *customer satisfaction* – which is mainly measured by intention to repurchase, asked of all customers shortly after order fulfilment;
- *financial criteria* – which includes both profit and loss and balance sheet ratios.

The Business Re-engineering within GBCS was extensive, and 19,000 of the 26,000 employees had their job content changed. The improvements to date have been encouraging:

- associate 'Extreme Satisfaction' increased to 63 per cent in 1993 from 38 per cent in 1989;
- customer satisfaction increased to 80 per cent in 1993 from 53 per cent in 1989;
- project management satisfaction increased to 90 per cent in 1993 from 41 per cent in 1989;
- receivables (debtors) reduced with 71 per cent payment in 30 days in 1993, instead of 69 per cent in 60–90 days in 1989;
- adjustments (write-offs etc.) down to 0.6 per cent of revenue in 1993, instead of 4 per cent in 1989;
- revenue increased and costs were cut – in the second quarter of 1992, GBCS posted their first profits, and had turned the corner, with 1993 being the first profitable year.

The process re-engineering teams and the culture change teams between them have run a successful Business Re-engineering programme which has put GBCS back into a strong position, and with a culture which will be increasingly able to embrace change and achieve continual improvement.

LESSONS LEARNT

According to members of the process re-engineering team, the following are considered critical to the success of the programme:

- keeping in touch with the customer;
- overall strategic plan developed before change introduced;
- sustained top-level commitment from the start;
- design teams included those people who actually did the work (not just managers);
- culture change activities were critical;
- good relationships with the IT support teams;
- constant communications with all those affected.

Lessons were learnt along the way, and these are being applied to other re-engineering programmes within AT&T. The four main lessons are:

- **Constant customer focus**. Input from customers at the very start provided good indications of problem areas, and also firm benchmarks. The customer interface continued throughout the process redesign to get feedback on the proposed changes and to validate the design. The new process also includes customer response mechanisms to allow continual improvement.
- **Timing of culture change programme.** The culture change programme in GBCS came on the coat-tails of the process re-engineering programme, more by dint of circumstance than by design. Teams working in other AT&T business units are making sure that the culture change runs alongside the process re-engineering effort.
- **Timing of inclusion of IT support team.** The process re-design team only included the IT support team well into the re-design process. It is now considered that the IT support people should be involved right from the start. However, the IT support needs to be open-minded and not tied to the concept of having to develop bespoke systems to solve problems. In the end 90 per cent of the needs of the new process could be met by off-the-shelf solutions.
- **Human cost to change teams.** The process re-engineering team worked very hard. This had a cost in terms of quality of life for those involved. As the head of the team put it: 'People worked 18 hours a day, often seven days a week. They lived away from their families for three years. If I had to do it over again, I would never allow some of the sacrifices that took place.'

Like many of the organisations in this Part, AT&T Global Business Communications Systems has learnt a lot from their Business Re-engineering activities. These lessons are being passed on to the wider AT&T corporation. GBCS have also learnt that change is not something you do just once – having gone through the process re-engineering and the culture change, they have learnt how to continually change to keep ahead in a competitive market.

SUMMARY

- **Know what you want**
  - Clear case for change.
  - Use of cross-functional change teams to formulate details.
  - Change teams include 'doers', not just managers.
  - Clear communication of vision, mission, values and objectives.
  - Agreement on 3–5 year strategic plan.

- **Make a plan**
  - Use of pilot to plan detail.
  - Cross-functional change team changed to reflect skills need.
  - Roll-out plan using standard template.
  - HR teams focus on HR policies to support cultural change.
  - Fully agreed deliverables from IT and training with agreed budgets.

- **Do it**
  - Pilot success used to overcome cynicism.
  - Constant and consistent leadership support.
  - Use of transition teams at overall and regional levels.
  - 'Communicate, Communicate, Communicate.'
  - Training of associates and coaches in their new roles, and in the new process overall.
  - Change teams offer support, expertise, encouragement and advice.
  - 'Coach, Coach, Coach, Change.'
  - Stick to initial design – consider changes after roll-out and learning curve cleared.
  - Empower ongoing process owners.

- **Monitor**
  - Frequent team meetings and updates.
  - Constant checking with customers.
  - Associate satisfaction is a key measure.
  - Other non-financial benchmarks used (as well as financial).

2

Banca d'America e d'Italia

INTRODUCTION

Banca d'America e d'Italia (BAI) dates back to 1918, when it was established as the Banca dell'Italia Meridionale. It gained its current name in 1923, and grew slowly to become one of the larger retail banks in Italy, with some $8.5 billion in assets and some 97 branches by the late 1980s. The branches were spread across Italy, over a 1,500 kilometre distance from Milan to Sicily. Owned primarily by the Bank of America, BAI provided the parent with a useful cash stream. In the late 1980s the bank was sold to Deutsche Bank, which now owns more than 98 per cent of the equity.

The case is interesting as it shows the detail of analysis and pre-planning the change teams went through to ensure a smooth implementation.

BACKGROUND AND THE IMPERATIVE FOR CHANGE

When Deutsche Bank took ownership of BAI, the new acquisition was beginning to return a lacklustre performance. Although it had a good branch network, it only had less than 1 per cent share of market. The deregulation of the Italian banking industry in 1988 resulted in increasing competition. BAI's performance began to suffer badly, with higher than average operational costs and dissatisfied customers.

The systems for managing the bank were antiquated, the processes were inefficient and it was difficult to ascertain which products, branches and customers were generating a profit and which were not. At that time a few banks were being subsumed by their competitors.

The bank's new CEO, Gianemilio Osculati, was in no doubt that either the bank underwent major change, or it would suffer.

The CEO had a sound background in managing change and introducing new IT systems to improve performance, having being a senior member of the consulting firm McKinsey. The knowledge he had gained in the mid 1980s with this firm (specifically concerning the introduction of IT and change into banks) was to prove invaluable for BAI.

FIRST STEPS – FORMULATING A FUTURE VISION: FIRST HALF 1988

The CEO recruited a top-level manager to champion the change. Andrea Giochetta had a similar background to the CEO, and had experience of managing change which was underpinned by new IT systems in banking. Together they formed a cross-functional multi-disciplinary team of some seven managers. These included three business analysts, two IT specialists, a software development manager and an accountant. They also brought in outside consultants to join the team and bring some complementary analytical and process skills.

The team first conducted an overall strategic review of the bank, focusing on customer needs, the competitive environment and the current ability of the bank to compete. They found that 90 per cent of their problems lay in the lack of any coherent information strategy, and that this presented a unique opportunity to completely re-engineer the branch processes to create a paperless bank. With over 80 per cent of the bank's revenues coming from the retail operations in the branches, the re-engineering effort had a strong chance of improving the bottom line dramatically.

By the end of the first half of 1988 the team had a very clear vision of the paperless bank that they wanted to achieve. The aim was for any teller in the branch to serve the needs of any customer, and that all transactions would need to be completed to the customer's satisfaction before he or she left the branch.

PLANNING THE IMPLEMENTATION IN DETAIL – SECOND HALF 1988 TO MID 1989

The central team of consultants/internal managers expanded. Two teams were formed, one focusing on designing the new branch organisation and processes, and one focusing on designing the new IT systems needed to support the processes. Needless to say they worked closely together. They did some detailed analysis including a detailed customer survey, as well as a value chain analysis, which helped in the detailed process redesign.

The organisation and process redesign team grouped every customer transaction into ten families. This included, for example, deposits, withdrawals, foreign exchange, money orders, etc. The analysis also covered in-house processes including closing branch balances and stocks/bonds closure. They then process mapped each current process including all of the inputs and outputs needed. With such detailed process and input/output mapping the team then worked to simplify the process. For example, the cheque deposit transaction required 64 process steps, nine forms and 14 accounts. It was simplified to 25 process steps, two forms and two accounts. The team worked closely with tellers and back-office personnel to ensure that their facts were correct, and also to start to build some commitment for the future changes.

Whenever a product family was redesigned by the organisation and process team, it was handed onto the IT team. This team worked separately from the organisation and process team, and focused initially on information requirements and data storage at branch level. The current mainframe system was operating to full capacity, and was slow and inefficient. The team designed a client/server architecture based on LANs in the branches linked to each other via a central host on a standard IBM protocol WAN. When the organisation and process team started to hand on redesigned processes, the IT team thus had already designed a platform and concept on which to write the software to support each customer transaction. The IT team used a CASE tool to help their planning and software development.

When all the transactions were redesigned, and the IT systems were in prototype stage, the teams then focused on what would be needed at branch level to implement the change. This included management structures, training and branch layout. By late 1989 the planning was complete.

IMPLEMENTATION TECHNIQUES – 1990/1991

A variety of techniques were used to support the implementation. These included:

- visible and active leadership;
- use of pilots;
- phased and planned roll-out;
- communications.

Visible and active leadership

As is clear from the details concerning the scope and planning of the change, the CEO played a very active role. In the initial phases he personally devoted up to 40 per cent of his time to the re-engineering programme, and often dropped informally onto the change teams to see how the progress was going. He kept the day-to-day running of the bank, and the concerns and distractions which that can bring, away from the teams. By placing a top-flight manager to lead the programme full time, he ensured that he could continue to devote his needed leadership to the bank as a whole, and not just to the re-engineering teams. At the same time, with Andrea Giochetta in full-time control, the re-engineering teams had the leadership they needed to get the job done.

Use of pilots

As with any radical re-engineering programme there existed a lot of scepticism concerning the proposed changes. And the changes were so radical that if they did not work, the bank would face disaster. In order to minimise the downside risk, and maximise the opportunity to demonstrate success to passive resisters, three pilots were conducted in mid 1990. The pilots were run in three branches, and were a great success. They enabled the IT team to fine tune the finalised versions of the software prior to roll-out. The customers loved it, and so did the staff. The pilots thus demonstrated to the more sceptical that the vision could work.

Phased and planned roll-out

The roll-out began in earnest in late 1990. Three branches a week were converted, using a detailed project management planned conversion process which was replicated for each branch. The roll-out included two weeks' training of the tellers in a converted branch. After this they returned to their home branch for further training. The branch they came from was converted into the new format, with the new layout and IT systems, over the week end (starting on Friday night and working through to early Monday morning). The new layout is open plan, with no traditional split between back and front office – the IT systems have removed the need. Even the branch manager's desk has been moved out to the front. The tellers sit in a line, with the branch manager facing the line. Each branch also has a newly created securities officer. The introduction of the software was also phased, with the basic systems introduced first (deposits and current accounts) which covered 90 per cent of the business. As new modules become available they are rolled out with the necessary training. The most recent roll-out was in the second quarter of 1994 to support the new insurance business.

Communications

Communications were key. In fact BAI learnt that perhaps they did not do enough (see below under 'Lessons learnt'). A few approaches were used:

- *Leadership behaviours booklet*. The re-engineering effort broke through traditional hierarchies and required more of a team-based approach to managing the branches. Their parent bank, Deutsche Bank, had several booklets aimed at managers, and BAI translated one of them for use internally. These were distributed in communication meetings to the managers.
- *Top management presentations*. Part of the branch conversion process included a presentation by top management. Top managers also ran a series of meetings with managers to explain the changes.
- *Quality training seminar*. During 1990, the bank ran a two-day seminar on quality, which was used to communicate the need for change, and the future state vision.
- *Programme monitoring*. Every month the re-engineering teams presented to the top management team of the bank the progress of the projects and issues they were still facing. This ensured that even those not directly involved with the change teams were kept up to date with what was going on.

MONITORING AND RESULTS ACHIEVED

The monitoring covered not only the progress of the projects but the results achieved. These results were impressive, especially from the customers' viewpoint. BAI customers can walk in with some cheques to pay into their account. These are scanned into the computer by the teller, and cleared by EDI with the relative correspondent bank. At the same time the teller can view the customer details and offer them a specific product (such as a Certificate of Deposit [CD]) which suits their needs. This whole process can take less than 30 seconds.

More numerate results include:

- increase by 50 branches with little headcount increase. The recruits for the new branches, as well as the new securities officers, were from staff no longer needed in the converted branches;
- average staff level in branches cut from 7–9 to 3–4;
- cash closing time cut from two hours to ten minutes;
- revenue doubled between 1987–1992 (24 per cent of which was specifically due to the re-engineering programme);
- securities customers increased by over 300 per cent 1987–1993;
- system reliability increased from 75 per cent to over 99 per cent;
- IT maintenance spend reduced by 20 per cent;
- operating costs (excluding depreciation) were reduced from 4.9 per cent in 1987 to 3.2 per cent in 1992 (which included new businesses – like-for-like percentage in 1992 decreased even more to 2.8 per cent).

In addition to the above, the staff morale has greatly improved. The tellers now are able to serve the customers more efficiently and feel more valued in so doing.

LESSONS LEARNT

Those involved in the re-engineering effort feel that the following were the critical factors for success:

■ use of outside consultants as part of joint change team;
■ deep involvement of CEO, together with dedicated head of programme;
■ a shared vision about how to maximise the use of IT.

If anything could have been different, it would have involved more time invested in building commitment in middle (especially branch) management The centre of the re-engineered process was the teller, and so the teams spent most of their time working and understanding their role, and how to enhance it. The IT systems effectively removed many of the traditional management roles. On the one hand many processes were centralised onto a file server, and on the other hand much decision-making and client development was devolved to the teller. So the branch managers initially felt threatened. The BAI re-engineering team thus hit a lot of resistance which might have been avoided if more time had been spent training and communicating with this level of management.

The bank continues to evolve. Having gone through a period of radical change, it finds it easier to continue to change. The systems are being upgraded, with a migration to OS/2, and new services with supporting systems continue to be rolled out.

SUMMARY

■ **Know what you want**
 — Joint external/internal team to do strategic review.
 — Clear and simple vision – 'the paperless bank'.
 — Formulation of two task teams.
 — Support of CEO.

■ **Make a plan**
 — Exhaustive process analysis and redesign.
 — IT systems to match redesigned processes.
 — Involvement of key staff (but not enough of middle management).

■ **Do it**
 — Pilots to prove and fine tune.
 — Planned and phased roll-out.
 — Continued support from top (initially up to 40 per cent of CEO time).

■ **Monitor**
 — Early successes communicated.
 — Action and results monitored.

3

Birmingham Midshires Building Society

INTRODUCTION

Birmingham Midshires Building Society is based in the Midlands in the UK. It is currently the thirteenth largest building society in the UK, with some 1,500 staff, £4.3 billion assets, 120 branches and 22 property service shops. The Society is in the middle of an ambitious re-engineering programme, which was started in earnest in late 1990. With a new management team on board, the culture of the Society has been changed dramatically. The main aim of the programme is to focus the whole organisation into delighting the customer. The service to the customers has been greatly improved, with commensurate financial results. The progress so far has been so impressive that a leading industry expert, an analyst for the stockbroker arm of UBS, wrote recently:

> Three years ago they were on the danger list. They are now on the prize winners list.

What is interesting about this case is the initial focus on culture, goals, strategy and behaviours to delight customers rather than on re-engineering processes themselves. It is only now, some three years into the programme, that Birmingham Midshires is turning its attention to radical BPR using IT. Having approached re-engineering this way, the chances of success are greatly increased as the organisation is fully able to adopt increasing change willingly.

BACKGROUND – THE IMPERATIVE FOR CHANGE

Birmingham Midshires's roots can be traced through some 50 mergers dating back to 1849. However, it was in the 1980s when the Society saw its most dramatic growth, from some £150 million assets in the early 1980s to over £3 billion by the end of that decade.

This growth was typical of the building society sector and was fuelled not just by the merger activity of the 1980s, but also by an explosive demand for mortgages and by diversification. The 1986 Finance Act liberalised financial services and allowed building societies (traditionally focused on savings and house loans) to expand into real estate agencies and insurance broking among others. There was a general scramble to enter these new markets by the building societies (and also a commensurate rise in acquisition prices as well).

Although Birmingham Midshires grew, its performance declined mainly due to internal control problems posed by too rapid growth and an unfocused strategy. Several mergers brought their own differing systems and cultures. The problem was compounded by the collapse in the UK of the property market at the end of the 1980s. Birmingham Midshires entered the new decade as one of the top 20 building societies, and one of the worst performers. The issue facing the main board in early 1990 was to either change, or be merged into a competitor and effectively disappear.

THE FIRST STEPS – LAYING THE FOUNDATION: SECOND HALF 1990

It was recognised that Birmingham Midshires needed a different type of leadership, with experience of change management in large organisations. A new chairman, Christopher James, was elected in 1990, as well as a new CEO who was given the executive responsibility of re-engineering the Society. Michael Jackson joined as CEO on 3 September 1990. His experience included significant spells at Citibank and Bank of America, and he also had run his own quality management consultancy. A charismatic and energetic leader, he is the youngest CEO of any of the top 20 building societies. His task was to improve the performance of Birmingham Midshires dramatically.

Early steps in laying the foundations included workshops with the existing executive team which were run by the CEO. These helped the team to come to terms with the malaise of the Society, generate the options they faced and to take the tough decisions needed. Their first priority was to decide to divest themselves of some of the acquisitions of the past, and unprofitable products and services. After the decision of what to divest had been taken, the next step was to re-engineer what was left.

DEFINING THE VISION AND VALUES – 1990/1

The executive team during the end of 1990 concentrated on formulating a vision for the future. They included all of the senior managers in their workshops, and staff drawn from all parts and levels of the Society. A variety of tools were used to analyse and diagnose the current situation, including SWOT, customer segmentation, investment profiles, growth/share matrix (BCG model), and an industry attractiveness/competitive positioning matrix (GE/McKinsey shell). Part 3, Appendix 1 has details of some of these tools. Many then novel techniques were also used by the CEO during their workshops. For example, he brought in some papers and magazines, and asked those present to cut out words and pictures which best described their current strengths and desired ones in the eyes of their customers. A montage was built up by those present. The words which seemed to appear most were the words 'first' and 'choice'. From this exercise, and detailed research into customer required values, the vision statement was formed. The key was to focus the whole organisation on *customer delight*. The vision statement reads:

> 'By being FIRST CHOICE for our customers, our people and our business partners we will grow, profitably'.

The 'business partners' were originally called 'suppliers', but this was changed to reflect better the nature of the desired relationship. The mnemonic FIRST reflects in more detail the values which customers said would cause them to make Birmingham Midshires their First Choice. It stands for: 'Friendly, Informed, Responsive, Service orientated, and Trustworthy'. The executive team then formulated a values statement, called the 'Pillars of Excellence', as a foundation for building a First Choice organisation. This reads as follows:

1. A belief in being the best at what the Society does.
2. A belief that people in the organisation should be innovators and should take calculated and communicated risks without feeling that they will be punished if they fail.
3. A belief in the importance of attending to details in doing a job.
4. A belief in the importance of people as individuals.
5. A belief in superior quality and service.
6. A belief in the importance of informality to improve the flow of communication through the organisation.
7. A belief in the importance of economic growth and profits.
8. A belief in the importance of 'hands on' management, the notion that managers should be 'doers', not just planners and administrators.
9. A belief in the importance of a recognised organisational philosophy developed and supported by those at the top.

10. A belief in the importance of having fun through one's work.

A measurement process was also developed concurrently with the vision and values statement, and this ensured that the focus on *results*, as well as action, was maintained.

In January 1991 the vision and values statements, decisions on divestments, a new organisation structure and quality-based strategy were communicated to all staff. They individually received a copy of a quality 26-page document known as the 'Rocket Document'. This was rolled out by a series of 17 top management road shows which all but a few staff attended.

After this communication exercise, nine cross-functional change teams were quickly formed. They worked on fleshing out the details of the strategy and goals derived from the vision statement, the behaviours necessary to support the values statement, and the front-line organisational structures needed. The top-down 'Rocket Plan' was thus rebuilt bottom-up through a process of change teams and the involvement of many managers and staff. Towards the end of 1991, the executive team viewed the plans of every manager and area of business, making decisions on where to invest, consolidate or withdraw further. The new policies covering the whole organisation were hammered out and packaged into three booklets, which were produced for every member of staff:

■ *Our Strategy and Goals*. This 43-page booklet explains the vision, strategy, positioning, goals and targets for the next five years. These include financial, product volume and customer satisfaction targets with the defined processes for how these are measured. Signed by each member of the top executive team, the booklet ends: 'Let's work together to turn our full attention on customers, turn the heat on the competition, deliver **First Choice** service and have some fun on the way.'

■ *Our Behaviours*. This 19-page booklet explains the Pillars of Excellence and includes charters covering the required behaviours for the Society, Management, and People, a Profile of a First Choice person, and attitudes towards the Environment and Business Partners. Communications are also covered, explaining how the staff will be regularly communicated with. All of this includes defined, measurable targets, as well as the current scores (i.e. each of the 10 Pillars of Excellence had been previously scored and benchmarked). This booklet ends: 'You'll always have a job as long as you're changing, adapting and growing and as long as there is meaningful work for you and you accept locational and role flexibility.'

■ *Our Structure*. This 47-page booklet describes the roles, responsibilities and key leaders of the various parts of the organisation. Target time allocation for how the CEO spends his time is detailed, and also the proposed (and actioned) changes in the structure. It also includes a description of the roles of the main board and executive team. The roles of the change teams are also covered, including their sponsors and the requirements for the rest of the organisation to work with them. This booklet ends with a description of the criteria for success for the organisational structure.

The booklets were distributed to every staff member during a series of cascade meetings, and by early 1992, everyone knew the direction of the Society and how it was going to get there.

PLANNING THE ACTION IN DETAIL –
END 1991 INTO 1992

After the details of the divestments were planned (and beginning to be implemented) and the vision and values statements were fully clarified, the various change teams then began to work on the detailed planning. Each team had a top member of the executive team as a sponsor to support, guide and motivate them. The vision statement and the three booklets are broken down into five goals, with supporting 'Mission Critical' and 'Secondary' objectives. These form the basis of the detailed Corporate Plan (which is reviewed and updated annually). Each team used project management planning techniques, and underwent team building training. Once the objective was achieved, the team disbanded (or moved onto a new objective).

Currently about a dozen multi-functional teams have been formed and disbanded, with 18–20 teams now active. Each objective has a nominated person responsible as sponsor, with target timings, phasing and priorities. On average each multi-functional change team spends two months planning the detailed action of their projects which support the objectives before they actually start. The teams which have delivered their projects so far include: Roll-out of the First Choice Vision; Required MIS; Credit quality process; Personnel and Training support; Sales and service – strategy and structure; and Sales automation. The teams that are active now include: Pendeford (new office move from six central offices into one total open-plan head office); Management Process; Insurance Strategy; Competencies; and a large and radical IT BPR programme.

IMPLEMENTING THE CHANGES IN BIRMINGHAM
MIDSHIRES – KEY TECHNIQUES AND ISSUES

A variety of techniques were (and still are) being used or invented to move the organisation forward. These techniques are seen as new enablers. These are, in no particular order:

- forming the right team;
- leadership behaviour;
- communications techniques;
- use of symbols and recognition;
- objectives setting and appraisal for each individual;
- generation of new training;
- management of success and resistance;
- new corporate governance procedures.

Forming the right team

The CEO played (and continues to play) a vital role. During 1991 he focused on ensuring the top team had the right skills and attributes to provide the Society with the leadership it needed. The top executive team's new roles were defined during 1991. Of the nine original team, only one remains on the team. Of the seven remaining posts (not including the CEO), one was filled by an internal promotion, and the remaining six were created by recruiting top executives who had previously been successfully involved in implementing radical change. Of those who left the top team, one retired, one bought back one of the divested businesses, three moved onto significant responsibilities elsewhere in the Society, and the remainder chose (and were given support) to pursue their careers outside the Society.

Leadership behaviour

The CEO and his team spent the majority of time communicating and motivating the managers of the organisation to achieve the vision and the needed behaviours to uphold the values. Currently the CEO has no dedicated office space. Instead he has a laptop PC and a mobile phone. He spends his time working actively with managers, coaching and mentoring, supporting and motivating, listening and helping to remove barriers to change. He also spends time on external relations, and thinking strategically about the next steps for the Society, and how to keep the organisation focused on customer service and working towards their First Choice vision. The executive team meet regularly in a series of formal and informal meetings. These include taking coffee together prior to the working day to talk through issues and keep each other informed, as well as formal update and planning meetings every two weeks. First names are used throughout the Society, another change introduced to implement the values statement.

Communication techniques

A variety of techniques were introduced to assist the re-engineering effort. These have ensured that everyone is fully informed as to what exactly is going on, and are also designed to be two-way. In addition staff feel fully involved in the change process, and readily take ownership to ensure successful implementation.

■ *'Listening to you first' programme.* A staff attitude survey was introduced, currently updated annually (but this may be increased). The survey resulted in a whole series of suggested actions put forward by the staff, and refined by staff Focus Groups. In 1992, some 165 actionable items were signed off by the executive team, originated by the staff. Each action has a nominated person responsible for implementation, as well as a time for implementation.

■ *FIRST Ascent meetings.* Each month, the top executive team reports to senior managers in the business how the change programme is going, and the results and performance of the business. The meeting notes are produced in hard copy, and cascaded down to the whole organisation. Managers also give change project and departmental updates which encourage cross-functional dialogue and understanding.

■ *First Edition, Newspoints, and News Review.* An internal monthly magazine, *First Edition*, was launched in early 1992. In addition *Newspoints* is produced each week giving progress and news of the change teams. On top of this, *News Review* is made up of news clippings about the Society and the world at large, and is distributed every day for all staff to see.

■ *Face to Face programme.* Each member of the executive team has a target to visit branches in the field and departments in the centre. The agenda is set by those being visited, and from these meetings members of the top team can learn, face to face, about the key issues and the things that still need to be changed. About 200 actionable items are collected a year from this programme.

■ *Celebrating wins.* Staff members receive individual communications to celebrate wins. For example, when the Society won a recent Customer First award (see below under results so far), staff members individually received a letter of thanks and a certificate personally signed by each of the executive team. They also received business cards with the award logo, presented in a personal silver business card holder with the vision statement engraved on the back. Each staff member also receives annually a small concertina card which has the vision statement and supporting goals, with the measures of progress for each goal as well as broader financial progress. This type of communication ensures a shared feeling of continued individual involvement with the goals of the Society.

■ *Customer communication.* Each customer receives twice a year *First Focus*, a magazine about the Society's products, services and activities. The Society has also redesigned its corporate identity logo, and is building a marketing campaign (including TV) on the theme 'We'll exceed your expectations' and 'I never expected that'. The Society uses its customer satisfaction scores to measure customer perceptions of 'exceeding expectations'. The advertising is designed to communicate the reality of what the Society is actually achieving in exceeding expectations, gained from the feedback of its customer expectations. In addition to these customer communication techniques, the CEO personally visits customers every month who have not received the service they expected. These visits are invaluable in helping the organisation continue to improve.

- *Brand character video*. A highly emotional and motivational video which lasts a few minutes was produced, reflecting the desired vision and values of the Society. It is played as an opener and scene setter at the start of any large staff conference or meeting, and is designed to show everyone what the Society will look like when it is a First Choice organisation.
- *Open Quality Day*. Every three months a large Open Quality Day is run for about 200 staff (15 per cent) at a time. Speakers include not only staff but also external speakers from best demonstrated practice companies. Business partners are invited to attend. The theme is very much about delighting customers with superb, quality service.
- *Hot Ideas*. A suggestion scheme was started to encourage staff to come up with changes themselves. About 1,200 ideas to date have been generated, 50 per cent of which have been signed off by the executive team.

Use of symbols and recognition

Symbols are used extensively, and revolve around the First Choice theme. For example, there is a First Choice award, where the recipient is presented with a First Choice lapel badge. This honour is proposed by customers and the staff themselves. If you go to the head office of Birmingham Midshires you will see a large frame which shows the photographs and testaments of those who have won the First Choice staff member of the year, as well as the First Choice staff members of the month. In addition to First Choice awards, each executive has a budget to use to award staff who deserve extra recognition. This is extra to the current pay for performance system (which was proposed and designed by the staff themselves).

Objectives setting and appraisal

For the main board and throughout the organisation, a Continuous Improvement Process (CPI) appraisal system operates. The documentation which supports this is straightforward and sets out the job purpose, key accountabilities and objectives which are set in a measurable way around the corporate goals. Everyone has a personal development plan. The CPI appraisal process enables *all* staff to identify, set and agree their objectives with their manager in line with the published corporate goals and objectives. Their personal development plans then document the new training and learning experiences to be gained in the next year. This formal system is also backed by a more informal system. For example, the top executive team often meets for a self-appraisal and personal feedback session. This behaviour is repeated all the way down.

Generation of new training

New training courses have been introduced, concentrating on behaviours and attributes, rather than just technical work skills. One of the most important courses run was the First Choice Leadership Training. Every member of the executive team, all senior managers and all the change teams were the first to go through. It was an experiential, outward-bound adventure-based training course with outside activities and many review sessions. Each member of the course assessed himself and his peers, and frank, but constructive, feedback was given. In addition, the course created common values, purpose and vocabulary to assist the re-engineering effort. This type of training is considered vital in Birmingham Midshires. Currently there is a planned yearly total of 8,500 training days for the year in 50 different types of courses, 75 per cent of which focus on values and attributes, and 25 per cent on work skills. Next year the Society plans to increase training days by over 16 per cent, and use more self-learning techniques. All the training is totally linked to each of the five goals of the Corporate Plan which evolve from the vision statement.

Management of resistance

Naturally a programme of change of this size and complexity met some resistance. The managers were regularly assessed and given feedback on their performance and adaptability to the changes. Each manager was set clear and agreed objectives, and was also measured against the Pillars of Excellence.

Those who found it difficult to change were counselled and given as much support as possible. Those who continued to fail to adapt (about 25 per cent) were assisted with counselling and moved out of the Society to new jobs where they could succeed. Much of the resistance in managers and staff was overcome through visible communications, and a focus on encouragement and support rather than punishment. Those who adapted well were given more responsibilities and turned into champions to help coach and provide an example to those who were having difficulties. The result of divesting non core businesses, re-engineering and natural attrition has been a reduction in staffing from 2,450 to just under 1,500, a 40 per cent reduction. In fact, just 900 people (37 per cent) still remain of the original 1990 workforce, while 600 new staff have been hired.

New corporate governance procedures

The shape of the main board of the Society was also changed and now consists of seven non-executive directors and three of the executive team (the CEO, Finance and Commercial Directors). Working closely with the non-executive chairman and board members the CEO has developed a very comprehensive process and approach to corporate governance. This is summarised in a Board Operational Policies Guide, and is considered by outside experts to be one of the most advanced in the UK. It is very comprehensive and includes processes which range from how directors are selected (including Belbin team roles and psychometric tests) to how the main board sets, measures and directs the future strategy of the Society. All members of the main board are subject to the same type of individual self-assessment and feedback as the executive team and staff members.

MEASURING THE RE-ENGINEERING, THE RESULTS SO FAR AND CONTINUING THE PROCESS

Once the vision and values had been set, a detailed measurement process was designed. This included a variety of themes, the most important being the measurement of customer satisfaction. Over 400,000 questionnaires have been sent to customers since the beginning of the re-engineering programme. Each returned questionnaire is analysed and recorded, with monthly figures reviewed at main board level. This measurement process itself has given rise to change projects. For example, customers expressed dissatisfaction over the management of MIRAS (tax relief for mortgages), and a team was set up specifically to deal with this issue to improve customer satisfaction. Customer satisfaction is the major driver for the Society, and all staff are included in an incentive programme that records measured improvement in customer satisfaction.

Action is measured by regular change team updates, which is then reported in *Newspoints* and First Ascent meetings. Key performance indicators are regularly monitored, including customer satisfaction (scored by the customer satisfaction survey forms mentioned above), staff satisfaction (scored by staff attitude surveys), volume indicators (new mortgages, arrears and repossessions) and financial indicators (assets to staff, ROCE, cost/income ratio).

The results so far have been very encouraging and include:

- ■ Customer satisfaction: Up from 88 per cent in 1990 to 97.0 per cent in 1993.
- ■ Profit per staff member: Up from less than £4000 in 1990 to over £20,000 in 1993.
- ■ Return on capital: Up from under 5 per cent in 1990 to over 15 per cent in 1993.
- ■ Cost/income ratio: Down from 71 per cent in 1990 to 49 per cent in 1993.
- ■ Revenue: Up by 33 per cent from £89.5 million in 1990 to £118.9 million in 1993.
- ■ Operating profit: Up 150 per cent from £15.9 million in 1990 to £39.7 million in 1993.
- ■ Assets: Up 19 per cent from £3.6 billion in 1990 to £4.3 billion in 1993.
- ■ Staff levels Down by 1,000 (40 per cent).

In addition to the numerate indicators above, the morale of staff members has greatly improved and the Society's external image is also much improved with many more favourable media articles about their changes and successes.

The programme continues. The Society's enablers of change to increase customer satisfaction for the next 2–3 years revolve around four key thrusts:

- ■ changing and replacing the core IT systems;
- ■ combining the six existing central offices into one technically facilitated modern open-plan head office;
- ■ establishing core competencies for every role (including the CEO). The board has already been completed;
- ■ re-engineering a second time around customer-facing processes, with emphasis on decentralisation to empowered staff members individually with state-of-the-art IT systems to support them.

For the past 18 months a team has been designing the future system requirements to support new radically improved processes with enhanced IT. This is to build on some IT developments which have already been introduced (which include laptops for sales people, leading-edge software for valuations and arrears collections, and software which has eliminated paper in the mortgage process). The output from this team has formed the basis for a detailed BPR programme. It is testament to the culture change that over 20 per cent (350 plus) of staff recently volunteered to serve on the new change teams to support the BPR programme.

The Society has won eleven awards over the past couple of years, an achievement directly due to the changes implemented by the re-engineering effort. The awards include commendations for the Annual Report (called The Progress Report) by Price Waterhouse and *PR Week*, and two awards for the staff member in-house magazine *First Edition*. More significantly, in 1993, Birmingham Midshires was voted the UK's Number One company for Customer Service by winning the inaugural Customer First award sponsored by First Direct (who compete in some products) and *The Daily Telegraph*. This award resulted in personal congratulations from the Queen. In 1994, the Society was awarded the coveted 'Investors in People' accreditation by the government for its concentration on developing people. It was also recently awarded the Service Excellence Organisation for the Midlands prize, by Arthur Andersen and *Management Today*, and is being put forward into the national awards. Birmingham Midshires is set to continue the improvement.

LESSONS LEARNT

The critical success factors which Birmingham Midshires attribute to their progress so far are:

- a deep desire and drive across the board and executive team to reach their First Choice dream;
- comprehensive and clearly formed plans;
- early communication to ensure all understand what is needed;
- early involvement of staff in how the change is delivered;
- open communication, informality and hard listening;
- early measurement of progress, communication of successes and feedback of learning experiences;
- continued communication and pursuance of goals.

The main things that Birmingham Midshires say they would have done differently would have been to get the top executive team sorted out faster, and to have concentrated earlier on the HR elements of the change. It is certainly intended to tie the next stage of BPR closely with new supporting HR policies and best practice.

SUMMARY

- **Know what you want**
  - Agree the need for change, and get leadership in place.
  - Analyse internal and external circumstances and needs.
  - Build an inspiring vision and supporting values and behaviours.
  - Use workshops to build commitment.

- **Make a plan**
  - Form cross-functional teams.
  - Use project management techniques.
  - Run team building and train change teams (following leadership).

- **Do it**
  - Provide visible, enthusiastic, energetic and inspirational leadership.
  - Use a variety of communications.
  - Generate new training.
  - Evolve supporting HR policies concurrently.

- **Monitor**
  - Monitor both action and results, and report progress regularly to everyone.
  - Report early successes quickly.
  - Celebrate wins.
  - Counsel failure.
  - Act decisively on repeated and constant failure.

4

Cigna International (UK)

INTRODUCTION

Cigna Corporation, with assets of about $60 billion is a leading provider of insurance and related financial services throughout the world. In the US it ranks amongst the largest investor-owned insurance organisations, and is the second largest US-based insurer active in international markets.

In the UK Cigna Corporation has a variety of subsidiaries. One of these, Cigna International, has carried out a major re-engineering programme, which started in mid 1990. This subsidiary specialises in health and dental insurance, and associated employee benefits. Their re-engineering programme has achieved dramatic results, with significant new IT systems and, as importantly, it has turned the organisation from a hierarchical one into a team-based one with significant re-training of employees and management. As is common in any successful re-engineering effort, the programme has not only transformed the organisation – it has allowed it now to embrace change readily and continue to strive for improvement.

BACKGROUND – THE IMPERATIVE FOR CHANGE

Cigna (UK) emerged from the changes made to the operation surrounding the business performance of Crusader Insurance, Cigna's previous name in the UK. Cigna (USA) had purchased Crusader Insurance a number of years previously with the intention of entering the UK and European market. However, although Crusader was known as an insurer which had presence in a number of product areas, they did not have a leading position in any of them. As it stood, Crusader found it difficult to grow in an increasingly difficult market. Hence, in the late 1980s, a strategic review was undertaken and it was decided to refocus the organisation, concentrating on its employee benefits products which were seen as a growth area. In addition, during 1990, the main office situated in Reigate, England, was closed and relocated to Greenock, Scotland. Later that year, Cigna divested itself of its life and pensions business.

With this change in strategy and subsequent opportunity to build a new business, Cigna considered the scope for a re-engineering programme in the UK, after having first-hand knowledge of the benefits achieved by other Cigna divisions in the USA. The re-engineering programme was started in earnest in the spring of 1991 and covered not only the headquarters based in Greenock, but also their offices in London, Birmingham and Leeds.

THE 'FLY-BY' – APRIL–MAY 1991

A small (i.e. 4–5 people) joint team of external consultants and internal managers did a very quick analysis of the company. All senior managers were interviewed, including the top management team of ten people (of which only four remain today). The fly-by lasted a couple of weeks, and was aimed at identifying what the key issues were perceived to be, as well as how ready and able the senior managers were for implementing radical change. A quick benchmarking exercise against the competition was also undertaken. At the end of this phase, the team presented to the top management team and it was agreed that there was scope for change. A workshop with all concerned planned out the next stage of more detailed analysis.

DETAILED REVIEW: MAY 1991 – SEPTEMBER 1991

A more detailed review of the business then occurred. The review focused on three areas: a strategic needs review, an operations review and a systems review. The output was aimed at defining business practices, organisational structure and systems needed. A variety of tools and techniques were used. The key tools included value chain analysis (including analysis of value verses non-value added activities, and effort to duration ratios), process mapping, SWOT, and a Comb chart of competitive positioning (details of these tools can be found in Part 3, Appendix 1). An economic model was also built projecting the possible benefits that change could bring against a do nothing scenario. The model used DCF and also payback techniques.

Internally a variety of interviews and workshops were run. The management team and the full-time change team (still a small joint team of consultants/managers) underwent facilitation training to ensure the best was got out of the workshops. Managers joined the workshops and 'revisioned' the company. Inputs into these workshops included 'A day in the life' papers which described what working in the future organisation should be like. These were written by the staff themselves.

Externally around a dozen key corporate customers were interviewed. Some of the results provided surprises. For example, the internal measuring system of the company showed that insurance claim turn-arounds took five days, but the reality for the customers was more like 15. This was because the internal measuring systems were measuring the wrong things (concentrating more on effort rather than duration). Customers also compared Cigna to competitors, which helped the competitive analysis.

Around this time the first of the management changes occurred, with a new CEO coming on board. Roger Dockett was the HR Director for the Cigna UK and European operations, and thus had the required skills in culture change and team building.

The output of this phase was a series of goals and supporting broad initiatives and project objectives. The three goals of the programme were:

■ To re-engineer business practices and organisation to grow as a value-added, low-cost provider of employee benefits.
■ To establish a culture of customer focus, continuous improvement, empowerment and teamwork.
■ To implement improvements to achieve at least £1 million of potential benefits annually.

Each goal was supported by a series of supporting projects. At this stage about a dozen project objectives were identified. Each goal was clearly benchmarked for subsequent measurement.

PLANNING THE ACTION IN DETAIL, AND MOVING TOWARD IMPLEMENTATION

A core internal re-engineering team was set up. This central team was full time and recruited from both inside and outside the organisation. It numbered 8–9 people, and included organisational change specialists with HR skills, business analysts and IT specialists. They reported to the VP Systems and Administration, Dick Lorenc, who was a member of the top management team and who took on the main responsibility for sponsoring the whole re-engineering programme. The core team set about planning the implementation in detail, working closely with staff at all levels. About half a dozen projects were planned, using project management techniques including Gantt charts. These plans were handed onto cross-functional process teams, who did the detailed implementation. The cross-functional process teams worked closely with the central re-engineering team during the planning phase.

Much use was made of setting clear measurable targets and benchmarks against which to measure not only the progress but also the results. Before each project got underway, the process team responsible for implementation had a clear and concise project plan. This made life easier when implementing as changes could be readily assimilated without the team losing direction or wasting effort.

IMPLEMENTATION

A variety of techniques were used to ensure smooth implementation. The aim was to move the organisation from a traditional hierarchical and vertical organisation into cross-functional teams serving specific clients, able to take on growth without having to increase resources. A variety of techniques were used to achieve this:

■ use of pilot teams – 'Do it, test it, fix it';
■ use of facilitation and team building training;
■ communication processes;
■ employment of rapidly developed IT systems;
■ 'water on stone' approach to build consensus.

Use of pilot teams

The principle of 'Do it, test it, fix it' was used to define in more detail how the new cross-functional process teams would work. For example, the first time this was used was in the post-sales process whereby individuals were taken from each department of administration, claims and accounts. They were seated together around different desks with the simple instruction to carry on with their work. After some difficulties, and within a couple of weeks, they were far more productive. The initial difficulties revolved around the 'chaos' and 'storming' phase of new teams. They went through some of the team dynamics discussed in Part 3, Appendix 1, Section 6 (Forming – Storming – Norming – Performing, or Chaos – False team – Conflict resolution – True team). When the group were moulded into more of a team, with team building training and facilitation, they became even more productive. This approach lay the foundation for forming the finalised cross-functional process teams (which focus on a specific set of customers and cover areas such as new enrolments, claims, renewals, information requests, etc.). The use of pilots allowed the organisation to learn the lessons of implementation, and apply them to the roll-out of the idea. It also allowed them to fine tune the concept. More importantly, the pilots demonstrated the practicality of the approach and helped win over the more sceptical.

Use of facilitation and team building training

As has been mentioned all the change project teams, as well as the new cross-functional process teams, had team building training and facilitation made available to help them through some of the more difficult aspects of team dynamics. The training involved workshops and simulations, where members played the roles of either participants, observers or facilitators. By concentrating the training on *how* the team were to operate, rather than *what* the team were to do, the organisation reduced the risk of implementation failure and also ensured that everyone was given as much support as possible to adapt to a new working environment. In addition to this, the entire management went through facilitation training and they were encouraged to use this approach in their actual roles.

Communication process

Communication was key to the success of the programme. A variety of techniques were used.

- *Presentations to staff.* There were frequent formal presentations to staff by both the re-engineering team and the top management team about the programme, its goals and progress.
- *The '11 O'clock'.* In addition to the more formal presentations, at 11 o'clock each Friday in the cafeteria, individuals from the senior management team would (and still do) present the progress of the company to the employees.
- *Notice boards.* Full use was made of notice boards to communicate the progress of the programme, and early successes.
- *The '8.05'.* Each day at 8.05 the re-engineering team would get together to discuss that day's activities and priorities. They would reconvene at 17.00 hrs to report back on progress and discuss issues arising from the day. Although this was mainly internal to the central re-engineering team, it ensured that facilitation to the remaining change project teams was consistent and efficient. Top managers also frequently took part in these meetings, especially the IT director who was the change programme sponsor. By doing so top management could be fully aware of the progress and barriers.
- *'Board sessions'.* Each change project team (and now, each cross-functional process team) has a flip-chart in their open area (the office is totally open plan), and they daily plan on the flip-chart what needs to be done, and who will do it.

Employment of rapidly developed IT systems

The divestment of the pensions and life business gave the company the opportunity to downsize their large mainframe systems. They re-designed their back office systems and brought in and adapted the same software that Cigna was using in the US (which had about a 70 per cent fit for the UK), onto an AS/400 platform. However, the front-end systems were completely overhauled. A Customer Information System (CIS) was put in. In each office around the country client/server systems (based on Sybase/ Microsoft SQL server on Novell LANs) were put in. These LANs were linked to each other through an AT&T WAN. The software was bespoke and splits into two: the 'Routing Engine', which tracks the move-ment of quotes and the 'Underwriting Engine', which automates a lot of the underwriting and does 'what if' analysis. The use of IT has allowed Cigna to form 'virtual teams', teams which work together but are not located together. For example, a sales consultant in the north can work closely with an underwriter based in London. The team training obvi-ously played an important role here, but the level of customer service through these virtual teams is greatly enhanced. The new system took a total of five months to develop and deliver.

Water on stone to build consensus

A great deal of preparation and patience was employed to build the con-sensus necessary to achieve such radical changes. For example, before any employee or manager was involved in the programme, they heard presentations about the new philosophy and also (at manager level) were individually interviewed to see how they felt about the changes. This was carried out up to two months before they became directly involved or affected. Their comments were carefully noted, and the subsequent training fine tuned to ensure that their needs for development were met. If resistance to change was met, the central re-engineering team took great pains and efforts (sometimes over months of time) to ensure that they understood people's fears, and showed/facilitated them through. This approach minimised the inevitable fall-out that change brings, and also demonstrated to the individuals in the organisation that they were being listened to.

MONITORING, AND THE RESULTS GAINED

Progress was monitored by the central re-engineering team, who facili-tated and monitored the progress of the individual change project teams. At the same time series of metrics were developed which covered

Productivity, Quality, Service and Premium in Arrears. These were developed as change was being implemented by the new cross functional process teams, and used as an initial benchmark against which results could be measured. Each of the four areas had a few distinct measures:

1. Productivity: Average units processed per person per week.
                      Average units outstanding per week.

2. Quality: A mixture of:
                      Team audit results (% correct);
                      Complaints received/units processed;
                      Claim cheques returned/claims paid.

3. Service: Combination of:
                      Renewals/new business policies processed;
                      Administration post processed.

4. Premium in arrears: Cumulative reduction in value and volume of arrears.

The results gained over the past few years at Cigna are dramatic:

- claims turnaround in four days instead of ten;
- quotation turnaround in two days instead of 17;
- annual savings of around £1 million;
- service levels improved from 52 per cent to over 90 per cent;
- quality level improved from 55 per cent to over 90 per cent;
- annual sales growth of 7–10 per cent;
- operating profit moved from loss to gain.

The benefits of the re-engineering programme, however, are much more than just the figures shown above. The whole organisational culture has changed to the extent that change can be readily taken on board for continuous improvement. Morale has greatly increased. And, more than anything else, the customers love it. In fact part of the selling process is to invite the customers to meet their proposed team, and the team go through how they actually work to serve the client's needs. They explain the re-engineering exercise and what it delivers for the customer – the visitors leave impressed.

Cigna International continue to re-engineer, and internal projects are still running. The central re-engineering team, however, now no longer operates in the same way as it did. The organisation has evolved into one based on teams, highly flexible and able to change. The core of the culture is team-based, and Cigna reckons a team takes about a year to really start to perform at their potential peak. From having to nudge and influence actively as a change team, the internal re-engineering team are now more integrated into the business and assist others in the organisation to implement their own discrete re-engineering/change projects. The transition to a new culture is complete.

LESSONS LEARNT

The following factors are considered by Cigna to be critical for the success of the programme:

- facilitation and team building training;
- presence of a strong overall sponsor at high level to 'break glass';
- full-time central team to coordinate and support all the projects;
- relocation to new site (from Reigate to Greenock);
- rapidly developed client/server IT system.

The relocation of one of the main offices allowed a recruitment effort of new blood into the company, and helped the programme gain a critical mass of acceptance.

Those involved in the central re-engineering team consider that they might have spent even more time on training (although there were costs constraints), and also more time with the senior management team to help them through the changes. However, the programme has succeeded and all the targets have been met. Cigna has been awarded the Service Excellence Organisation for Scotland (and are being put forward for the national prize).

SUMMARY

■ **Know what you want**
— Analysis to include willingness/ability to change.
— Small core team with consultants.
— Use of workshops to gain consensus.
— Clear goals and measurements.

■ **Make a plan**
— Formation of internal re-engineering team.
— Increasing involvement of newly formed cross-functional process teams.

■ **Do it**
— Central team supports process teams with facilitation techniques.
— Use of team building training for newly formed teams.
— Top leadership involved, and top-level sponsor (to 'break glass').
— Rapid development of IT systems.

■ **Monitor**
— Clear targets up front.
— Designed measurement system.
— Measured action and results.
— Results monitored include many non-financial as well as financial indicators.

5

Digital South Pacific

INTRODUCTION

Digital South Pacific is the subsidiary of the US-based Digital Equipment Corporation, which has a worldwide presence and employs over 94,000 people. The South Pacific region includes Australia, New Zealand, Fiji, and Papua New Guinea. With annual revenues of just over AUS$613 million, Digital South Pacific is the second largest Australian exporter of information technology. The company offers the full range of computer products and associated services.

Digital South Pacific are in the early stages of a major re-engineering programme. The first phases of implementation covering only a part of the business has only just occurred. Although their programme is run entirely within the subsidiary, the original momentum was from the parent company in the USA.

The case shows how a foreign subsidiary can pick up and run with an initiative originally generated many thousands of miles away, and the time it can sometimes take to plan and prepare radical change in a large functionally driven organisation.

BACKGROUND – THE IMPERATIVE FOR CHANGE

Although Digital was very successful in the 1970s and 1980s, towards the end of the 1980s the increasingly competitive nature of the computer industry was beginning to make itself felt. By early 1991, the company was losing US$3 million a day. By 1992, the daily losses climbed to over US$7 million. Although some of the losses could be attributed to costly mistakes such as the failure of the VAX 9000 mainframe (aimed at IBM's core business) to achieve its target sales, the processes within Digital were not efficient. In July 1992, the founder of the company, Kenneth H. Olsen, was replaced by a new CEO, Bob Palmer.

The situation in Digital South Pacific reflected the general malaise of the overall company. The processes to serve and deliver to customers had been designed ten years earlier, but products and services had changed. The IT systems to support these processes themselves were antiquated and inefficient. It became clear that if Digital did not do something to change and improve, the steady decline would tip the company into an abyss.

INITIAL STEPS – FORMULATING THE VISION AND THE PROCESS FOR CHANGE: 1991

The re-engineering initiative started in the USA in 1991. Bob Palmer, then VP Manufacturing, brought a cross-functional team together to look at where the major problems were. Palmer then initiated a major project called Supply Chain Re-engineering which was aimed at re-designing the ordering, manufacturing and supply processes.

The vision statement which the project was designed to achieve was as follows:

> *Fast, Flawless,* and *Simple* delivery of *Value* as perceived by our customers such that Digital becomes the benchmark towards which others strive.

Each of the words Fast, Flawless, Simple and Value were underpinned by series of metrics which measured Time (for 'fast'), Quality (for 'flawless'), Ease of doing business (for 'simple') and Meeting customer needs (for 'value'). A Core Re-engineering Group was established at Digital in the USA to prepare a methodology for BPR which was designed for use by the corporation to drive the re-engineering efforts to implement the vision. In addition to the methodology (how to get there), a consulting company had been hired to produce a set of world-class benchmarks against which Digital could measure itself, and its success in re-engineering. For example, the best-in-class commodity (PC and peripherals) companies could commit themselves to a lead time when taking the order, and be 95 per cent relied on to meet the stated delivery time.

SETTING THE PROJECT UP IN DIGITAL SOUTH PACIFIC AND INITIAL ANALYSIS: 1992

In Australia, the Director of Manufacturing, Logistics and Operations, Mohamed Haddadi, became the sponsor of the local re-engineering project. In March 1992, he recruited Maggie Alexander to head up the overall programme as the Regional Operations Manager. Maggie had experience of managing entrepreneurial change, including establishing a direct marketing organisation.

Two project teams were set up. The first team was outside the main re-engineering effort and was aimed at gaining quick wins in a Productivity Programme, by improving how the current process ran. The team was headed up by a project manager and consisted of twelve part-time functional team members who were serving different functions and business groups. The second team concentrated on the main re-engineering project which was called Quantum. This BPR team consisted of a joint team of external consultants and internal managers from across the functions. The external consultants numbered three, and came from an IT consultancy experienced in implementing BPR. The internal team consisted of the sponsor, Mohamed Haddadi, and the project leader, Maggie Alexander. Seven other team members were drawn from the finance, credit, warehouse and logistics, operations, service and sales departments. They had their own room, a conference room which was turned into a project room to house them all.

The Quantum Project Team started in August 1992, and was full time. They were overseen by a ten-person review board which was drawn from functional heads and some of the top executive team. The Quantum Project Team (which became known as the Q-Team) began to analyse the situation in Digital South Pacific. They looked at all the core processes in the subsidiary, and mapped them out using techniques which had been developed by the US corporation. These included TOP, which was a mapping technique using pictorial symbols to represent tasks and relationships. They also conducted a survey of 120 customers, and followed up with a detailed 45 minutes interview with 50 of them. They also looked in detail at the current IT systems.

Their findings highlighted many problem areas. The order management process had been developed many years previously, and was focused on the more complex systems business side of the company. The commodity business (which sells PC and peripherals) and the service business, however, had grown considerably and were ill served by a process which was cumbersome and not suited to the needs of their customers. It took 6.8 days to expedite a PC delivery order. The average process time for a maintenance order took 6.6 hours just to enter the contract, and 9.3 hours to add any amendments. A new service contract took 4.2 hours process time (effort) with an average cycle time of 64 days (duration). With such inefficient processes, it was not surprising that externally the customer perceptions of Digital South Pacific were not flattering. For example, there was a 20 per cent level of dissatisfaction with the ordering process. Customers stated that Digital took too long to serve their needs, were unreliable and produced confusing invoice documentation.

The aim of the initial analysis was to gauge the extent of the problem, and the size of the opportunity, as well as the initial scope for the detailed re-designs and implementation planning. The Q-Team reported monthly to the review board to ensure that all functional managers, and the top executive team, were kept informed. They also kept their sponsor, a member of the top executive team, informed on a more regular, informal basis.

On 19 October 1992, the Q-Team presented their initial findings to a joint meeting of the top executive team and the review board. The aim of the meeting was to communicate the findings and agree the next steps and the budget it would need to carry the initiative forward. Just about all areas of the business needed to be re-engineered, but it was decided to focus at first on one of the core businesses which was growing rapidly, the commodity business. At the same time, a ten-point action plan with defined benefits was agreed which focused on fixing some of the issues discovered in the analysis.

DETAILED REDESIGN OF COMMODITY BUSINESS: 1993

During the end of 1992, Maggie Alexander spent time in the USA to share the Australian experiences with the US core team. She also picked up more tools and techniques that would be needed for the detailed redesign. In Australia she began to canvass and gain commitment from top managers to provide the necessary people (some full time and some part time) which would be needed for the next phase.

In January 1993, the Q-Team changed some of the personnel to ensure the skills needed were in place, and also to release people back into the day-to-day running of the business. The next few weeks were spent planning how the next phase of the re-engineering projects would proceed. This plan was signed off by the review board in March 1993. An internal Digital Organisational development consultant, John Harradine, joined the team part-time as a facilitator and to train the team in the skills they needed to take the project forward. This included training in team building, workshop skills, project management techniques and RAMS (which creates a process model using cards which can be easily displayed on the wall and moved around). The team also learnt how to use modelling flowchart software on which the new redesign could be carried out (ABC Flowcharter and DECmodel).

The Q-Team began to prepare for their five-day workshop with cross-functional managers to focus on the commodity business. They also worked with the top management of the commodity business to help them finalise their strategic plan. This was needed to dovetail in the re-engineering programme. The workshop was run in early April with 20 people. The current process maps were put up, and the team worked with the managers to come up with a very broad top-level new redesign. They used the RAMS process mapping tool to help build a top-level future design. The Q-Team, assisted by John Harradine, also ran team building exercises, and gave presentations on change management techniques and dynamics.

The top-level design which came out of the workshop now needed to be detailed and this was done by the Q-Team, working closely with the commodity business managers in small meetings and half to full-day workshops. Matters were complicated by the business having a financial year end in June, and all that implies for management time. However, by July the design was sufficient for the detailed specifications to be planned.

During the summer, the Q-Team organised customer focus groups to share with them what the new processes would look like, and what the level of service would mean for them. Their reactions and opinions were closely noted. This exercise was very valuable as it allowed the team to fine tune the processes, as well as gauge the effectiveness of what they were proposing. It also communicated Digital South Pacific's commitment to improving their level of service.

All the plans of the Q-Team used full project management techniques (including PERT and Gantt charts – see Part 3, Appendix 2 for full descriptions), and they also used Microsoft Project to help track the critical path and produce project update reports. The implementation planning resulted in a full migration plan for not only the processes, but also the people (HR policies), structure and culture, as well as the IT systems.

Towards the end of 1992, one of the major problems was that the IT systems applications were not yet ready from the US. The new worldwide applications for the order administration and fulfilment process were modified off-the-shelf applications, Point and SAPR/3. They were being developed and prototyped by the corporation in the USA and Germany. The Q-Team leader spent weeks going backwards and forwards to the USA to get an early release, but to no avail. In the end it was decided to go ahead, making do with modifying the current systems until the new applications could be released.

IMPLEMENTATION – KEY TECHNIQUES

The Q-Team had a difficult job. They had received a broad direction from the USA and the sponsorship for change was in place. However, the subsidiary needed action fast, and great pressure was put on them to come up with quick fixes. The effort had to be underpinned by new IT systems and applications, the production of which was out of their control. They employed a variety of techniques to ensure the implementation moved forward as smoothly as possible:

- frequent communications;
- use of a dual tracking productivity programme;
- involvement of top management to continue sponsorship;
- use of outside facilitator;
- phasing the implementation.

Frequent communications

The use of workshops and frequent review meetings meant that the Q-Team could keep the key decision-makers informed and involved in what was happening. This educated them in some of the complexities of re-engineering. In addition to this, the Q-Team put out a monthly/bi-monthly newsheet to all employees. They also used a standard presentation and gave frequent talks about what was happening.

Use of dual tracking productivity programme

The needs of Digital for improvement were acute, and a long re-engineering programme would not deliver the required benefits fast enough. The short-term productivity programme looked at how the current system could be improved without changing the processes themselves. The ten-point action plan resolved process issues and coordinated functions more effectively. The gains within a year were helpful: contract administration was improved by 54 per cent, order administration by 18 per cent and regional operations by 9 per cent. The productivity programme ended in December 1993, and was incorporated into the regional operations department.

Involvement of top management to continue sponsorship

The Q-Team spent a lot of time briefing top management and preparing for them presentational material for further dissemination. Top management themselves were thus able to give presentations to employees explaining the changes and what it would mean for them all.

Use of outside facilitator

Similar to any full-time re-engineering team given the task of managing complex change, the Q-Team had its ups and downs. They went through the positive reaction to change a few times (see Part 1, Chapter 4, Section 2.3.1 for a description of this curve). When they were in the check out phase, at the nadir, an external facilitator was useful to help them regroup and sort out their own internal issues and problems that 'informed pessimism' can often bring. This helped the team to keep its morale and keep moving forward.

Phasing the implementation

It was clear from the initial analysis that to re-engineer the whole of Digital South Pacific all at the same time would have been very risky and expensive. To ensure a smooth implementation it was decided to phase the work, and concentrate on one major process/business at a time. Within the commodity business re-engineering programme, the same approach occurred, with a three–phase implementation. Phase 1 occurred in September 1993, when the business started to move towards cross-functional process teams by moving some previously separated employees in different departments to sit and work together. This move was also accompanied by the introduction of some new functions in the IT systems (i.e. automatic fax of order information), and some elimination of non-value added activity within the process. Phase 2 occurred in March 1994, and included the introduction of a new credit management process, a new warehouse picking process, EDI for purchase orders, on-line credit authority and automatic delivery calculation with an overall information track-back capability. Phase 3 will occur later in 1994/early 1995, and will involve the completion of the new IT systems on a net-worked client/server platform, and the process will be linked into the worldwide new processes which are being implemented elsewhere.

MONITORING AND RESULTS ACHIEVED SO FAR

The action was monitored against clearly defined project plans updated using the project planning software of Microsoft Project. The results are monitored against the key indicators tied to the vision statement of a Fast, Flawless, Simple delivery of Value.

The Q-Team are currently analysing the results of the first two phases of the re-engineering programme of the commodity business in Digital South Pacific. Although this exercise has not been completed fully, early indications are encouraging:

- Fast: PC delivery times cut by 38 per cent.
- Flawless: Errors in order processing reduced by 75 per cent.
- Simple: Order entry time reduced by 30 per cent.
- Value: Customer dissatisfaction reduced by 15 per cent.

The final phase of the re-engineering programme for the commodity business is currently being planned. After that, the team will move onto the rest of the core processes/businesses in Digital South Pacific.

LESSONS LEARNT

The following factors are considered critical for success by Maggie Alexander, the Q-Team leader:

- visionary leadership, with a simple, well–communicated vision;
- use of consultants with re-engineering knowledge and facilitation skills;
- understanding of customer needs and focusing on them;
- use of analytical and planning tools for objectivity;
- full-time central re-engineering team;
- courage in management to slay 'sacred cows';
- communication, communication, communication.

The early experience with Digital South Pacific has taught the organisation and the central Q-Team some valuable lessons to be applied in the future. The first lesson is the importance of continued, uncompromising sponsor commitment. At one stage of the re-engineering programme, a crisis occurred elsewhere in the organisation and a key member of the Q-Team was taken out to deal with it. That set the programme back weeks, and the member concerned left the company due to the lack of commitment the move showed.

Another key lesson learnt is the need to focus early on in getting relevant data. Typical of many functionally driven organisations, the cross-functional data and key performance indicators were very hard to get hold of.

The final lesson is to focus the re-engineering effort, wherever possible, on areas within the control of the organisation and not rely too heavily on outside dependencies. Much time was wasted waiting for application releases which were outside the control of the re-engineering team. This highlights the problem for large, multinational re-engineering efforts. The Q-Team in Australia went faster than the US Team prototyping the software applications, and thus the Australian team had to introduce short-term measures (modifying existing applications) in order to keep the momentum up. On the other hand, the experience of the Australian team will benefit the corporate re-engineering programme as much of the work done by the Q-Team can be replicated elsewhere. Maggie Alexander has spent time in the USA passing on this knowledge, and at the time of writing, two members of the Q-Team are working with their US counterparts to ensure all the Australian lessons are passed on.

SUMMARY

■ **Know what you want**
  — Simple clear vision.
  — Vision tied to measurable indicators.
  — Joint consultant/internal team.
  — Budgets agreed up front.

■ **Make a plan**
  — Change team trained in project management.
  — Project management software to help with complexity.
  — Full involvement with workshops of those affected.
  — Checked and fine tuned with the customers.

■ **Do it**
  — Phased and manageable approach.
  — Use of external facilitator and specialist to help central team.
  — Regular consistent communications.

■ **Monitor**
  — Use of project management software to assist tracking and reporting.
  — Results tied directly back to the vision statement.

The Digital re-engineering programme is continuing, and in many areas is still in its infancy. With competitive pressures still mounting on the corporation, the Australian experience has shown so far that re-engineering business processes can improve performance. The question is now not so much how Digital can re-engineer itself, but how fast can it re-engineer itself.

6

Ford

INTRODUCTION

Ford Motor Company needs little introduction. Incorporated at the turn of the century, the company currently employs over 322,000 people worldwide. It produces vehicles in North America, South America, Asia and Europe (with factories in the UK, Germany, Belgium, France and Spain, and further facilities being developed in Eastern Europe). In 1993 its worldwide volume was 6 million vehicles, 30 per cent of which were accounted for by its European operations.

The case of Ford differs from others in this Part. In many ways the re-engineering history of Ford reflects the wider history of re-engineering itself. It shows that re-engineering theories are not so much revolutionary as evolutionary, even if the application of such theories can be revolutionary. The case study tracks this evolution. It shows how, and why, Ford evolved through employee participation schemes, quality management approaches and gradually into process improvement and business process re-engineering.

BACKGROUND – THE IMPERATIVE FOR CHANGE

Until the 1970s, Ford in the USA saw little reason for change. In the 1960s and 1970s, the US automobile market lacked a strong sense of competition, dominated by the three giants of Ford, GM and Chrysler. Although the 1960s saw a growing tide of consumerism and increasing sophistication of demand, the US auto industry did not respond in any concrete way. Although warranties were extended, there were no large and radical product developments. In the late 1960s and early 1970s the only real pressure for change was provided by the US government, spurred on by consumer pressure groups and activists like Ralph Nader, which motivated the government to introduce legislation mainly focused on emission and safety standards.

However, the oil crisis of 1974 sent the first real shock waves through the automobile industry. The US market moved rapidly to small cars, giving the Japanese an advantage and wrong footing Ford which had overcapacity in large cars. Ford's only stop gap was the Pinto, and they started to move manufacturing capacity towards it. Then in the mid 1970s the US government froze oil prices, consumer confidence increased and bigger cars came back into fashion, leaving Ford with an over-capacity in the Pinto.

By 1978, Ford was back in step with the US market. Record profits were announced, but the euphoria was short-lived with another oil shock in 1979. Small cars came back into fashion, hitting Ford's over-capacity in large cars. The Japanese had meanwhile improved their small cars, offering the US consumers overall excellent quality and features which they had previously associated with large cars. For the first time in their history, the US automobile giants were faced with credible outside competition. Meanwhile, the economy nose dived, and inflation soared with the prime rate at over 18 per cent. This hit the dealers hard. At the same time Ford in the US was suffering from a poor quality image, with hardly a week going by without Ford being lambasted by the press for either emission problems or safety standards. The situation was compounded by the problems of the Pinto, and the subsequent case against the main board directors by the State of Indiana, which alleged the Pinto was prone to catch fire in rear-end collisions (the case was eventually decided in Ford's favour). The only small cars that Ford had in the USA at the time of the second oil shock in 1979 were the Pinto and the imported European Fiesta.

The early 1980s saw Ford closing three assembly plants, with the US company actually having to borrow from the European company to meet payroll obligations. From the last quarter of 1979, Ford was running in the red.

The 1970s had shown Ford that it lacked a certain degree of flexibility and market responsiveness. It was seemingly continually wrong footed by the large car/small car swings. Its product development cycle was slow, and concentrated on adding minor revisions to keep abreast of legislation. Quality was a concern, not helped by the recalls necessary to add the minor revisions. Ford's reputation was suffering. At the same time the Japanese car manufacturers, who had moved from 'joke status' to serious competitiveness, were beginning to make serious inroads into Ford's traditional markets, particularly in the USA. It became clear to Ford that either it changed, or it would continue to decline.

THE FIRST STEP – BREAKING THE
MANAGEMENT/EMPLOYEE PARADIGM: PM/EI

In late 1979, Henry Ford II announced his replacement, Philip Caldwell. His appointment as Ford's chairman was to break 20 years of family rule at main board level. Caldwell became seriously concerned by Ford's seeming inability to be flexible and responsive to market needs with quality products. He seized on quality and it was to become a rallying cry for Ford. Many senior executive visits were made to Japan. It became clear that if Ford was going to compete well, it needed to break the traditionally acrimonious and confrontational relationships between Ford's workers (staunchly represented by their unions) and Ford's management. The visits to Japan showed not only the size of the threat that the Japanese posed, but also showed that Ford would never be able to begin to be a quality company with the current internal culture of 'them and us'.

After a series of meetings between senior executives and the unions, it was agreed that Ford needed to engender a more participative style. A core team, mainly from the employee relations department, was pulled together and they formulated the basic and, for some, radical policy of Participative Management/ Employee Involvement (PM/EI). PM/EI philosophy was based on teamwork to identify problems and solutions. It called on workers to become more involved in their work environment, and management to become more participative in their style. It was the start of Ford's move towards being able to form teams to work on problems (a vital ingredient for re-engineering).

The core team rolled out the concept across the company at senior levels (as well as union level), and this was cascaded to lower levels. The aim was to break the former adversarial relationship between worker and manager, and to begin to build a culture of teamwork. Joint full-time teams were formed to work on particular problems. The management opened the books to the unions and employees to show them the full seriousness of the problems faced by the company.

The approach, and the success of PM/EI, differed from place to place. It showed that an idea can be brilliant and logical but at the end of the day it boiled down to the quality of the local management and ability of the workers to cooperate to put it through. However, the PM/EI initiative was just the beginning.

THE EVOLUTION INTO QUALITY AND THE IMPACT OF DR
EDWARDS DEMING – EARLY 1980s

Participative management and employee involvement was great, but in itself did not guarantee quality. Ford's approach to quality was based on inspection rather than prevention, and it needed deeper surgery. In the early 1980s an NBC programme entitled 'If the Japanese can, why can't we?' impressed Ford's president Donald Petersen. The programme talked about the 'Japanese Way' which in fact was not so Japanese after all, but American – an American who was ignored by American industry, but revered by the Japanese. Dr Edwards Deming was an extraordinary man, who will go down in history as the man who shook up traditional attitudes of management, especially where quality is concerned.

Ford sent the corporate Director of Quality, accompanied by some senior managers, to visit Deming in Washington. They spent a day with him and were impressed. A dozen senior managers also visited the few US companies that he had worked with, and this impressed them even more. It was very apparent that Ford's quality systems were wrongly directed. The first problem was that quality in Ford meant inspectors and this meant cost – but factories which had the lowest cost base were traditionally the best regarded in Ford. The second issue was that the systems were geared towards picking out (and punishing) poor quality, rather than putting in preventative systems.

Deming was hired in the early 1980s to work with Ford. He never accepted work with a company unless he could start at the top, because he felt that quality was as much a state of mind as anything else, and if the minds at the top are not in tune then the chance of success is diminished. His view was that quality systems were the responsibility of management, and this responsibility started at the top. So Deming started meeting and passing on his philosophy to those at the very top of Ford. He was more than a quality consultant, as he passed on a whole new philosophy and management attitude. Quality became a leading issue, and was cascaded to all levels. The attitude gradually changed from a hierarchy picking holes and pointing out mistakes to a more open attitude involving more open communication.

The effect on Ford was radical. Previously unheard of decisions were made. For example, the US automatic version of the Ford Escort was held back by Caldwell and Petersen because they were concerned about some of the quality issues. As automatic cars typically accounted for some 80 per cent of sales of new models, and as Ford had been at that time running at a loss, the decision surprised many. Before in Ford, such a decision would have been very unlikely. Holding back the Ford Escort sent a *very* strong signal to the rest of the organisation. It also demonstrated that leaders were prepared to 'walk the talk', and maintain constancy of purpose. Quality slowly became an important issue in a company traditionally driven by cost considerations.

THE SHARING OF A VISION – MID 1980s

In 1984, Henry Ford II (who had handed over chairmanship to Caldwell a few years earlier) retired from the main board. However, before he left he pulled together a small team headed by a senior vice president to work on a vision for the company. It was the first attempt by the company to explain who the company was and what it was about. It was taken to the main board and the top 60 senior executives. Henry Ford then delivered Ford's Mission, Values and Guiding Principles (MVGP) to his farewell meeting attended by the top 400 managers of the company from around the world

MVGP described not only the mission of Ford but also the culture it needed. Statements included: 'Continuous improvement is essential', 'Quality comes first', 'We are a team' and 'People are the source of our strength'. No one present, indeed no one to whom MVGP was cascaded to, could disagree with the underlying philosophy. Putting the vision into practice was an altogether different matter. Be that as it may, another key cornerstone of Ford's evolution into re-engineering was in place.

THE CEMENTING OF QUALITY – FTQE: MID TO LATE 1980s

The effect of Deming was beginning to make a difference. The mid 1980s saw good profits and for the first time since the late 1920s Ford generated more profits than General Motors worldwide. However, the gains were becoming harder to achieve – the low hanging fruit had been picked, and more sophistication was needed to continue the gains. At that time Ford was launching new products such as the Granada and the Taurus. They were voted car of the year in the mid 1980s in the USA and Europe. However, the launch of the Taurus had been delayed because the development was not completed on time.

A team was pulled together to look at Ford's quality systems. The team was mainly from the Corporate Quality Group, and it included cross-functional input from review meetings. Although Ford's quality systems had improved thanks to Deming's influence, they were focused on the manufacturing and engineering side of the business. Ford had achieved a shift from quality based on inspection to one using prevention. However, the cross-functional processes (which included many outside manufacturing and engineering) were too slow, and not of high quality. The current quality strategy of providing parts that met specifications was too limiting. Once specifications had been met, there was no motivation to improve further. The team formulated a new quality policy which was to focus the organisation on customer needs rather than engineering specifications. Quality was thus redefined as providing products and services which a customer needs, and meeting expectations at a price that represents value. The new quality policy also recognised that all work is a process to provide these products and services, and thus the issue of quality was extended to all employees, not just engineering and manufacturing.

The new initiative was called Ford Total Quality Excellence (FTQE). On 10 January 1986, at a one-day retreat, the new policy was launched to the top 60 executives in the company. The new policy, philosophy and approach was explained in detail. The FTQE team also rolled it out to top management in Europe, South America, Australia and Asia. The exercise was then repeated for middle management.

THE EMERGENCE OF CROSS-FUNCTIONAL TEAMS: MID 1980s

By the mid 1980s the three initiatives of PM/EI, MVGP and FTQE were running along together. In some areas they had a great impact, in other areas very little. The areas which benefited most were invariably those which found it easy to form cross-functional teams and had good support from top local leadership. The programmes themselves were formulated and rolled out by teams, and were really designed to spawn more teams at local levels to sort out quality issues.

One of the cross functional teams which came out of these programmes was called 'Concept to customer'. The Taurus had taken too long to develop and a cross-functional team was formed in the mid 1980s to look at the product development process and redesign it. A lot of IT was beginning to make an impact on the working processes of Ford, including networked systems and CAD/CAM. Led by Dan Rivard, the team redesigned the product development process. It also redefined the way programmes such as new product development should be managed, by using cross-functional process teams co-located together. Putting the team's recommendations into action cut the US development time on the new Mustang and Explorer by 25 per cent.

There were other early examples of process re-engineering in Ford. The move to reduce Ford's central accounting accounts payable (creditors) department by 20 per cent, from 500 to 400, was initially enthusiastically planned by rationalising the processes and introducing new IT systems. However, when Ford looked at Mazda it was amazed to find out that they had only five people in their accounts payable department. The team involved then looked at radical re-design, and achieved a 75 per cent reduction instead of 20 per cent.

It was clear to Ford that the three initiatives had sparked off some good local initiatives themselves and that these had produced results. However, what was missing were the actual methodologies for the job. Many understood what was meant by the initiatives, but few understood how to actually go about making things happen. There was a frustration in many managers, generated by the fact that although many could not argue against principles such as FTQE, there was no clearly defined methodology to help put it in place and integrate it with the culture change and teamwork. This led to large patches of cynicism in the company at lower levels, the evidence of people who heard all the great words from those higher up but saw little sign of anything actually happening. There was a clear need to integrate the disjointed approaches of PM/EI, MGVP and FTQE into a single and coherent methodology which would enable delivery.

FORD'S PROCESS IMPROVEMENT METHODOLOGY: LATE 1980s – EARLY 1990s

In 1988 a cross-functional team was formed to look at the current implementation of the PM/EI, MVGP and FTQE initiatives and to learn from successful examples such as the Concept to customer team, and the team which redesigned the central accounts payable department. The result was a methodology which, when passed onto managers, assisted Ford in implementing the changes it needed to stay competitive.

The methodology takes a cross-functional team through outlining the scope of the change and contracting with the receiving managers, project planning and implementing change. It provides analytical tools and change management techniques, and guides the team through seven stages of process improvement starting with 'Identifying the Opportunity' through to 'Continuing to improve'.

The methodology was launched in 1988. An external consultancy was hired to assist in the design of the training programmes and to help roll the methodology out. Two courses now run in Ford. The first, lasting a day, is an overview for senior executives. It concentrates on the role of sponsorship, and the new management attitudes needed to ensure a sound and supportive environment within which a re-engineering project can work. The second course, lasting four days, is aimed at training managers to lead cross-functional re-engineering teams. The course delivers training in the application of Ford's seven-stage Performance Improvement (PI) methodology. As importantly, the course also develops the inter-personal individual leadership skills needed to form and lead cross-functional teams. The course ends with the various teams who attend making broad action plans and being committed to action back at their localities. The workshops and seminars have been run every month since their launch, and to date over 4,000 team leaders in the USA and some 900 in Europe have been trained.

MULTIPLE RE-ENGINEERING PROJECTS

The result of Ford rolling out a methodology (within an organisation well used to PM/EI, MVGP, and FTQE) was the emergence of a whole variety of discrete process redesign projects. Due to using a defined and high quality methodology, Ford's success rate with its re-engineering projects runs at about 80 per cent. Successful re-engineering projects include:

- the engine factory in Spain which redesigned the casting process and eliminated the need for an entire shift, and also improved up time on line by 15 per cent;
- the process for managing dealer claims for returned service parts redesigned with large savings accruing to both Ford and their dealers, and a dramatic reduction in errors;
- the process for selecting and testing new paints redesigned resulting in the process time being cut in half.

The PI methodology is backed not only by the training courses, but also by full-time teams in the USA and Europe which provide leadership and assistance/support for teams using the approach. They also act as a body of knowledge and learning. About 60 re-engineering projects are currently running in Europe, in addition to those in the USA.

The evolution of Ford continues. A new reorganisation has just been announced, moving Ford to organise along product support centres, consisting of full cross-functional process teams with all their own support. A new 25-person senior cross-functional team has been set up to design the detail, plan the transition and implement the new vision. The team includes the newly created position of VP of Process Leadership (which has also recently taken on IT systems from its traditional home of finance). The changes at Ford are set to continue.

LESSONS LEARNT

The case study above shows that a large organisation's move to using re-engineering techniques does not necessarily have to involve the start of a large radical programme. Re-engineering projects for organisations which have already implemented mission statements, quality circles and more employee participation, are not so much revolutionary as evolutionary.

The critical success factors for re-engineering projects (according to Richard Lindner, the head of the European Process Improvement support team) are:

- change does not happen easily without crisis, or without perceived pain of the status quo;
- acceptance and visible support from the very top is vital – without it, initiatives die;
- participation in designing and planning of those affected by the changes in the process chain is vital;

- constancy of purpose is a *sine qua non*. Re-engineering is a long-haul process, which does not work with changes of direction half way through;
- the balance must be right between short-term action (to reduce the pain of the status quo and achieve the gain of the change), and long-term risk of failure due to a too rapid implementation.

Ford has learnt from its mistakes. To some degree it still remains a functionally driven organisation – there is a frequently stated view that those who are on cross-functional teams should be appraised annually on how they do on the team, rather than have the normal functional appraisal. The new reorganisation should help to overcome such a functional approach.

Ford's PI methodology is thorough and sometimes slow. However, those who go through it once are more able to manage change faster and at far higher quality than those who have not. If nothing else the methodology gives Ford managers the vital tools and techniques to manage radical change. These tools and techniques will be the most important for the managers of the next century.

SUMMARY

- **Know what you want**
  - Understand the need for change, and ensure top-level sponsorship.
  - Keep in touch with outside management development.
  - Ensure employees are involved in redesign.

- **Make a plan**
  - Cross-functional team to re-design.
  - Frequent reviews with those affected.
  - Frequent feedback to top-level sponsor vital.

- **Do it**
  - Central workshops and seminars, with additional cascades.
  - Use of a structured, logical approach.
  - Training with commitment to action at end of course.
  - Full-time PI teams on call to give support to part-time re-engineering teams.

- **Monitor**
  - Learn from successes and failures.
  - Keep developing approaches to suit circumstances.
  - Keep updating knowledge.
  - Pragmatic actions get pragmatic results.

7

Kingston Hospital

INTRODUCTION

Kingston Hospital is situated in the south London metropolitan area in the UK. It was founded just over 150 years ago, and has delivered health care ever since. It has done this in various guises, ranging from being a poor law institution to a TB sanatorium. Like the rest of the hospitals in the UK, it was subsumed into the newly formed National Health Service (NHS) in the late 1940s. In the 1950s it had up to 600 beds, but has shrunk in size since then to a current level of some 330 beds and 1,400 staff members.

In 1991, Kingston Hospital became one of the first newly formed self-governing hospital trusts. This move was part of the controversial health policy changes made by the government of the day. The idea of these reforms is to improve the quality of care, whilst ensuring the best value for taxpayers' money. The move to trust status is a large step for any hospital. It involves, firstly, preparing a business plan which demonstrates managerial competency, financial stability and a clear strategy for health provision, and then applying for trust status using the plan as justification. Becoming a trust allows the unit to be self-governing with a vastly increased balance sheet and profit and loss responsibility. Revenue is generated by bidding for health provision contracts from those who control the flow of health spend, namely district authorities (purchasers) and general practitioner fund holders (GPFHs). GPFHs are those general practitioner practices which have applied for similar privileges in primary care that trust status affords to those who provide secondary care. Trust costs are controlled within guidelines set by government, but the managers of the units have far more freedom to make and implement their own decisions than they ever had before. This in principle allows them to be more responsive to the health care needs of the communities they serve, increasing the quality of health care delivery, and also to manage costs more tightly to ensure better value for money.

Kingston Hospital currently provides all the normal standard services that one would expect of a modern acute hospital unit. It competes for health provision contracts from six district health authorities and from GPFHs. The latter also includes the newly formed Kingston and Richmond multi-fund, the first of its kind, consisting of some 112 general practitioners based in 33 practices which have come together to form a central purchasing body for secondary health care.

BACKGROUND AND THE IMPERATIVE FOR CHANGE

When the first wave of trusts were formed, Kingston immediately found itself in direct competition with two neighbouring hospitals each within an eight mile radius. Kingston was fairing well, being in the top 10 per cent of the most efficient hospitals in the country prior to becoming a trust. It enjoyed a good relationship with the Department of Health, and a sound reputation for being innovative and creative. However, the newly recruited CEO, John Langan, realised that the move to trust status was only the start of the changes that were necessary to improve service delivery. The market was becoming more competitive, and patient needs were more demanding. It became clear to him that Kingston would need to remain at the cutting edge of improvement if it was to compete efficiently with the hospitals around it. In addition to the two immediate competing hospitals, Kingston faced over 20 more within a 15 mile radius. If Kingston did not compete efficiently, the purchasers and GPFHs would place their service needs elsewhere, and this would deny a revenue stream. A decreased revenue stream would raise doubts about the future survival of the hospital. The CEO had great faith in his highly motivated team and quality staff and he was determined to keep moving Kingston forwards.

He had come across the idea of 'Patient Focused Care' in the USA. This approach was an innovative way of providing superior quality care to patients in hospital, and involved forming flexibly skilled, multi-disciplinary teams which each focused on about a dozen patients. The US experience had shown patient care could be demonstrably improved, and he wondered whether the concept could be translated into the UK health sector. He persuaded the main board of the trust, as well as the regional health authority, to invest in a management consultancy assignment to see what the options were.

INITIAL ANALYSIS – MID 1991 TO EARLY 1992

An international management consultancy, one of two which had first-hand experience of Patient Focused Care in the USA, were retained to undertake a study for the hospital. This lasted several months, and the team of consultants numbered between three and nine at any one time. They studied both the external health care market, as well as the internal structures, procedures and processes.

The consultants reported to a small steering committee consisting of the CEO, the Director of Medical Specialities, the Director of Nursing and the Director of Finance. The team used a variety of analytical tools and techniques including high-level process mapping, patient satisfaction surveys and market trends and segmentation of needs. This analysis was conducted by holding interviews, observing work movement, self-measurement, activity reviews and benchmarking against international comparisons. The findings were not very complimentary. For example, the process to do the simplest X-ray required a minimum of ten people involved in a total of two hours of effort, of which 22 minutes were value added, and the remaining 82 per cent involved communicating, coordinating and scheduling. These inefficiencies had nothing to do with those involved in the process, who themselves were often frustrated. It was more to do with an organisation whose processes had become so ingrained they had become part of daily life. The study pointed to significant areas of opportunity to improve service delivery quality and enhance value for money, all of which involved moving services closer to the patient, rather than the patient closer to the service.

It was clear from the consultants' report that Kingston Hospital would benefit from a re-engineering programme the type of which Patient Focused Care could provide. The initial small steering group was expanded to eight and included all the executives and one or two other key personnel. Between February and April 1992 the steering group held a series of meetings to discuss how to take the action forward. They also met with the main board and the Department of Health, as it was clear that to re-engineer the hospital and implement Patient Focused Care would need a considerable investment and would represent a radical departure from some closely guarded beliefs in the health sector as a whole.

A vision statement was formed with some supporting goals:

'To improve the quality of the care provided by Kingston Hospital and ensure we deliver best possible value'.

This was formulated by the steering group. The supporting goals revolved around three themes of, firstly, improving the quality of care, secondly, achieving a flexible workforce and, finally, increasing value for money.

The CEO and his steering team convinced their higher authorities to sponsor the change. Although naturally requiring a large investment in the major organisational changes needed to improve patient care, they demonstrated the anticipated benefits would justify such expense.

DETAILED CLARIFICATION – APRIL TO JULY 1992

Once the go ahead had been gained, the change process picked up a gear. The steering group remained intact, but in addition a full-time Patient Focused Care Team was recruited. This was headed up by Margaret Conroy, who had previously worked at the Department of Health. It included three others: a qualified sister, who had previously run a day surgery unit; a general manager, who had wide NHS experience; and a training officer who specialised in training and organisational change. The first month was spent normalising the relationship between the consultants (who were thinned down to assist on the IT development only), the steering group and the Department of Health.

The immensity of the task ahead dawned on them, and they quickly came to the conclusion that the only way to so radically re-engineer the hospital was to do it one chunk at a time. (The re-engineering programme is still going on at the time of writing.) The acute wards of the hospital were arranged on three floors of the building. It was decided to focus exclusively on one floor which held four medical acute wards. This totalled 114 beds. The medical acute wards were chosen for a variety of reasons. All the wards were located on the same floor, and the clinical consultants already worked well as a team. In addition, Kingston would be the first to apply Patient Focused Care into such an area, as at that time the philosophy in the USA had not been fully applied to such wards.

In addition to the central Patient Focused Care Team, three part-time working groups were quickly set up to carry on the detailed design. Each group was multi-disciplinary in its area. The Care Group, for example included nurses, physiotherapists and doctors, whilst the Administration Group consisted of accountants, HR managers, secretariat, etc. The third group looked at the 'Hotel' area which included ancillary services such as catering and domestic management. These working groups met every two weeks, and worked in detail with the full-time Patient Focused Care Team in clarifying the detailed implementation issues of the vision. The groups also did project work between their meetings, interviewing colleagues and identifying issues. Much of this work was done by them after their shifts ended. There was frequent feedback to the overall steering group.

The focus at this stage was still on the what, and not yet on the how. The main effort was spent on the detailed processes and new job design.

A watershed workshop was run in the early summer of 1992 involving the steering group and the working groups, facilitated by the Patient Focused Care Team. The main output of this workshop was the agreement of what the final design would be like – multi-functional Care Teams caring for all the needs of a dozen or so patients. The Care Teams would be responsible for 90 per cent of the care needs of the patients, the cleanliness of their environment and simple maintenance tasks. Some of the specialist support (such as X-ray and laboratories) would be moved closer to the patients in direct support of the Care Teams, and the wards would be changed to facilitate the enhanced care being delivered. It was a massive undertaking to change just about everything including job descriptions, responsibilities, reduction of hierarchies, use of IT, refurbishing the wards and new HR development policies.

PLANNING THE IMPLEMENTATION – JULY TO SEPTEMBER 1992

After the workshop, the Patient Focused Care Team and the CEO got to work with a white board to begin to plan the implementation. The team focused on designing the layout of the new medical acute ward (merging the four wards together), and the exact numbers and make up of the Care Teams. Eleven such teams were planned, looking after an average of ten patients each (with the least cared for being eight and the most 14).

The detailed implementation planning included the full involvement of the ward sisters, the nurse manager, the business manager, a senior clinical consultant (who was also the chairman of the Clinical Management Group), as well as the Directors of Nursing and Finance. The planning also included the phased withdrawal of contracts with outside providers for portering and cleaning (as this would be taken on by the new Care Teams). Layout design and building activities, recruitment and training plans were made.

Because much of what the Patient Focused Care Team were planning was so new, there was not sufficient detail to use computer-assisted project management tools. The plans were drawn up on graph paper into a Gantt chart format. There was pressure to deliver demonstrable benefits, as the Department of Health wanted to see change implemented quickly. Some of the time scales and milestones were very tight. The implementation began in earnest in the autumn of 1992.

IMPLEMENTATION – KEY TECHNIQUES

The Patient Focused Care Team used (and continue to use) a variety of techniques to help the implementation:

- phased roll-out;
- newly trained cross-functional Care Teams;
- new supporting IT systems;
- communications;
- management of external resistance;
- active and visible leadership support.

Phased roll-out

The four wards on the medical and acute floor were merged and refurbished two at a time. Patients were moved onto another floor into two overspill wards to allow the work on one half of the floor to be done. When the first half of the floor was completed, the two untouched wards moved across to allow completion of the whole floor. When that was done, the two overspill wards were freed up for future patient movements needed to facilitate further changes. The approach of doing one floor at a time has the advantage of not only being manageable, but also highlighting lessons for future floor conversions. When the patients moved into the newly converted care areas, they were immediately cared for by the newly formed Care Teams.

Newly trained cross-functional Care Teams

The newly formed Care Teams average 18–20 members each, working around the clock in shifts of about five. Team members consist of two types: Qualified Carers and Unqualified (but trained) Carers. To support the introduction of the eleven new teams on the medical acute floor, 40 people were recruited. All members of the team are trained to achieve core competencies which cover patient confidentiality, how to assist a patient in washing and toiletry, resuscitation techniques, making a patient comfortable in bed, cleaning the patient's bed space, etc. The Qualified team members also have individual competencies which can range from how to administer an ECG, take blood, insert drips, etc. The Unqualified (but trained) team members undertake, in addition to their core competencies, minor maintenance activities and know, for example, how to change a washer on a tap. Each member is trained and encouraged to extend his or her own individual competency beyond the core competencies. Core competency training is also extended beyond the Care Teams, and is organised to include managers and administrators.

New supporting IT systems

Client/server networks are being extended across the hospital. These will, in time, hold all the information of the patients being cared for. As part of this exercise, the hospital is currently piloting a new electronic case note system (Kingston Case Notes™), which includes standard procedures and core protocols which recommend action whenever a diagnosis is made. So, for example, when the patient diagnosis is entered onto the system it will show what recommended drugs should be used, how often the patient should be checked, etc. This system is still being developed and rolled out, and when completed it will reduce the documentation considerably. It is also planned to link up into two general practitioners' surgeries in the community to test the benefits of EDI.

Communication

The Patient Focused Care Team used a variety of techniques to keep people informed and to build commitment to the changes. These were started a few months before the implementation began:

- *Large staff seminars.* Two large staff seminars, for up to 100 staff at a time, were conducted to communicate the change. The presentation was done by the CEO, members of the top executive team and also by members of the Patient Focused Care Team.
- *Weekly 'Surgery'.* Each week the Patient Focused Care Team held a voluntary briefing session for about 14 staff members at a time. The groups were controlled to ensure a cross section of staff from differing functions were involved at a time. The meetings were two way, so that the team could not only communicate what the changes were all about, but also listen and understand what the main fears and concerns were. The weekly surgeries were run for some eight months before they became monthly. They are still run today, and are fully attended.
- *Mobile information board.* A four-piece concertina bulletin board is used by the change team to communicate progress and the philosophy of the programme. It is put outside locations with high footfall (such as the entrance, the canteen, etc.), and moved when it is updated at regular intervals.
- *Information leaflet.* A leaflet was distributed to all staff members explaining the broad scope of the programme, and the details with photographs of each of the four members of the Patient Focused Care Team. This was useful for the team, as they could be readily identified by people when walking around the hospital.
- *Newsletter and Kingston Hospital Khronicle.* The team distributes a newsletter whenever something major regarding the progress of the change occurs. This is useful to keep those not yet affected directly by the change in touch with what is going on. In addition the team provides articles for the in-house magazine, the *Kingston Hospital Khronicle* (sic).

The team have a well-communicated open-door policy, and a lot of informal communication about the programme occurs with people simply dropping in for a chat.

Management of external resistance

The changes in Kingston Hospital are radical as they cut across closely and sometimes jealously guarded frontiers of job demarcation. The idea of qualified staff attending to some of the more basic needs of patients (such as a clean environment) engendered a lot of debate in various professional journals. The new approach also went against the received wisdom of contracting out from hospitals activities such as cleaning and portering. The CEO and the team spent time adding to the debate, and eliciting support from similar like-minded external people, encouraging them to enter the debate in a positive way. This lobbying helped to ensure that the external debate was as balanced as it could be.

Active and visible leadership support

The role of the CEO was crucial. He spent up to 30 percent of his time in the initial phases of the programme. He continues to be involved spending around 10 per cent of his time on the re-engineering project. The Patient Focused Care Team reports direct to the CEO and so ensures that any major issues which need resolution can be sorted out quickly. The support of the main board and the Department of Health is also crucial, and helps to protect the changes in Kingston Hospital from being obstructed by outside influences. The Secretary of State for Health, Virginia Bottomley, opened the newly re-engineered floor of Kingston Hospital in person at the formal opening in November 1993.

The first floor was operationally completed, with the new refurbishment, layout, diagnostic facilities, Care Teams and IT network, in October 1993. The formal opening followed closely after. The hospital is now busy introducing the new approach to the maternity ward, which will be ready for opening in December 1994. This consists of a new ward custom designed and built using Patient Focused Care principles. It is anticipated that the whole programme will take two to three more years to complete. The core Patient Focused Care Team is still playing a central role, with the training specialist, George Kempton, heading it up. The previous team leader has gone to another hospital to head up a new team formed to put the same programme into action.

MONITORING AND EVALUATION

It would be imprudent and premature at the time of writing to divulge the detailed gains of the re-engineering effort to date, given both the relative recent implementation into only one area of the hospital, and the wider political context of UK governmental health care reform. The project is to be evaluated by Kingston Hospital and, independently, by the Department of Health commencing in the summer of 1994. It is anticipated by then that the new working arrangements will have become sufficiently embedded to ensure reasonably valid results. A comprehensive picture of the benefits arising from the re-engineering will become more available later in the year through the evaluation reports.

Be that as it may, and although the medical unit has only been delivering Patient Focused Care for less than six months, it is becoming apparent that a range of benefits are resulting from the restructuring:

- X-ray time has been reduced by over 1.5 hours, with the process steps cut by 66 per cent. More significantly, only two people are required to carry out the new procedure, instead of the ten needed previously.
- Confirmation of diagnosis and amendments to treatment can be made much more quickly as pathology reports are now available in two hours.
- Staff satisfaction has improved with the increase in time and care they can devote to their patients.
- Patients appreciate the quicker responses to their requests for help or information.
- Patients also find the atmosphere less intimidating as they very quickly get to know and trust the staff who will be looking after them, and can see them constantly in the area in which they are being cared for.
- The morale and commitment of staff working on the unit has been manifested by their not wishing to return to work on conventional wards.
- More patients are receiving a higher quality care than previously.

Given the early indications of success, one can assume that Kingston Hospital is well placed to continue to roll out the concept further across its other wards.

LESSONS LEARNT

The current head of the Patient Focused Care Team, George Kempton, considers the following three points critical for the current success of the programme:

- public commitment and leadership of the CEO;
- independent full-time transition team;
- external high-level political support and funding.

The team have learnt a few lessons from the programme so far, and looking back they might have done some things differently:

■ **More detailed and accurate implementation planning**. For example, the conversion of the floor took much longer than anticipated, which had a knock-on effect.
■ **More communication**. The team consider that they missed the opportunity of taking the communication effort more directly to the staff members. This could have included, for example, making presentations to the day-to-day staff meetings which already occurred.
■ **More training**. This should have been provided up front for the Care Teams, as the competencies took longer to be achieved than originally thought.

These lessons are currently being applied to the implementation of the new maternity ward and the continuing roll-out.

SUMMARY

■ **Know what you want**
   — Strong new leadership.
   — Detailed analysis.
   — Importation of best practice from abroad.
   — Gradual and increasing involvement to get consensus of vision.
   — Use of part-time cross-functional working groups to input into a full-time core team.

■ **Make a plan**
   — Bite-sized chunks.
   — Detailed planning for first part.

■ **Do it**
   — Phased roll-out.
   — Training of new cross-functional teams.
   — Varied and open communication.

■ **Monitor**
   — Regular and open reviews.
   — Fears and concerns listened to.
   — Outside stakeholders kept informed.

8

National Vulcan Engineering Insurance Group Ltd (UK)

INTRODUCTION

National Vulcan is wholly owned by the Sun Alliance Insurance Group and has been in business for 130 years. Its core business is the inspection of commercial and industrial equipment (for statutory safety purposes and insurance) and the provision of engineering insurance. These inspections, and writing of insurance policies, cover a large market from the corner garage to nine of the UK's 13 nuclear power stations. It is the leader in the sector, with 23 per cent share of market.

The core activities of Inspection, Insurance and Plant Database Updating include over 2,000 on-site inspections every day, resulting in over 500,000 reports sent to customers every year. Over 75,000 insurance policies are issued annually. A detailed record of over 2.5 million items of plant inspected or insured must be kept. The company has around 1,100 employees including some 500 home-based engineers.

THE IMPERATIVE FOR CHANGE

National Vulcan became a victim of its own success. Long-established and successful, it had a deep-rooted conservative culture. Rigidity and complacency had crept into every corner of the organisation. Staff expected (and got) jobs for life, there were 55 grades of staff, and messengers of change were quickly shot. However, their market became more competitive, and customers (operating in a deep recession) became more discerning.

National Vulcan began to lose customers (even long-standing ones), and cost ratios escalated out of control. In the scramble to keep revenues some poor risk decisions in underwriting were taken. The result was catastrophic. Annual profits dropped from £9.6 million in 1989, to just over £6 million in 1990, and then to a loss of £6 million in 1991. Without radical change it became clear that the company was heading for a collapse.

INITIAL STEPS – CHANGE OF LEADERSHIP: EARLY 1991

The holding company, Sun Alliance, took rapid action. In early 1991 they replaced the incumbent managing director with a new one, Ken Sinfield, and told him to turn the situation around. Ken Sinfield had previously managed Bradford Pennine, the specialist motor insurance arm of Sun Alliance, and had also held responsibility for Electronic Marketing, as Director of Sun Alliance Management Services Ltd. He thus had the skills of general management with a firm knowledge of IT. He also had the right circumstances to re-engineer National Vulcan, because, as he says himself, 'There is nothing like the prospect of death to focus the mind.'

FORMULATING THE VISION – SPRING 1991

The managing director took just over two months to get to understand the business, the people in it and the issues it faced. He spent time walking the processes with his management team. This included, for example, walking the process to issue the lowest priced new insurance policy. The walk round took the best part of a day, and included meeting 30 different people in ten different departments scattered around the building. There was a backlog of many weeks. One manager had been involved in the process for over 40 years, claiming proudly that it had never been changed in his time. This was fairly symptomatic of the entire organisation. The plant database updating included over 10 million pieces of paper which needed to be chased, a mind numbing and lengthy task which achieved lots of mistakes, disgruntled customers and a 30 per cent staff turnover. The Inspection process was little better, with home-based engineers typing reports using several pieces of carbon paper (and a lot more snopake), which were posted second class (to save money) for checking by more senior engineers at head office who returned the reports for correction and a repetition of the cycle.

By doing some effort/duration analysis it became clear that the whole situation was grossly inefficient. For example, the insurance process consisted of three days' effort which took three month's duration to achieve. Of the effort itself, only three hours were real value added, and of that three hours, two hours 57 minutes could be automated. The remaining three minutes represented less than 0.01 per cent of the total and was called 'The *Valuable Difference* – performed by valuable people'.

Concurrently with the internal analysis, an external Customer Satisfaction survey was commissioned. This made dismal reading. When presented to senior management one comment was: 'I don't know what's wrong, we have not changed; the customers must have.' On top of the customers being analysed, so was the competition. It was clear that as National Vulcan got weaker, the competition got stronger.

At the end of this period, the new managing director formed a mission statement, supported by some stretching goals:

> We will be the highest quality and lowest cost operator in the UK Engineering Insurance sector.

The stretching goals included:

- All customer transactions must be processed within 24 hours of receipt; this included policy issue, inspection report dispatch and plant database updates.
- Only one pair of hands must be involved in the processing of those customer transactions, no matter where within the company they were received.

The vision was to focus each employee onto the valuable difference, with each individual able to be the window into National Vulcan for any customer. IT was visioned to be the key enabler by acting for each employee as a window into the rest of the organisation. This focus on the 'valuable difference', and the philosophy of a window into a window, was the underlying idea of the vision.

The initial reaction to the managing director's presentation was disbelief. In fact, after his presentation to senior managers, the stunned silence was broken only by a muttered 'Hans Christian Anderson'. It was clear that the transition was going to need decisive, clear and supportive leadership.

MAKING THE DETAILED PLAN AND FORMING THE CHANGE TEAMS – SUMMER 1991

During his initial ten weeks and his various walk abouts, the managing director had identified the change team leaders he needed to drive the change forwards. These cross-functional teams were now rapidly formed and reported direct to the managing director. These teams were tasked to re-engineer the three key processes of Insurance, Inspections and Plant

Database management. The teams were not headed up by managers in charge of the current processes, as it was felt that it would be hard for them to be effective as they would have the most to lose in any new changes.

The change teams worked quickly to draw up the detailed plans needed to move the organisation towards achieving the vision and goals. They focused on not only the key processes, but also the IT needed to change them. At the same time the top executive team worked with the managing director to prepare the detailed business plan. This plan was used by the project teams as the basis for timing (and costing) the actions needed to meet the targets. By the middle of 1991, the managing director was able to present the plan to the Sun Alliance group. There followed some hard debate, as National Vulcan were asking for over £2 million to support an IT strategy on top of the current IT annual spend of £2 million. The current spend was not very effective, with a mainframe system covering only 20 per cent of the business which had taken three years just to get to the pilot stage. To compound the problem, 1991 was not exactly the most successful year for the Sun Alliance Group, and money was very tight. The group had lost £466 million, one of the largest losses ever recorded by a private company in the UK. Happily the managing director managed to convince the group that what was presented was what was needed, and in the autumn of 1991 implementation began in earnest.

IMPLEMENTATION KEY TECHNIQUES – 1992/3

A variety of techniques was used by National Vulcan to ensure that the changes were implemented:

- strong, yet informal, unremitting leadership;
- use of cross-functional teams with power;
- centralisation of dispersed activities;
- fast and courageous decision-making;
- rapidly developed IT systems.

In essence the implementation took just over a year. The focus was on survival, and a strict prioritisation of action was undertaken to ensure focus on the valuable difference that the re-engineering effort could itself produce.

Strong, yet informal, unremitting leadership

Not only was Ken Sinfield's vision a shock for the organisation, so was his style. The organisation was as hierarchical as it was formal, with 55 different job grades and the new managing director initially being addressed as 'Sir' or, more informally, 'Mr Sinfield'. Wherever he went he told people to change this, and to call him simply 'Ken'. Despite initial generally negative reactions, he persevered and slowly people around him began to change. He provided the central leadership that the crisis demanded. There was not much time to go for a slower consensual approach (as in other cases in this part). However, his door was always open. Whenever people reported that things could not be done, the reply was 'Change the process so that it can be.' Despite the shaking of heads, solutions were found. He also provided firm leadership for the rapid development of the IT systems (where his previous experience of developing some of Sun Alliance's IT systems was invaluable). Of the original ten-man top management team, only two remain today (and these two were only in the company a couple of years before the new managing director arrived).

Use of cross-functional teams with power

The cross-functional teams which were formed to re-engineer the three core processes of Inspection, Insurance and Plant Database Updating, were given the power to act. Apart from the IT teams, who were full time, most of these cross-functional teams were part time. Some of the new process team leaders were taken from relatively junior ranks of the company, and in some cases previously direct subordinates became superiors. This was hard medicine for some managers, but it demonstrated that the change was the priority.

Centralisation of dispersed activities

The insurance business was a nightmare of administration spread across 24 sales offices. The sales staff spent more time on administration than selling. The managing director decided that this had to change. Seventeen of the best staff in the field were made a 'godfather' offer to relocate to a centralised Customer Service Unit, based in the head office in Manchester. On top of that new staff were recruited locally. At the same time, the 24 offices were condensed into nine.

Fast and courageous decision-making

The structure of the change programme allowed for fast decision-making. The managing director personally spent over 50 per cent of his time on the programme. Courageous decisions were taken. For example, the Customer Service Unit reorganisation took just three weeks, by closing down the operation and stopping all customer processing. The hope was that the backlog was so long that none of the customers would notice – they didn't. The CSU was achieved within six months of the new managing director arriving.

Rapidly developed IT systems

Without IT systems, the vision would not be possible. IT systems were fully developed to support the new processes in the three core activities within a year. The normal approach of development, with the resultant thousands of person days development, was abandoned. Instead small teams of IT professionals worked alongside the change teams to develop the supporting IT systems needed. The Plant Database eliminated the need for paper altogether, and took just nine months to develop from scratch. The process was designed in such a way that the large amounts of paper-based information did not need to be scanned into the system – over time they simply became redundant. The Inspection process has been enhanced with field engineers using laptops with some intelligent software able to generate whichever of the 200 different report forms are needed. The 2,000 reports daily are now turned around in 24 hours, and are managed by a central team of twelve (instead of the 140 clerks needed previously). The Insurance process uses a SUN Workstation system with easy-to-use graphical user interface software. The work of ten departments is now done by one, and the old three-month process now takes less than 24 hours. The IT allows the staff to focus on customer needs, rather than administrative routines.

MONITORING AND THE RESULTS ACHIEVED

The monitoring of the change programme was carried out through frequent progress reports via the change teams to the managing director and a cascade to all staff concerned. The results achieved were dramatic:

- Insurance process: Three months to issue a policy cut to less than 24 hours. 40 steps, 30 people, 10 departments cut to two steps, three people and one department.
- Plant Database: From months out of date, to 24 hourly update. 35 process steps cut down to two. Staff turnover cut from 30 per cent to 2 per cent. 10 million paper documents reduced to none.
- Inspection process: From seven weeks to 95 per cent within 24 hours. Thirteen process steps and 18 people cut to three steps with three people. From thin carbon copies, reports are now quality laser printed.
- Customer reaction: Complaints reduced from an average of 15 a month to less than one a month. Loss of customers stopped, with new customers being attracted.

■ Financial benefits: From a loss of over £6 million in 1991, profit was achieved in 1992, which rose to £6.2 million in 1993. Per capita income has increased by over 49 per cent. Cash flow has improved by 35 per cent.

There are many other benefits of the programme. Staff headcount has reduced from 1,341 to 1,100 with a non-compulsory redundancy policy. Many staff now find themselves working in higher value areas as old jobs have disappeared, and as a result staff morale has greatly increased. They have been transformed from administration clerks into insurance professionals, and are able to focus on the 'Valuable Difference' and in so doing are delighting their customers. They have also achieved the position of being the lowest cost provider of their services.

In December 1992, and again in December 1993, National Vulcan won the accolade 'Top Engineering Insurer' awarded by the Institute of Insurance Brokers. In 1993 they were awarded the *Computer Weekly*. 'IT Performance' award, and *The Sunday Times*/Anderson Consulting award for 'IT for Business Excellence'.

LESSONS LEARNT

National Vulcan admit that the communication process put in to support the change programme relied too much on cascade. Although one can never communicate too much, they feel nevertheless that they should have invested more time in communication. They also worked initially with an IT consultancy – this did not work very well as the consultants concerned were too tied to a more traditional (and slower) approach to IT development.

SUMMARY

■ **Know what you want**
  — Need for change and pain of status quo clearly identified.
  — Detailed understanding by top leadership of current process change needs.
  — Understanding of customer perceptions, through independent analysis.
  — Clear vision with stretching goals.

■ **Make a plan**
  — Use of cross-functional change teams with IT expert support.
  — Clear plans and milestones.
  — Capital approval up front.

■ **Do it**
  — Focusing on priorities (not trying to do everything – claims process was relegated for further work after first three core processes had been fixed).
  — Strong and involved support and direction from top leadership.
  — 'It can be done' mentality.

■ **Monitor**
  — Measure cycle times and inputs, not just financial results.
  — Share achievement outside, as well as inside.

The programme continues, with around half a dozen change teams working on all aspects of the organisation to keep the momentum up for continuous improvement. As in other cases in this book, National Vulcan have learnt that after going through a radical re-engineering programme, they are far more able to change and adapt than before. The re-engineering programme has not only delivered results, it has also allowed the organisation to start a never-ending process of change and improvement.

9

Oticon

INTRODUCTION

Oticon is a Danish company, based in Copenhagen, which specialises in the manufacture and distribution of hearing aids. It is a privately owned company, and was founded in 1904. It includes 14 subsidiary companies around the world, and numbers just over 1,100 employees. In the 1960s and 1970s the company was in its heyday. It was the world's leader in hearing aids, and enjoyed a worldwide 15 per cent share of market. It was unparalleled in its sector by size, product quality, distribution network and reputation.

The interest of this case lies in the way in which its President, Lars Kolind, re-engineered the head office. The programme is unusual in its formulation and in its implementation which happened at 08.00 hours on 8 August 1991. It also shows how one can move an organisation from 'chimneys' to 'bubbles' (see Part 1, Chapter 1).

BACKGROUND AND THE IMPERATIVE FOR CHANGE

Oticon became a victim of its own success. At the end of the 1970s it was the undisputed leader – there was no perceived need for change. Indeed any radical ideas and proposed changes were quickly buried and stifled. But the 1980s began to highlight the cracks in the armour. New technology in the market was making an impact, especially 'hidden in the ear' hearing aids. Oticon's products were all behind the ear hearing aids, and were standard. The new products were mass customised, i.e. the same electronics but with a customised shell fitted in the individual's ear. Due to the growing market of hearing aids, Oticon's revenue line did not suffer, but its share of market declined from 15 per cent to 7 per cent.

Oticon's decline of market share problem was joined by a financial crisis in 1987. The costs had risen during the 1980s and profitability had slowly declined. This was compounded when the Danish kroner strengthened against the dollar, and in 1987 30 per cent of the equity on the balance sheet was wiped out. Change was needed quickly.

FIRST STEPS – NEW LEADERSHIP

Lars Kolind was recruited by the main board to sort the company out. He had an unusual background. He had managed a family business in Denmark, Radiometer, and had demonstrated good experience in managing change. He had held a senior post in the Danish Government National Research Centre, and had been an associate professor in planning theory at the University of Copenhagen for several years. He was also very active in the scout movement, having worked in the movement as a volunteer for many years and had achieved senior posts. He joined Oticon in September 1988. The first two years were spent reducing costs by 20 per cent to return Oticon to the same level of profitability (5 per cent of sales) which it was used to.

THE FORMATION AND SHARING OF A NEW VISION

In late 1989, the results of a hard year's cost-cutting was beginning to show some returns. However, it was clear to the new CEO that Oticon did not have any sustainable advantages, and that this would mean long-term decline in an increasingly competitive marketplace. Many of the electronic giants (i.e. Philips, Siemens, Panasonic, Sony, etc.) had hearing aid divisions and these were becoming more and more sophisticated. To compete effectively, Oticon needed to be highly responsive, creative, innovative, fast and flexible. Over the Christmas and New Year holidays of 1989, the CEO pondered the possibilities.

The field organisation and distribution were sound, and the manufacturing operation still quite competitive. The basic strategy (product, price, place and promotion) was secure for at least a couple of years. The company had a high degree of competency. The problem lay in the brains of the organisation, its head office. Although representing only 30 per cent of overhead costs, the 150 people in the head office controlled significantly more. Its day-to-day decisions and activities affected significant costs throughout the organisation. It also set the culture and the way the organisation thought and behaved. This was a conservative, slow-moving, unresponsive culture, a dinosaur facing extinction. It was highly departmentalised. To compound the situation, the head office was actually split into two different sites, several miles apart. It was clear a new and radical change needed to happen in the head office first. It was the re-engineering of the head office which became the CEO's priority.

At the end of 1989, he held a series of informal discussions. These discussions only confirmed what he feared and led him to write, over the Christmas holidays, a four-page document entitled *Think the unthinkable* (which later became the rallying cry of the re-engineering programme, and of the newly created head office the programme gave birth to). The document itself became known as the '1,000 Birch Trees' document. He had a vision of a seamless, borderless head office without internal walls or partitions. The head office vision had no titles, grades or departments, no job descriptions or the normal paraphernalia which conventional management wisdom dictates for control and efficiency. He described as a metaphor a large room with 1,000 birch trees on castors, which would move to form groups when needed, before moving again to form new groups. It was a radical and, to some, 'crazy' vision.

In early 1990, the CEO distributed the document for discussion with his top management team. This consisted of some five senior managers who had been in the company for many years. It would be an understatement to say that the vision met with a high degree of scepticism. His team were defensive about their departments, grades and offices. All that they had held dear was proposed for destruction. Over the next few months, with a series of patient discussions and explanations, the CEO managed to get one or two to accept, in principle, that his vision might just be possible.

On 18 April 1990, the CEO called together a meeting with all 150 employees in the head office. He described his vision. He also said that he understood if people did not want to be part of it, and that those who wanted to go would be fully supported and assisted. (In fact, remarkable as it seems, no one left during the transition to the new state.) The reaction of his audience followed the classic initial reactions to change – shock, disbelief and anger. At the end of the presentation the CEO was in no doubt that over 95 per cent of the head office were against the idea. However, he had won his spurs in the company and the previous year's efforts had earned him a high degree of respect and goodwill. It was this goodwill on which he was to capitalise.

PLANNING THE ACTION IN DETAIL – ENERGISING CHANGE

During the next three months, the CEO slowly began to energise and empower the head office organisation into action. He spent up to 30 per cent of his time doing this. He approached individuals informally, and invited them to plan one of the details, and subsequent implementation, \of the vision. This gave rise to several informal groups which worked on various aspects of the vision including, for example, the IT systems needed, the location and design of, and move to, the new head office (a disused drinks factory nearby), the training needed, the type of furniture needed, etc. How did he do this? He enthused and motivated individuals, and this was passed on by those he touched to others who quickly formed the *ad hoc* groups. To ensure coordination and consistency he also recruited one of his previous students Steen Davidson, whom he knew from his days at Copenhagen University. Steen became the overall full-time project manager.

Within three months about 50 people (30 per cent of the head office) were working on designing and planning the change. These people were the opinion leaders, and rarely managers. The central coordinating team, for example, numbered six. Headed up overall by the newly recruited project manager, the central team consisted of a secretary, a product development engineer, a personnel assistant, a marketing assistant and an export assistant. The CEO spent a lot of time with the central team, which coordinated the action of the *ad hoc* groups.

The only person full time on the re-engineering programme was the project manager. The CEO made it quite clear to those involved that participation could only be part time, and all involved still had to fulfil their normal roles and responsibilities. All projects in Oticon had a number – the number for the re-engineering project became 330, standing for 30 per cent improvement in 3 years. The goal was set.

MANAGING THE DYNAMICS OF CHANGE – KEY TECHNIQUES USED

Apart from the use of *ad hoc* cross-functional teams to carry out the detailed design and planning, the CEO used a variety of other techniques to ensure the radical programme would result in a realised vision. These included:

- late afternoon seminars;
- 'dialogue shop';
- extending the stakeholding;
- computer Christmas;
- counselling resistance;
- all staff values conference;
- burning bridges and building ambassadors;
- a new enabling environment;
- disengagement auction.

Late afternoon seminars

These were run by the CEO and the project manager, and were carried out every month from mid 1990 up to the move in August 1991. He invited professors and external experts to speak about the principles of a knowledge based, learning organisation. The seminars were attended by 50–70 people at a time, and thus individuals would have gone to several by the time of implementation. This helped to prepare the people mentally.

'Dialogue shop'

From his days in the Danish army, the CEO borrowed a technique which can be used to build commitment (although not under fire!). He arranged a two-day off-site workshop for all managers (just over 30 in all) to work in detail on the future design. The first day he ran the 'dialogue shop'. This consisted of a brief presentation in plenary session by the senior management team to the whole group, which was then split up into five groups. Each group then had the opportunity to question, in detail, one of the five senior managers. After 45 minutes of questioning, there was a 15 minute break when the senior managers quickly compared notes. The senior managers then rotated each to be questioned by a new group. This happened five times, so that each group individually questioned each senior manager for 45 minutes. The challenge was for the groups to find major inconsistencies and to bring these back to the plenary session. Needless to say they found very few, if any. The senior management team, when told about the task a few weeks before, made sure they were all in agreement about what the vision meant. And at the end of five 45 minutes question and answer sessions, the middle management were in no doubt as well. The second day was spent discussing the key difficulties and concerns regarding the actual implementation.

Extending the stakeholding

In the October of 1990, the CEO purchased 17 per cent of the equity from the private foundation which had held 100 per cent. This was a very visible and public statement of commitment to the radical changes being planned for the next year. The foundation also offered the right to buy shares to all employees. This was done over a phased three – year period, totalling another 8 per cent. The shares were fully subscribed.

Computer Christmas

It was clear that in the new organisation of the head office each and every person would need to be fully computer literate, especially using graphic user interface software such as Windows. Just before the Christmas of 1990, Oticon purchased 130 state-of-the-art IBM PCs with 386 processors and full Windows-based office software (including spreadsheets, database, word processing and drawing). Each PC had a state-of-the-art printer. The CEO told every employee that for a nominal rent (about US$15 a month), each employee could have a PC and printer for his or her own personal use at home. If an individual accepted, the obligation was to teach himself or herself how to use it proficiently. Although such hardware and software is outdated now, back in 1990 it was very desirable. The uptake was over 90 per cent and the computers were taken home for introduction into family life over Christmas. Naturally whoever took a computer home became the PC champion of the family, and by the time of the move to the new office, everyone had gained computer proficiency (which was subsequently improved by specific application training in the new head office's IT systems). The other unplanned benefit from this approach was that many people started to carry out some of their work at home. This was useful in freeing up time at the office to work on the re-engineering programme.

Counselling resistance

One of the largest sources of resistance to change were the middle managers. This was understandable, as the vision had no middle managers, just a small management team and 150 staff. The main fear was typified by the question 'What will *I* be doing?' The CEO held many one-to-one counselling sessions. The response was invariably the same: 'What do you *want* to do?' The middle managers were encouraged to analyse what their own individual skills were and what contribution they could make. Many had risen to their current rank as they had very good technical skills in a particular area, so they could contribute by acting as technical specialists. Others had risen because they were very good people managers, and so they would could contribute by acting as project managers. The CEO fully expected at least 15 per cent to drop out – but due to the way the change process was managed, not one dropped out or was moved out during the transition.

All staff values conference

In early 1991, a two-day conference was held for all staff. The design and plans were nearing completion, and these were shared with all present. The conference focused on the values of the new organisation. A values statement was drawn up. The basic philosophy was that all staff members would in future be treated as adults. When the new move was complete in August, a lot of the old systems would simply be thrown away. The values focused on the way employees would view each other. They would be trusted to make sensible decisions. Work hours would be abolished. Appraisal would be done by their peers and by what their projects achieved. The organisation would be team based, with people serving on a variety of projects when the need arose.

Burning bridges and building ambassadors

In the spring of 1991, news of the new organisation reached the press. The whole approach and design of the new future state was described in detail. It provided a media sensation, with many full-page articles appearing (in 1992 these numbered over 100). With such a public commitment, there was no going back – the bridges of retreat to the past were well and truly burned down. Needless to say, the changes invoked a lot of external curiosity. And employees were soon besieged by their unions, trade and professional associations, old schools, etc., to come and talk in more detail about the vision of a head office with no walls, departments, job descriptions and hierarchies. The employees became ambassadors. There was no company produced slide show or script. Employees were trusted to tell the story without a centrally controlled prompt.

A new enabling environment

The new head office was designed in an old drinks factory. The previous owners liked classical art, and the large open-plan space is surrounded by towering marble columns. A lot of greenery was put in (shades of the birch trees). There are no owned desks. Each workstation has a networked PC and a mobile phone. The desks have no drawers. Each employee, including the CEO, has a caddie to hold papers and files (not that there are many – all mail is scanned into the IT system and then shredded, and paper has been much reduced). The only rooms are 'dialogue rooms', each with a circular sofa and small low coffee table. The table is not large enough to hold paper or to sit behind, but is deliberately planned to encourage open discussion. White boards are included to help groups communicate, plan, discuss and brainstorm. The IT systems are based on a client/server system, and to date a total of some US$6 million has been invested. Most of the software is adapted off the shelf. All fax communication is electronic. Apart from confidential personnel files, all information is open to anyone who wants it.

Disengagement auction

To help the organisation 'de-learn' the old culture and disengage from the past, all the old furniture in the old offices was auctioned to the staff after the move into the new offices. The auction was announced several weeks before the move, and staff were encouraged to visit any office to look at the furniture. Oticon had done very well in the past, and the furniture reflected the opulence the company had once enjoyed. The higher the rank in the company, the better the furniture, and this in itself became an item to joke about and ridicule. All the furniture was auctioned off to the employees to take and use at home.

After all the preparation above, the employees all moved into the new office building at 08.00 hours on 8 August 1991.

MONITORING AND THE RESULTS GAINED

Monitoring the action was achieved as explained above – frequent and informal communication with some large meetings thrown in. The initial results were far from satisfactory. The new head office moved, in a very real sense, into a chaos similar to that described in Cigna's Team Progression Matrix (see Part 3, Appendix 1, Section 6 for a description of this). This was not helped by a bad result for 1991 and for early 1992, and the head office had to be downsized from about 150 to 112. Needless to say all those made redundant were helped in every way to find new jobs, but morale was not improved.

It took several months for the organisation to settle down into the new ways of doing things. Former managers have become specialists or project managers (depending on what they are involved in). Administrators are more involved in the running of the mainstream business (as there is less administration to do). People discuss what opportunities exist and team together to bid for company resources to fund projects. Once funded the projects organise their own training to ensure the team formed has the right skills. This training also includes project management techniques, team building and inter-personal skills.

People are actively encouraged to participate in projects outside their traditional skills area to help them develop. Each individual is involved in more than one project at a time, as well as carrying out tasks in more than one of the old traditional functions at a time. All the current project plans are kept on the IT system, and everyone can key in and see what everyone else is doing. Appraisals are by peers, which is put into the pay system to decide who gets rewarded what. Abuse of such a free atmosphere is therefore avoided, as those who do not perform as well as they could are soon found out by their peers. The only formal hierarchy is the top management team who decide which of the employee-generated projects should be awarded a budget to go ahead. This top team currently numbers ten (it varies as some people rotate through it for development).

After the rocky start in late 1991 and early 1992, things began to happen. People began to 'think the unthinkable'. For example, Oticon bucked the conventional wisdom that hearing aids should be marketed as something almost to be ashamed of, as attractive as an artificial limb. The market trend was thus moving toward hidden-in-the-ear hearing aids. Behind the ear aids were flesh coloured. Despite market research to the contrary, Oticon introduced a silver-grey coloured aid to be marketed as a state-of-the-art communications enabling device: the new product was a success. Oticon also marketed a 'multi-focus' hearing aid with automatic volume adjustment, the first of its kind which gave birth to a whole new technology, multi-focal technology. Needless to say Oticon is also developing hidden mass-customised hearing aids as well, to meet the particular preferences of some customers.

The results are impressive (all figures shown from 1990 to 1993):

- revenue up by 45 per cent from DKK455.9 million to DKK661.2 million;
- operating profit up by over 400 per cent from DKK 16.9 million to DKK85.5 million;
- net earnings up by 500 per cent from DKK 10.4 million to DKK62.3 million;
- annual revenue growth up from 1.4 per cent to 22.7 per cent;
- return on equity up from 6.7 per cent to 36.9 per cent;
- R&D as percentage of turnover up from 3.5 per cent to 6.7 per cent.

In 1993 Oticon was the only European company to be nominated for The Computerworld Smithsonian Award in the USA. It was awarded the IT award in Denmark in late 1993.

The re-engineering programme continues with an extension of the philosophy in the head office being extended to two factories in Denmark. The IT systems between these factories and head office have been linked by a WAN for data and telephone communications, and over the next few years the network will be extended to cover all Oticon's companies throughout the world. It is also planned to roll out the new philosophy. Danish culture is characterised by informality and equality. It will be interesting to see how well such a managerial philosophy extends to other cultures. Whatever the result Oticon has a place in history in what it has achieved, and shows that there are many more radical and 'unthinkable' ways to re-engineer a company.

LESSONS LEARNT

The CEO feels the following were key to success:

- initial compliance approach, and use of power by CEO;
- change founded on communicated and shared set of values.

SUMMARY

■ **Know what you want**
  — Strong visionary leadership.
  — Debate with top management team.
  — 'Think the unthinkable'!

■ **Make a plan**
  — Informal empowered ad hoc groups.
  — Go around resistance, and empower opinion leaders not rank holders.
  — Central project coordination.

■ **Do it**
  — Lots of patient communication.
  — Burn bridges, build ambassadors.
  — Link change with an event (i.e. office move).
  — Counsel, counsel, counsel.

■ **Monitor**
  — Data available to all.
  — Communicate, communicate, communicate.

10

The Progressive Corporation

INTRODUCTION

The Progressive insurance organisation began business in 1937. It was co-founded by Jack H. Green, and Joseph M. Lewis (the current CEO's father). The co-founders were graduate law school colleagues, who decided to set up an insurance company after being involved together as lawyers investigating a company which was selling a dubious automobile service contract. From those early days, Progressive slowly grew. The Progressive Casualty Insurance Company was founded in 1956. The Progressive Corporation, an insurance holding company formed in 1965, owns 52 operating subsidiaries and has one mutual insurance company affiliate. The companies primarily provide personal automobile insurance as well as other speciality property-casualty insurance and related services. These are sold mainly through independent insurance agents in the United States and Canada. The 1993 estimated industry premiums, which include personal auto insurance in the USA and Ontario, Canada, as well as insurance for commercial vehicles, were US$115 billion and Progressive's share of market, with total revenues at US$1,954.8 million was 1.7 per cent.

This case is similar to that of Ford in that the re-engineering efforts within the company were more an evolution of change initiatives rather than a specific re-engineering programme. There was no grand plan, but rather a series of discrete initiatives which, like the pieces of a jigsaw puzzle, slowly combined to form the picture of a 're-engineered' company that Progressive represents today. As the CEO, Peter Lewis, himself admits, the company has been employing a variety of re-engineering techniques for some time now. It is only the recent emergence of business re-engineering as a recognised and defined approach which has led the company to write in its annual report for 1993: '"Re-engineering" is what we have been doing to respond to ... threats and opportunities, as well as to the changing environment. The result is Progressive's new strategy for the 1990s.' This case outlines the main themes of that re-engineering effort and how it was, and continues to be, achieved.

Many of the changes which Progressive have implemented were mainly started by the initiative of the CEO, Peter Lewis. He joined the company in 1955, after graduating from Princeton, and became the CEO ten years later, when the turnover was some US$6 million with 100 people. He has since guided it to the current position of over US$2 billion revenues and around 6,500 employees. Unlike some of the other cases in this book, the changes in Progressive were thus driven by a leadership which had been in place for some time.

BACKGROUND – THE IMPERATIVE FOR CHANGE

At the end of 1987, Progressive's results, and their people, were on an all-time high. They were confident that they could sustain their growth and profits by just carrying on the way they had been going. However, 1988 was to provide some shocks. Two main issues arose: the general dissatisfaction of consumers with the auto insurance industry, and increased pressure from competition.

The dissatisfaction of consumers towards the auto insurance industry was well known, but in California in November 1988 voters passed Proposition 103. This was a citizen's law which placed punitive conditions on auto insurance companies, demanding a return of 20 per cent of the premium to customers. Progressive decided it was too difficult, and too risky, to do profitable business in California, and they decided to pull back from the Californian market.

At the same time, the leadership of Progressive were shocked to find out that one of its main competitors, Allstate, had passed them in total US volume on their own speciality of non-standard auto insurance. After 25 years of observing Progressive's success, Allstate and other competitors like Penn Central (now called American Premier Underwriters) recognised that Progressive's high expenses ratios and wide profit margins gave them a perfect opportunity to take market share by providing similar services with a lower cost base. Progressive realised that Allstate, with its distribution and data advantages, could quickly overwhelm them unless they acted fast and decisively.

In 1989 Progressive suffered a decline in operational profits. It was clear that the company needed to change.

INITIAL STEPS – 1989/1990

The CEO, Peter Lewis, and COO, Bruce Marlow, recognised that they needed to pursue a variety of actions almost concurrently. Progressive needed to concentrate on delighting customers to overcome the current hostile view which the consumer generally held toward auto insurers. A variety of initiatives were started in 1989 and 1990, each employing different tactics. These included:

- improving the claims process;
- matching corporate values with a meaningful vision;
- TQM programme to empower change lower down.

Improving the claims process

One of the major areas of customer dissatisfaction with the auto insurance industry was the lengthy claims process employed. Although Progressive was faster in settling claims than its competitors, typically within a few days, they still suffered from this poor customer perception. In early 1989 the CEO (to back his new vision statement) said that he felt Progressive needed to provide a 24 hour, seven day a week, Immediate Response® service. The initial reaction to the idea was not exactly enthusiastic. The CEO kept talking about his vision, and also recruited one of the most successful and respected executives in the claims department to head up a small team to look at the process. This they did, and redesigned it to cut down the cycle time. The number of customers contacted within nine hours of an accident has increased by 54 per cent, and payments made within two weeks has increased by 45 per cent. The improvements were greatly enhanced in 1992 by the introduction of Process Leadership (see below). Claims are now processed far faster, with Progressive representatives often on site with the customer within four hours.

Values and vision

Progressive has a values statement, which was formed in the mid 1980s. The values statement, which is still very much part of Progressive today, are called 'Core Values'. These are described as 'pragmatic statements of what works best for us in the real world', statements which govern decisions and behaviour, and are understood by all Progressive people. They are the standards by which Progressive stands, and they consist of five key elements, which are called:

- *Integrity* – 'We revere honesty ... and encourage disclosing bad news and welcome disagreement';

- *Golden Rule* – 'We respect all people ... and deal with them in the way we want to be dealt with ...';
- *Objectives* – 'We strive to be clear and open about Progressive's ambitious objectives ...';
- *Excellence* – 'We strive constantly to improve ...';
- *Profit* – 'The free enterprise system rewards most those who most enhance the health and happiness of their customers, communities and people ...'.

Although these values served (and continue to serve) Progressive well, it was clear to the CEO that the vision of the company needed clarifying. During the Christmas/New Year break of 1989/90 he formulated a vision statement which changed the emphasis of Progressive from just selling auto insurance to meeting the needs of its key stakeholders (the customers, shareholders and employees). On his return in early 1990 he shared his vision statement with his senior executives and the statement was finalised:

> We seek to be an excellent, innovative, growing and enduring business by reducing the human trauma and economic costs of auto accidents in cost-effective and profitable ways that delight customers. We seek to earn a superior return on equity and to provide a positive environment to attract quality people and achieve ambitious growth plans.

TQM programme

In 1989, the COO walked into the CEO's office and gave him a book on quality management by Dr Edwards Deming. After two hours of going through the book, the CEO realised that Deming's philosophy and approach was what Progressive needed. At that time there were many consultants using Deming's principles and Progressive selected one, a sole trader. She worked across the organisation, typically with current management and staff teams and departments in groups of 6–20. The training continued through 1989 and 1990, and gave rise to internal trainers which helped to roll the approach out. The organisation was told that staff were empowered to change what they wanted in order to save money or provide better customer service. There were two caveats: firstly, staff needed to recognise that they operated in a work chain, or process, and that if any changes affected others in the chain, these changes had to be agreed by those affected. The second caveat was that the changes needed to be measured in a quantifiable way. Through this programme the organisation got used to forming cross-functional teams to address process problems, through it took some time to have an effect, with some parts of the organisation using it more than others. In particular, the North Atlantic geographic division ran with the programme in earnest and within a year were demonstrating good results which served to encourage the other, more sceptical, parts of the organisation. The TQM programme introduced other benefits, not least a new discipline to solving problems. In the past, when a problem arose, Progressive executives would leap straight into action and quickly implement the first solution that came to mind. This often compounded the original problem! The TQM programme introduced a new discipline of analysing the problem soundly, and testing one or more potential solutions. The solution(s) would then be assessed and fine tuned for roll-out. This approach was to be vital in the future changes which Progressive introduced.

CONSOLIDATION – 1991

The various initiatives in 1989 and 1990 began to bear fruit, and the organisation slowly evolved from a hierarchical one to a team-based one, focused on delighting customers. These initiatives were consolidated with a few others, which included:

■ new distribution methods for customers;
■ new Express Quote service;
■ team training: 'Breaking New Ground'.

New distribution methods for customers

Progressive had traditionally distributed its services through independent agents. With a new culture of team-inspired change from lower down, one of the divisional executives in charge of Florida started to experiment with offering Progressive insurance direct. This included opening branches in shopping centres which dealt exclusively with auto insurance, as well as offering a free phone number. This free phone number was to include, a few months later, another innovation – Express Quote. The experiment worked well in California in 1991, better in Florida in 1993, and in 1994 the concept is being extended to Ohio and Texas.

New service – Express Quote

Despite some of the gains in 1989 and 1990, the CEO was still aware that consumer attitudes to auto insurance generally had not improved. He set up a meeting with one of the more active consumer pressure groups to listen to their concerns, organised in cooperation with Ralph Nader, one of the more energetic consumer activists in the USA. The group representatives told him that they viewed the auto insurance industry as a cosy, non-competitive cartel. This surprised the CEO, as he viewed his industry as extremely competitive. However, he realised that his views did not matter – the views of the consumers did. So he recruited one of his senior executives, Glen Renwick, to head up a cross-functional team to see what could be done. They came up with Express Quote, a free phone service which gives consumers a Progressive quote as well as four competitors' quotes (gained from quotes filed with State authorities). In many cases the quotes from their competitors are lower than their own, but 20 per cent of consumers who call become customers. This was initially tested in California (combined with the new distribution initiative outlined above), and is now being tested further in other states.

Team training: 'Breaking New Ground'

It became clear through the various initiatives which had started in 1989 and 1990 that teamwork was going to be vital for Progressive to re-engineer itself from an inward-looking hierarchy into a customer-focused organisation based on flexible teams. To help the teamwork, Progressive ran a series of eight-day experiential courses for over 1,000 managers in the summer and autumn of 1991. The courses were designed to teach the managers about team dynamics and to help them develop the interpersonal skills that they needed. In hindsight, the programme was expensive (over $10 million) and did not generate the value it could have. This was because it was too luxurious, and those who went on the courses did not belong to the same teams back at work. However, the exercise did teach Progressive how to undertake such training in a more value creating way. The courses are still being run, with shorter 1½ day courses. Those who participate go on the course with the same people that they normally work with, and in this way the course is tied directly back to the workplace. This training is valuable – not only does it develop individual interpersonal skills and organisational culture, but it also provides a common language and basis of understanding of how to work together.

MORE RADICAL SURGERY – 1992

Despite the various initiatives above, progress was not as fast as was hoped for. Progressive's initiatives to date had been aimed at externalities, and as yet no hard internal decisions had been made. To some extent the company had been in a stage of denial of the seriousness of the situation, but by 1992 it was clear that deeper surgery was needed. To this end three key initiatives were implemented:

■ process leadership;
■ cost reduction through staff reduction by flattening the hierarchy;
■ gainshare and teamwork.

Process leadership

Of all the initiatives which were introduced, process leadership was one which really changed the way the organisation was run. Progressive was organised like many companies, with a field geographic divisional structure and a central staff. Working with the divisional executives, the CEO and COO redesigned the running of the company. The central staff suffered from typical problems: they were not line managers, and thus were viewed as being out of touch, and they also were a source of resistance to the field initiatives, changes generated by those who were closer to the customer. The corporate staff were thinned down, and formed into process teams headed up by a divisional executive, who became a process leader in addition to his or her geographic responsibilities. This change took time to implement, using workshops and meetings, consultation and discussion with all concerned. To assist the implementation, it was agreed that the process leader's decision regarding his or her area would be respected by the other field divisional executives. A new compensation plan was put in place for the divisional executives, split 75 per cent for field geographic performance and 25 per cent for process performance.

Cost reduction through staff reduction by flattening the hierarchy

Progressive had grown fat during its successful years in the 1980s. This had led to a hierarchy which was more oriented to issues of ambition, turf and control than concentration on delighting customers. In addition the cost structure had become uncompetitive. The TQM initiative had shown the value of a team-based culture, and it became clear that the levels of hierarchy were a barrier preventing the change moving forward. The COO was given the task of solving this and, working with the senior executives, he flattened the hierarchy radically. Simply put, whole levels were removed which reduced the employee numbers from 7,600 to 6,000. This meant that staff lower down needed to act in a more empowered and responsive way, and this was helped by the TQM programme. The other process improvements and reductions in staff generally also helped to reduce costs. Of the savings achieved 30 per cent was through the flattening of the hierarchy, 40 per cent through process improvements and the remainder through other general staff reductions.

Gainshare and teamwork

During 1992, the organisation had got used to working in teams, and to cement the process, a gainshare scheme was introduced. The previous traditional salary compensation scheme did not encourage employees to take an interest in the company's performance, or to take risks and innovate. The new scheme linked compensation to performance on two levels: company and division. The gainshare element is a bonus paid out according to how well the company has performed, and how well the individual's geographic division has performed. In 1993, US$23.4 million was paid out to Progressive employees as part of the gainshare scheme. The scheme has helped motivate change, which is managed through teams. Whenever a team comes together to design, plan and implement changes they (as part of the original TQM initiative) have to measure current performance as a benchmark against which gains can be subsequently measured. To assist team dynamics, they agree who in the team (normally the most senior) is to decide the way forward if the team themselves cannot reach a consensus. Team incentive schemes include a discretionary award to teams which over-perform. This can include a cash bonus, or extra holiday time, and on average about 100 awards are made to teams each year. On top of this there is also a discretionary award scheme for individual employees who excel.

MAINTAINING THE MOMENTUM AND CONTINUOUS CHANGE: 1993 – PRESENT

The changes made during the period 1989 to 1992 provided a solid foundation for Progressive to improve performance. The company began to grow faster, and customer satisfaction improved as did employee retention. The last two years has seen Progressive continue to re-engineer itself. Much of what had been done in the few years previously had changed the culture and the way the organisation was run, and those initiatives were consolidated and continued with some recent additions:

- continued experimentation;
- enhanced IT systems.

Continued experimentation

Progressive continues to experiment to gain improvements. Sometimes the experiments work, sometimes they don't. However, by having such a culture, Progressive keeps moving forwards to delight customers. Sometimes the ideas outstrip available technology to support them. For example, a recent study looked at radical ways to improve the Immediate Response® service introduced some years earlier. The experiment looked at ways to settle customer needs totally after an auto accident. This included using in-car sensors to sense a collision, which would alert a patrolling van to arrive within minutes. The van operatives would video the damage, which would be sent via mobile communications in the van to a central computer for assessment, resulting in a cheque being printed in the van within minutes for delivery to the customer. At the same time, a pick-up van would arrive, as well as a replacement car. Within an hour of the accident, the customer would have a cheque to pay for the damage, and a replacement car while his or her car was towed away for repair. The technology, however, did not prove advanced enough to deliver this vision – but the study helped speed up some of the processes, and also serves to show Progressive's continued dedication to experiment, using teams, to improve services to delight the customer. And when the technology does become more readily available, Progressive will be very well placed to use it. Most of the debate that normally surrounds such radical ideas would have already occurred!

Enhanced IT systems

Over the past few years, the IT systems of Progressive have been updated to include client/server systems on LANs, linked together using WANs. This has been vital to support the new process leadership system which was implemented in 1992. New software has been introduced recently, such as Lotus Notes, which allows the formation of 'virtual teams' (teams working together but in different locations). Lotus Notes also helps all staff to communicate and keep in touch with the variety of changes and improvements being implemented.

MEASUREMENT AND RESULTS ACHIEVED

Every team agrees its own particular relevant measurements, and set up a process to ensure objective measurement is achieved. In addition the company monitors volume and financial indicators monthly, as well as customer satisfaction and employee attitudes. The results gained in the last five years have been very encouraging:

- ROE increased to 36 per cent in 1993 from 17.4 per cent in 1989;
- revenue increased by 54 per cent to $1,966 million in 1993 from $1,287 million in 1989;
- net income increased by 242 per cent to $267 million in 1993 from $78 million in 1989;
- operating profit increased to $120 million in 1993 from a loss of $9 million in 1989;
- underwriting margin increased to 10.7 per cent in 1993 up from 3.5 per cent in 1992;
- customer satisfaction improved by 18 per cent in 1993 from 1989.

The efforts at Progressive continue – given their current achievements, they have a sound base to build on. Like many other cases in this book, the Business Re-engineering projects of Progressive have not only proved successful, they have engendered a willingness to embrace change and continually improve. This will serve them well in the future to overcome the challenges facing them. The two main challenges the leadership consider important are, firstly, to maintain quality during rapid growth (currently at 30 per cent a year). The second challenge is to increase the level of customer service and quality of customer awareness and perception, as Progressive moves more to selling their products direct instead of exclusively through third-party insurance brokers. Some 40,000 calls a day are handled and each of these has to be perfect – dealing with customers direct is very different to dealing with knowledgeable brokers. Progressive intends to continue introducing changes and new skills to ensure it can continually improve.

LESSONS LEARNT

The CEO considers the factors below as vital for current success:

- clear, well communicated objectives;
- recruitment and retention of good people;
- excellent communication;
- willingness to change;
- sensitivity to consumers;
- 'killing the sacred cows' – and experimenting to learn.

Lessons have been learnt on the way. The CEO feels the main lesson is to watch the timing when a variety of initiatives are underway at once. For example the 'Breaking New Ground' programme occurred just before the middle managers were mainly cut out. This created problems when the very middle managers who went on a course to learn about teamwork suddenly found themselves no longer wanted as team members. This damaged the effect the training had for the company.

The COO feels that Progressive was too slow in the late 1980s to realise the extent of the need for change. When he first mentioned the theme of delighting the customers, his words were met with a fair degree of derision. Looking back, the COO reckons that if the three key initiatives of process leadership, flattening of the hierarchy (as part of cost reductions) and gainshare had been introduced in 1989 (instead of 1992), Progressive would have been further along the road. The reason it took time for these initiatives to come to light was because Progressive went through a time of denial, which prevented the re-engineering initiatives from achieving as much as they could.

The final lesson that the case shows is the positive effect a CEO can have by employing leadership skills effectively. Rather than telling and directing, the CEO should ensure that everyone knows the objectives and that with only a few ground rules, the organisation has the processes to get on and achieve the objectives in its own way. The CEO should manage only by veto, occasionally using it to keep people on track. To this end, he should display the type of crucial leadership behaviour needed in re-engineered organisations, detailed in Part 1 Chapter 4. The quotation of Lau Tsu is repeated in part:

> A leader is best when people hardly know he exists ... when his work is done and his aim fulfilled they will say 'We did it ourselves'.

SUMMARY

- **Know what you want**
  - Simple clear vision and values.
  - Listen hard to the customers.
  - Keep track of competitors.

- **Make a plan**
  - Build consensus for action through teams.
  - Agree measurements and processes to measure before implementation.

- **Do it**
  - Use experiments to learn, improve, reduce risk and gain consensus.
  - Use process leaders and cross-functional teams.
  - Use enhanced IT to keep communicating.
  - Empower leadership.

- **Monitor**
  - Objective measurement as part of the projects.
  - Non-financial indicators used as well as normal financial criteria.
  - Achievements linked to gainshare and discretionary awards.

11

Siemens Nixdorf Service

INTRODUCTION

Siemens Nixdorf Service (ITS) specialises in providing a full range of computer-related services including installing, servicing, maintaining and networking computer software and hardware. It has some $2.1 billion revenues worldwide. The operation is the result of the merger of two large high-tech giants in the late 1980s – Siemens DI (based in Munich) and Nixdorf (based in Paderborn).

The operation is in the midst of rolling out, across the world, its re-engineering programme which was started in late 1991. The programme is interesting in that it throws up common lessons from a variety of different cultures.

BACKGROUND – THE IMPERATIVE FOR CHANGE

With a large multi-billion dollar turnover, and multi-million dollar profits, ITS would not appear to be a likely candidate for a radical re-engineering programme. However, by the early 1990s the need for change was becoming more pressing. The recent merger of Siemens DI and Nixdorf did not initially result in efficient integrated processes. At the same time the industry was changing, and service was becoming more important. New entrants, which specialised in after-sales servicing, were beginning to make an impact, and the market was thus becoming more competitive. The projections of ITS showed that, without change, the operation would begin to incur losses by the mid 1990s.

THE INITIAL DIAGNOSTIC ANALYSIS –
SEPTEMBER – DECEMBER 1991

Gerhard Radtke, the head of the service business, formed a team with the brief to look at the business and come up with recommendations. The team worked with an outside consultancy, and thus a joint team (numbering ten) of internal managers and external consultants conducted the initial diagnosis. They were told to focus initially on how to reduce the head office headcount of over 1,600 people by 50 per cent.

The team quickly confirmed the loss projections, and also quickly realised that a reduction in head office headcount would not alone be enough to offset the projected losses which the operation was potentially facing. They began to analyse the field operations. This included 30 support centres around the world, with over 20 customer call points in Germany alone. The field base organisation numbered 11,400. The system of servicing customer needs was generally inefficient. Only 10 per cent of service problems were sorted over the phone, and repair technicians would usually have to make two trips – one to diagnose the problem and one to return with the necessary spares to fix it. There were also too many levels of management hierarchy.

The team reckoned that a redesign of the customer-facing processes would result in a 20 per cent increase in efficiency. It was clear that a significant re-engineering programme was needed. Radtke formulated a series of clear goals which the programme would need to achieve:

- 20 per cent reduction in headcount with increased customer service levels;
- remain profitable and avoid the decline into long-term loss;
- increase customer satisfaction, and avoid the loss of customers to competitors.

Before the programme moved on to detailed analysis and planning, Radtke presented the findings and recommendations of the diagnostic team to the main board of Siemens Nixdorf. His aim was to get fully sanctioned support for the programme, as well as a budget from central resources to use across the various locations across the world. This was crucial, and would save time haggling when the implementation began in earnest.

DETAILING AND PLANNING THE CHANGE –
JANUARY–JUNE 1992

The diagnostic team now became the 'CORE' team and acted as the overall coordination and control of the programme, which was called the

CORE project. Five other cross-functional teams were also set up. These looked at the detailed processes and customer needs for Materials Management, Field Processes, Support Processes, Head Office Processes and Additional Services. The first four focused on process efficiency and cost reduction, whilst the last team, Additional Services, looked at new service products which could be introduced to enhance revenues. Supported by the CORE team, the new teams analysed in detail what the current processes were, and how they could be redesigned to improve customer service and reduce costs. The internal tools and techniques included process mapping, cash flow and productivity analysis. The external analysis included customer and competitor interviews.

Each team produced its own detailed plans, using project management techniques. These plans were initially oriented towards two pilots which were set up to begin the implementation.

IMPLEMENTATION – TECHNIQUES USED: 1992/3

The implementation of the re-engineering programme relied on a number of techniques to ensure success:

- flattening and simplification of organisation structure;
- use of pilots to learn and gain commitment;
- leadership support;
- communications.

Flattening and simplification of organisational structure

The 30 previous regions were restructured into five areas, with two less levels of managers. Specialists who were previously ensconced in head offices were moved into these five new areas, and hence closer to the customers. At the same time the new processes at head office were introduced to support the more radical redesign of the field-based processes.

Use of pilots to learn and gain commitment

The newly designed field processes were first implemented in two of the new regional offices – Frankfurt and Brussels. New diagnostic processes increased client service over the phone, and field engineers with specialist support were grouped into teams. Some of these specialists were moved from head office (which was reduced from 1,600 to 800 people). The measurement and incentive systems were changed to focus the new teams more on customer needs and the new processes were underpinned by information technology. The new processes effectively cut the previous need for two trips to the customer down to one. These pilots helped the cross-functional change teams to learn lessons which could be used to fine tune the roll-out into the rest of the field-based organisations. These lessons also covered the training aspects, which were vital to successful implementation. The pilots also achieved dramatic results (see section on monitoring below), and this helped overcome resistance to change.

Leadership support

The support and approved budget of the main board demonstrated to the organisation that it was serious about implementing change. Gerhard Radtke spent much of his time (over 60 per cent) personally involved with the CORE team (who reported direct to him). He also spent time with the other cross-functional change teams, and (more importantly) communicating the change to line managers. His support was vital to ensure the change teams had the standing and credibility when dealing day to day with the head office and field managers. It was also vital to ensure that the resistance to change was understood, and managed proactively.

Communications

A few effective techniques were used to ensure that the organisation would embrace the change. These included:

- *Champions in Service booklet and posters.* A booklet was produced on the theme of fitness and training. The nature of increased competition was explained, and the need for change. As in athletic competition, it was explained that the organisation needed to get fitter, and reduce fat. It stated 'Champions are made. Not born', and began 'Let's become Champions in Service'. The booklet was easy to read, included many drawings and cartoons, and was distributed to each employee to build up awareness of the need, and the scope, of the re-engineering programmes. The motto was 'Closer, Faster, Stronger'. The back of the booklet included a 'Champion Check', ten questions for the reader to check the understanding of what was now needed, and the aim of the CORE project. The booklet was backed up by a variety of internal posters to assist further the communication of the new approach. A booklet was also produced for the customers, to keep them abreast with what ITS was doing.
- *Leadership presentations and discussions.* The top leadership spent much time presenting the need for change, and the scope of the re-engineering programme. Discussions with managers and employees were held to get feedback. The leadership spent a lot of time listening hard, to understand fully the fears and concerns of individuals in the organisation. This understanding helped formulate actions designed to overcome such fears and concerns. In Germany particularly, the

leadership spent a lot of time working with the workers' councils to ensure that they would embrace the changes and help to implement them. Without such support from staff and managers, the re-engineering programme would have been very difficult to implement. One of the main problems was that the middle and lower managers did not associate pain with the status quo. The top leadership spent much time in sharing with them the findings of the diagnostic review, and the medium-term crisis which was looming.

- *Visits to pilots.* In order to ensure that the managers of the organisation across the world would associate gain with the change, visits were arranged to the two pilots. This allowed engineers and managers to interact with their peers, and to see for themselves the clear benefits which the new field and support processes were bringing. Such visits allowed the leadership to position the rest of the organisation so that when the roll-out occurred (which began in early 1993), the need for change, and the benefits it brought, were already fully understood.

- *Fireside chats.* The changes introduced were traumatic for some, who had been comfortable in the way things had been run. The programme had also upset traditional boundaries of control, power and influence. To help people get over this, a series of 'fireside' chats were run, using external facilitators. These gave the organisation the ability to 'let off steam' and disengage with the current state, as well as provide the change teams and leadership with some frank feedback about how they were performing in implementing the changes.

- *Project updates, reviews and best practice identification.* The cross-functional change teams were working across national boundaries, especially when the pilots were rolled out. The CORE team acted as the main transition management group, and through regular feedback and review sessions ensured that they remained coordinated and that the top leadership was informed of progress. The teams themselves were often brought together to interact in a workshop environment in order to fine tune the quality of the implementation and identify best practice across the teams. These sessions were often held on the pilot sites themselves so that those not directly involved in that particular pilot could learn and apply the lessons elsewhere.

The hub of the re-engineering programme was the CORE team, with the leadership provided by Gerhard Radtke and his top team. The CORE team had their own project room, where anyone needing an update could go to find out how things were progressing. This method of transition management, together with the techniques above, ensured that the implementation (never easy in any circumstance) went as smoothly as possible. The open communication helped to ensure that the organisation became as comfortable as it could with the radical changes being implemented.

MONITORING AND THE RESULTS GAINED

One of the lessons of the pilots showed that the monitoring and measuring systems were not up to delivering the information needed to keep track of progress and the results achieved. Prior to roll-out, the measuring systems were overhauled and renewed to ensure that the CORE team and the top leadership could be kept abreast of progress. New measurement systems were also introduced early on, including customer Satisfaction which is monitored continually by an external agency which phones customers and produces a monthly report on findings, as well as conducting a more detailed annual review by mail. Operational monitoring is carried out by both normal direct reports within the current management structure (assisted by new systems), and reports via the change teams in the transition management structure. The full roll-out across the world is still in hand, but the results achieved by those who have implemented the changes are impressive and include:

- 20 per cent reduction in headcount;
- 35 per cent reduction in field costs;
- first-time fix rate up from 80 per cent to over 90 per cent;
- number of customers served per day by an engineer up from two to four;
- problem-solving by telephone up from 10 per cent to 25 per cent;
- one manager to 35, instead of to ten;
- customer satisfaction increased by 10 per cent;
- revenue decline halted, and expected to grow as new services are rolled out;
- operating costs reduced by 20 per cent.

The benefits of the re-engineering programme, however, do not just rest in the numbers achieved above (impressive though they may be). Having gone through such an exercise of re-engineering, using cross-functional teams and implementing radical change, the organisation is now much more flexible and responsive to customer needs. This has enabled the operation to serve customers using computer products which are not of Siemens Nixdorf origin. It will also allow the organisation to be closer to the customer, and when the customers' needs change and evolve, ITS will be able to change and evolve with them.

LESSONS LEARNT

The leadership of ITS feel that the following were critical to their success in re-engineering the organisation:

- *Use of joint consultant/managers team.* The use of external consultants, working as members of a change team which included managers from a variety of functions, ensured that the skills and techniques needed to achieve effective change were passed on. The support and guidance given by the consultant members of the teams to their inside counterparts in analytical techniques, facilitation and project management was crucial. The outside consultants could also act as a 'neutral' party and so help the organisation weather the inevitable political behaviour which any radical change engenders in an organisation.
- *Funding up front.* The up-front agreement to the capital and resources needed to drive the change through was also important. This allowed the change teams and leadership to focus on getting it done, instead of having to justify themselves all the time. By having a separate cost centre number, the agreed budget also prevented any field/head office squabbles during implementation.
- *Use of cross-functional teams.* The involvement of specialists from across the functions and across field/head office boundaries (including national boundaries), ensured that the process redesign was of a high quality and could be successfully applied.
- *Leadership support.* The time spent by top leaders proved vital. The communication was two way, and a lot of hard listening was also involved.

There are three areas where the ITS leadership feels that the programme initially could have been done differently:

- *More ruthless and transparent management in overcoming resistance.* There was no transparent assessment of managers regarding their active support for change. This allowed some to disrupt it, and perhaps they should have been counselled in a slightly more active manner. The problem the change teams found with less than enthusiastic managers was that this feeling cascaded down to all levels. If the manager was enthusiastic, so were his or her people – if the manager was not, then the barriers to change were significantly raised.
- *More communications.* More interactive sessions (such as the fireside chats, which only happened in Germany), and workshops could have been carried out. A more extensive use of workshops and facilitated sessions would have helped to build more commitment to change (and saved extensive follow-ups).
- *Improved measuring systems.* The measurement systems were initially not sophisticated enough, and the change teams learnt that they should have spent time planning and implementing measurement systems as well as new processes.

The three lessons above are being incorporated into the roll-out, which is still going on. And they will be incorporated with the future changes that the new flexible structure and culture will allow ITS to pursue.

SUMMARY

- **Know what you want**
  - Small joint external/internal diagnostic team.
  - Budget and targets agreed up front.
  - Diagnostic team evolved into CORE team.
  - Clear goals and objectives.

- **Make a plan**
  - Use of cross-functional teams, coordinated by the CORE team.
  - Common techniques used across teams.
  - Close work with line managers.

- **Do it**
  - Clear, demonstrable, committed leadership support.
  - Transition management by CORE team.
  - Use of pilots to build success.
  - Communication to listen as well as preach.

- **Monitor**
  - Measurement systems improved to meet demands of new processes.
  - Monitor action and results.

Part 3

Appendices:
Tools and Techniques

Appendix 1

Analytical and Process Tools and Techniques

---

1. INTRODUCTION

The analytical tools and techniques in this appendix have been used before by organisations to help senior management teams clarify a situation in order to facilitate decision-making. Most of them are not original, and I have tried to give credit to those who first formulated them. They will be recognised by many as everyday strategic business analysis tools. A few points should be borne in mind:

- Never lose sight of the fact that the best way to analyse the needs of the key stakeholders is to actually talk to them, and listen with an open mind!
- The tools presented together form a 'tool kit' of techniques you can employ to build up a sound picture of what is going on and what needs to be done. Like any tool bag, the situation will determine which the best tools are. Be wary of using just one approach – if the only tool you have is a hammer, then all your problems tend to get treated like nails! On the other hand don't think you have to use all the tools in the tool kit – this can lead to paralysis through analysis.
- The tool kit is primarily organised to assist you to understand fully the needs of the key stakeholders in the organisation (typically customers, suppliers, employees and shareholders). However, there are also a few which are 'general' which can also be employed to help with the process itself.
- Use a variety of approaches. No one approach will give a complete picture, so use a number of techniques to get a full feel of what is going on and what the options are.

Many of the tools are based on a matrix approach of looking at life. Some consultancies have in the past made a lot of money by selling a particular matrix approach. The Boston Consulting Group, for example, invented their famous 'Growth/Share' matrix (which we look at later in the appendix). But there is nothing magical in such tools. You can invent your own matrix. If you are faced with an uncertain situation, and you want to get a feel for the options (and thus the type of strategy you can pursue) then if you can identify the key variables which directly affect the situation, you can build a conceptual matrix to clarify your options.

Take, for example, the simple situation of going on holiday – the two key variables here are normally time and money. And you either have a lot of each or some of varying quantities. So you can see four basic options emerge:

■ Lots of money and lots of time – a world cruise or world tour.
■ Lots of time but little money – a camping holiday.
■ Lots of money but little time – go for a quick break in the Caribbean.
■ Little money and time – stay at home, read a book, go for walks or watch some old videos!

So our holiday options 'matrix' would look like Figure A1.1.

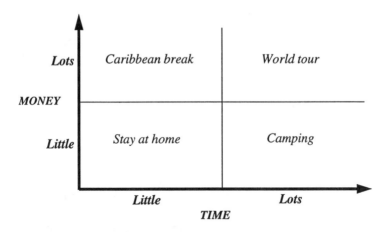

Figure A1.1 Example of a conceptual matrix.

Using two key variables, situations can be 'mapped out' to show what the options are, as well as what the current (and possible future) situation is. This approach can also be used to map out individual units (from people to different companies) onto a matrix showing, for example, a market analysis of competitors on price/quality variables. Other variables can be included, such as size variables of the units, by changing the colour or size of the 'bubble'.

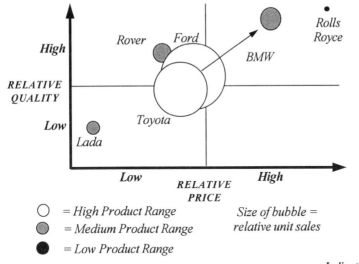

= High Product Range   *Size of bubble =*
= Medium Product Range   *relative unit sales*
= Low Product Range

Indicative example only

Figure A1.2 Example of a conceptual map.

You need to do some research to get the quantitative values for each plot. You can also use arrows to show unit movement. Figure A1.2 shows an indicative example of a map of the motor industry.

The examples above simply demonstrate what you can do: there are not many situations which you cannot show using a matrix approach. The advantage of the approach is that a picture paints a thousand words! However, be aware that the matrix approach gives indicative options, and that life is normally more complex than a simple two-by-two matrix.

2. TOOLS FOR CUSTOMER ANALYSIS

2.1 Five 'Cs' and 'Ps'

The five Cs and Ps (Figure A1.3) are just a checklist of things you should look at and understand when considering the needs of customers, the environment in which they exist, and how well their needs are matched by you (both by your products and people) and by your competition. They are useful tools for comparing with the competition, and also for comparing your current state to the future state you wish to achieve. The gap between the two will indicate the scale of the change you need to achieve.

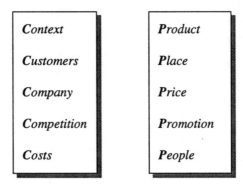

Context	Product
Customers	Place
Company	Price
Competition	Promotion
Costs	People

Figure A1.3 The five 'Cs' and 'Ps'.

2.2 SWOT analysis

A SWOT analysis (Figure A1.4) is a good summary of research into how customers and others view the organisation. The use of SWOT should be done with care, as it gives perceptions (which may not be facts). However, assuming that people's perceptions are their reality, it is a useful tool. It is worth using across a variety of groups so comparisons can be made – for example, comparing senior management's perceptions to those of customers in a SWOT format may show how 'in tune' the top of the organisation is with the customers! And further comparisons with staff perceptions may highlight internal issues as well.

S	Strengths
W	Weaknesses
O	Opportunities
T	Threats

Figure A1.4 SWOT Analysis.

2.3 'HPV' versus 'LDC'

The two general ways of competing are either by delivering High Perceived Value (HPV) or by achieving Low Delivered Cost (LDC). In reality most organisations try to achieve a degree of each. There is also the option of moving from being an LDC operator to an HPV position, whilst maintaining an LDC base (Figure A1.5).

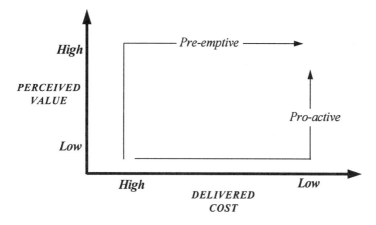

Figure A1.5 Value versus cost.

This in effect is what the Japanese car manufacturers did against the West, entering the market at the LDC end (remember when Japanese cars were perceived as a joke?). They then maintained their LDC position by investing heavily in product technology and quickly took market share from others. This forced Western manufacturers to invest in product technology and improve their marketing to keep their HPV position but achieve an LDC base.

Like any analytical tool, this can give a too simplistic picture. However, it is useful to plot competitors on a price/product quality matrix to see how the competitive market looks. One can also introduce a third dimension, service, to complete the picture. This can be achieved by using shaded bubbles for competitors with different shades to show the different levels of service.

2.4 Market versus product

To expand market share and increase revenue the four options shown in Figure A1.6 are possible. Moving into new markets with new products straight away is the riskiest, and should be avoided – the equivalent of 'Here there be dragons' on an old map!

2.5 Competitive Position versus Market Attractiveness

The matrix in Figure A1.7 is known as the GE/McKinsey Shell, named after the organisations who developed it – General Electric in the USA, and the management consultancy McKinsey & Company.

It is a useful tool if your organisation has a number of sites or differing product sectors/businesses. As shown in figure A1.7, six broad options emerge for consideration. You need to 'score' a range of criteria grouped under both variables. The kinds of criteria you can use are shown in

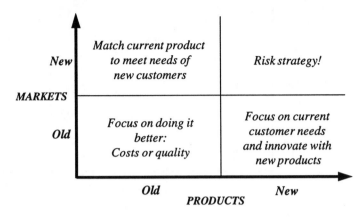

Figure A1.6 Market versus product strategies.

Figure A1.8, with each variable of 'market attractiveness' and 'competitive position' split into two sub-categories.

You should score each criterion out of 3 (1 being low/weak, 3 being high/strong). If you think that there is a large range of differing importance in each criterion then each can be weighted to get a more even score. As long as these assumptions are reasonable then the tool is of great indicative use, enabling you to plot elements of your own organisation operating in a variety of differing locations/markets.

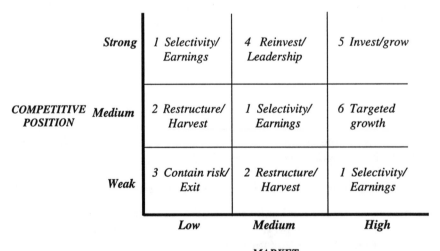

**Figure A1.7 Organisational competitive position
versus market attractiveness.**

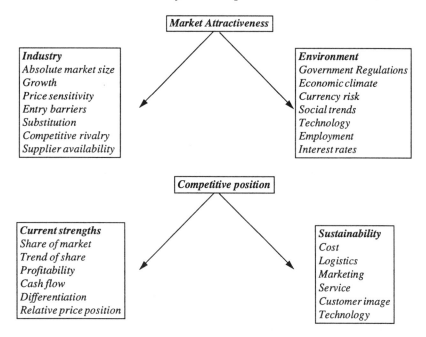

Figure A1.8 Examples of criteria.

2.6 Growth/Share matrix (the BCG model)

This matrix (Figure A1.9) was invented by the Boston Consulting Group (BCG), and is used to assist clients to formulate strategies if they have a portfolio of businesses/investments. The two variables used on each axis are the extent to which the market (within which the unit is operating) is

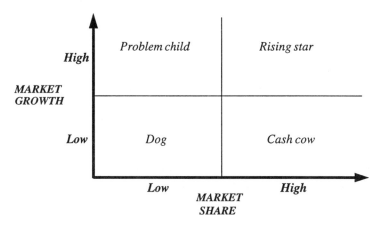

Figure A1.9 Market growth versus market share.

growing, and the market share which that unit has (compared to the other competitors).

Using this matrix you can see that one should 'milk' the 'Cash cows' to fund the 'Rising stars', review the marketing approach/strategy of the 'Problem children' and restructure or sell the 'Dogs'. Or should one? A rigid application of this model can cause more problems than it solves.

The drawback with this approach is that it can be too simplistic! Many difficulties arise from the very use of the tool – not many units within an organisation would like to be viewed as a 'Dog', and even the 'Cash cows' might have a problem with seeing all their hard-earned cash being siphoned off to feed others. In the past, some of the recommendations proposed by consultancies using this kind of approach often fell foul of organisational politics.

However, this analytical tool can help to shed an interesting light on a portfolio and is useful when used together with other tools.

2.7 Dynamics of competitive initiatives

For every successful change initiative which brings a new product to market there exists a 'strategic window' within which you have time to operate before others realign themselves to take some of the hard earned competitive advantage, and resultant sales you are generating, away from you. This is shown in Figure A1.10.

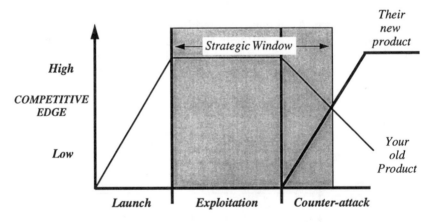

Figure A1.10 Dynamics of competitive initiative.

If the choice is to go for a new product, then be aware of the dynamics of competitive innovation. If it's such a brilliant new product, then rest assured, others will follow. However, there will be a window of time during which you can keep the advantage, but you need to think ahead to counter competitor response. This 'strategic window' covers the

'Exploitation' phase of a new product launch, and lasts until a competitor's counter-attack gathers sufficient force to take the competitive edge away from you.

By understanding the evolution of customer needs and the competitive environment within which your new product fits, you will keep ahead of the next moves. Failure to do so can result in long-term disaster. An example of such a disaster is that which befell the computer company Wang. They introduced office automation and word processing, but did not continue to innovate and lost out to others such as IBM. And this occurred despite pressure from those below senior management within Wang for changes to match IBM.

So just because your current product is the 'bee's knees', it does not mean that someone is not going to introduce a new product which will meet customer needs better. A typical response by some is to invest more time and effort in updating their own product to compete against a new one. Such companies are more focused on the product than the customer, with inevitable results. Many passenger sailing ship manufacturing companies which served the trans-Atlantic market simply added more sails to compete against steam – the final result was the capsize of a ship with too many sails, and the demise of trans-Atlantic passenger sailing ships! So focus on *needs*, and not on products.

This is worth bearing in mind when you look at the objectives which meet the customer's needs – how long will it be before your competitors counter-attack, what will they be likely to do, and what will your response be? These questions will need answering before you move!

2.8 Porter's five competitive forces

No analysis of a market would be complete without bearing in mind the competitive forces identified by the leading Harvard strategist, Michael Porter (Figure A1.11). While the lateral forces of suppliers, competitors and customers are often looked at, substitute products and new entrants are not normally given as much attention. Yet these two forces do pose serious threats, as banks found out with the mortgage companies, and

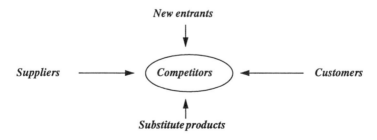

Figure A1.11 Porter's five competitive forces.

the record industry found out with cassettes! It is vital to gain an understanding of what the future and substitue products and new entrants are, and how much of a threat they pose (using the criteria of meeting customer needs).

2.9 Product quality (what you sell) versus service delivery (how you sell it)

In Figure A1.12 the obvious box to avoid is the loser's box! The way to use this matrix is to map yourself on it compared to your competitors. To get the data you will need to interview customers using qualitative means (structured questionnaires that can be scored) and qualitative means (focus group discussion with customers using trained external facilitators/market researchers). You can plot using bubbles to denote market share, and shading to denote profitability.

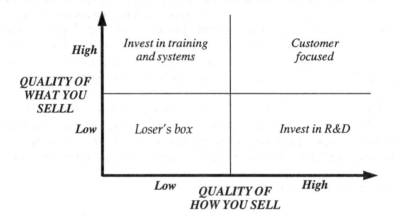

Figure A1.12 What versus how you sell.

3. TOOLS FOR SUPPLIER ANALYSIS

3.1 Value Chain

Unless you are a fully integrated business, your final end product/service to the customer will depend on suppliers. It is worth understanding what value the supplier adds to the overall business system. If one takes the final price paid for a service/product as 100 per cent, then working back through the business system you can construct a value chain as shown in Figure A1.13.

Once a value chain is constructed it is useful to see exactly what 'value added' is provided by the various parts of the business system. There are two ways of using this information:

- **Do it better.** This can be achieved by entering into closer relationships with your suppliers, and jointly exploring options to reduce lead times/costs. The savings can either be used to reduce prices (to become more competitive) or invested to increase quality.
- **Change the rules.** This is what IKEA effectively did in the furniture industry. They lowered the price of furniture by sourcing high quality (but lower cost) part constructed furniture, going for large edge of town warehouse sites, and letting the customer do the final construction. The savings gained from suppliers, distribution and production were mostly passed on to the customer who could purchase high quality furniture at a lower price.

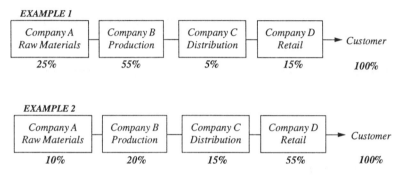

Each Company's % value added can be further broken down to show the value added of each company's activities - ie operations, marketing, administration etc

Figure A1.13 The 'business system' – value chain analysis.

Changing the rules of the game gives a competitor more sustainable advantage, as others cannot typically respond without fundamentally changing as well. As the 'build your own' furniture segment of the market was somewhat new in a traditionally conservative industry, not many thought it worthwhile responding. This gave IKEA time to carve a new niche and develop it.

3.2 Supplier availability versus value added

Once the value added of your suppliers is established, various options can be studied by checking the availability of suppliers. The suppliers can be plotted onto a standard matrix as shown in figure A1.14.

The fact that you are using an outside supplier implicitly suggests that you have made the make/buy decision. This decision should be revisited if the value added is low and supplier availability is limited. Integration is always an option. If there are many suppliers then either quality or cost

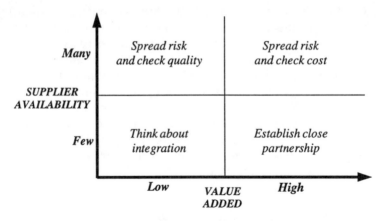

Figure A1.14 Supplier availability versus value added.

(depending on the value added) would be the primary concern (although both need to be borne in mind!), and it is worth spreading the risk to guard against supplier failure.

4. TOOLS FOR EMPLOYEE ANALYSIS

4.1 Introduction

Employee analysis can be broken down into two areas: 'Hard' analysis, and 'Soft' analysis. The latter is often ignored, but is no less important. The tools which one can use in both areas, and which are detailed below, are as follows:

- **Hard analysis:** employee turnover, days sickness, employee productivity, organisational structures, process analysis and business process re-engineering;
- **Soft analysis:** culture, competitive energy, strategic acceptance, values versus strategy, behavioural influences, leadership style, McKinsey Seven S, opposition versus support, three Rs.

Although the soft side may seem difficult to get a solid fix on, one can turn soft concepts into hard figures to ease understanding and analysis. This is explained in more detail in section 4.6.

4.2 Staff productivity, turnover, sickness

These are common statistics which are used to analyse employees. They are fine as far as they go, but are greatly enhanced when they are compared to those for other organisations (especially competitors). For many managers, the employee analysis frequently stops there. This is a mistake, and some of the tools below (depending on circumstance) should be used to get a broader picture.

4.3 Organisational structures

There is always a great temptation to reorganise reporting structures and responsibilities. This is a difficult task and must be managed with sensitivity – 'revolutionary in thought, evolutionary in implementation' is a good catch phrase. Be wary of going for 'standard' solutions. Flat hierarchies to replace stacked ones is a common approach but can lead to a loss of control. The answer is to get the balance right – it is not so much the way the organisation is set up (i.e. flat versus hierarchical) which is important as the *counter-balances* put in place to guard against the pitfalls. These pitfalls can vary according to the levels of hierarchy and degree of centralised control, as shown in figure A1.15.

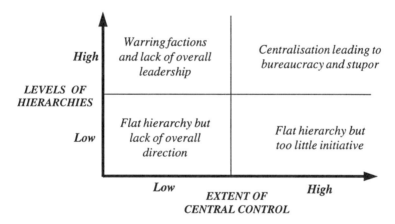

Figure A1.15 Organisational pitfalls.

If the organisation has many layers of hierarchy, what processes are in place to enable cross-functional cooperation? How fast is the organisation to react? What use is made of short-term multi-disciplinary teams? If the organisation is flat, how are employees motivated with a career path? How are objectives defined, linked to an overall strategy and monitored? How is feedback from key stakeholders communicated and how effective is the reaction?

The secret of organisation has as much to do with vision, values, culture and cross-functional *lateral* processes as it does with vertical reporting structures! The following two tools are very helpful in this respect.

4.4 Process analysis

Most organisations have an 'organigram' showing who reports to who, and what the functions do. Very few organisations analyse the flow of work across the functions or even within them, but this kind of analysis is a powerful way of spotting how the organisation could can work more effectively and either save time/costs or increase quality, or both! The types of symbols used in such flow charts are shown in Figure A1.16.

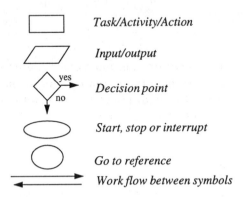

Figure A1.16 Process flow analysis – symbols.

An example showing a process flow is shown in Figure A1.17. The flow is an indicative example (and not very customer friendly!). It includes a very powerful analytical technique: effort duration analysis. For every task calculate the amount of effort needed per item (in the example in Figure A1.17 the effort was calculated as an average per order). Then calculate the total duration the whole process takes and divide the effort by the duration to get the level of efficiency. The example in Figure A1.17 is only 4 per cent efficient. You can add further value to such analysis by highlighting the 'value added' activities (i.e. only those which are truly valued by the customers). If this is deducted from the effort and redivided by the duration, you will gain a percentage value added for the process. Such analysis can be startling! Using such analysis, National Vulcan discovered it had less than 1 per cent real value added in its insurance policy process (see Part 2).

The flow chart boxes can also be colour coded to show the interdependencies between departments. It can be used for any series of events, from how a customer complaint is reacted to, to how long it takes to get a new product to market. It can be a very powerful tool. The secret is to think inductively rather than deductively. You should concentrate on cutting down on inputs and adding value to outputs. When a variety of people get involved in a lateral process, look for opportunities to lump

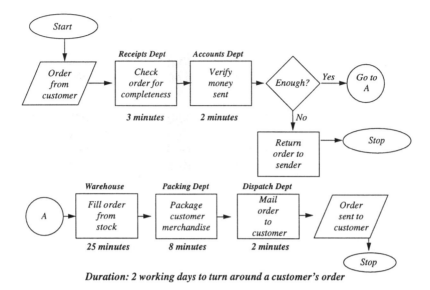

Figure A1.17 Example of work flow analysis – 96 per cent non-effective.

tasks (and people) together – this forms the basis of process re-engineering. Process analysis can be a major task, and off-the-shelf flow chart software packages exist to help speed up the analysis.

4.5 Business process re-engineering

The process analysis flows above are particularly effective when overlapped onto organisational structures. Companies are typically organised into functional, vertical hierarchies such as Marketing, Operations, Distribution, Finance, Human Resources, etc., and organisational charts typically reflect this functionality, with a high degree of hierarchy. Small wonder that status, turf, power, control, ambition and rank are often more important to the people than efficiency, lateral cooperation and customer service. Looking at what an organisation actually delivers to its customers, it becomes clear that it often depends on a few key processes in order to ensure that the customer is satisfied. And these processes often cut across functional vertical hierarchies (see Figure A1.18). Business process re-engineering suggests that organisations which put in a lateral management structure to manage the lateral processes often gain advantage over slower competitors. Such structures are different to vertical ones – they call for teamwork rather than rank.

The aim is to put in place task teams (under a key process manager) using the methodologies above, which take control and ownership across the functions to deliver a specific process. This can get rid of inter-depart-

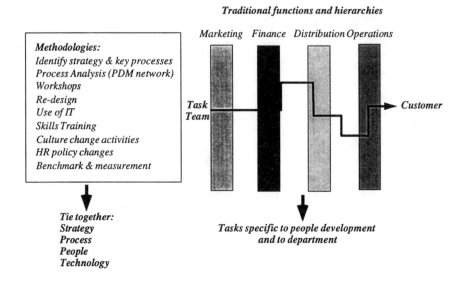

Figure A1.18 Process re-engineering moves away from hierarchies towards teams.

mental delays, inefficiencies, internal competition and slow expensive service. Backed with information technology, this kind of approach can boost morale, productivity and customer satisfaction at the same time as saving costs. The hierarchical vertical structures can be thinned down to concentrate on those tasks which have no cross-functional impact, and also on developing and training its members of the task teams. Although generally new to business and industry, such an approach is not new in other walks of life. For example, it is the way armoured warfare is waged. Although the various infantry, armour, artillery, engineer etc. regiments train and look after the careers of their own soldiers, they form 'Battle Groups' in war. These are essentially component parts of the various regiments reformed into cooperative task teams working under one commander. Like all approaches, business process re-engineering needs to be put in place only when it can have an impact, otherwise chaos can ensue!

The outline above has been very brief – a book well worth reading on the subject is called – 'Re-engineering the Corporation' A Manifesto for Business Revolution, by Michael Hammer and James Champy.

4.6 Turning soft into hard

Many of the tools which follow look at 'soft' things like culture, commitment, motivation, morale, etc. On first impression, the problem with these indicators are that they are hard to measure. However, there is a way to turn 'soft' into 'hard'. That is by asking defined questions of a good selection of people, and giving them a multiple choice to score their feelings. An example of some questions, and possible score analysis, is shown in Figure A1.19.

1.How satisfied are you with your pay?	Very happy	Happy	Neutral	Unhappy	Very unhappy
2.How supportive are your managers?	Very good	Good	Neutral	Poor	Very bad
3.How good is co-operation in your department?	Very good	Good	Neutral	Poor	Very bad
4.How good is co-operation with other departments?	Very good	Good	Neutral	Poor	Very bad

Example average scores

Q1 = 3.2

Q2 = 2.2

Q3 = 4.2

Q4 = 1.8

Example A of distribution to Q1   Example B of distribution to Q1

Figure A1.19 Turning 'soft' into 'hard'.

Each question is scored 1 to 5 (with 5 being 'very good', 3 being OK, and 1 being 'very bad'). The questionnaires can be collated and then each question averaged to get an overall score.

While the average score is important, so too is the distribution of scores. In the example above, question 1 scored just above average at 3.2 – so one could conclude that pay is being seen as acceptable. However, the distribution could tell a different picture. Example A shows that the distribution reveals that 50 per cent found pay acceptable, with the remainder split. Example B shows that people either thought it very good or very bad!

Remember that these answers are perceptions – but people's perceptions are their reality. So (in this example) a straight comparison with industry averages for compensation will show what gap exists between 'objective' external reality and the 'subjective' organisational perceptions. Any gap will show the scale of communication which is needed to bridge the perceptual gap. Obviously pay is only one part of how people feel about their work, and a broader questionnaire should be designed to capture all the angles.

Using questionnaires like this can get emotions stirred. It is important to do this independently from line managers, with a process set up to get the questionnaires to and from the respondents in a confidential way. A letter should also accompany the questionnaire stating what the objective is, and how valued the replies are. It should also be stated that the questionnaires should be filled in anonymously, although asking the respondents to identify their departments can give an interesting cross-functional comparison.

Don't forget to feedback the results of the survey and, more importantly, what you intend to do about it!

4.7 Organisational culture

You can measure culture in many ways. One way is to see the extent to which the organisation is loyal to itself versus loyal to outsiders. By using the 'soft to hard' type of questionnaires, you can plot the organisation (and even the various departments) on the matrix shown in Figure A1.20.

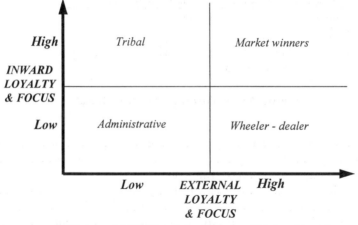

Figure A1.20 Organisational culture mix.

Typical 'one liners' and summaries of the four types of culture are:

■ **Administrative.** 'It's just a job.' People come into work, hang their personalities on the coat hook, don't feel any loyalty to their team, and feel that outsiders (either departments or end customers) are an evil necessity. They do not think either up or down stream. This culture is exemplified by what people might think typically exists in a bureaucratic governmental Civil Service organisation.

■ **Tribal.** 'We've a great team, with a great product – our customers don't appreciate what we do for them.' The organisation is more loyal to its products and own people than it is to the needs of the customers. This culture is typified by what people might think existed in an engineering led organisation.

- **Wheeler-dealers.** 'My clients like me, but think the rest of the company is rubbish – the other guys can't understand what the customer wants.' The focus is too much on the customer, with little internal cooperation and synergy. The sad thing is that in the long run, the customer does not get as good a service. This culture is typified by what people might think existed on the trading floor of a bank.

- **Market winners.** 'We really work as a team to exceed the expectations of our customers.' These companies win – they have processes in place which engender a high inward loyalty to the organisation and colleagues, while focusing them onto understanding and exceeding their customers' expectations and needs. They are innovative, responsive and fast. Typical organisations like this are small entrepreneurial companies, and large market leaders like 3M.

An example of a company which started in the 'Administrative' box and moved itself into the 'Market winner' box is British Airways. The company was privatised, and had a typical nationalised 'civil service' mentality. After drastically reducing waste (which resulted in many redundancies and even less loyalty!), the company slowly introduced a series of change programmes to move the culture of the organisation. To increase inward loyalty, 'A day in the life' programme was conceived. This explained to employees what each other's roles were, by visits, videos and presentations. This allowed the employees to see their part in an overall process to deliver service to the customer, and to appreciate how important each other's role was. To increase external loyalty the 'Customer First' programme was introduced, which encouraged all staff to take ownership of problems, not only of external customers, but also internal ones. Later on, a national TV advertising campaign portrayed the BA staff as 'supermen', going to extraordinary lengths to help customers. This not only helped external loyalty, but also helped to engender pride in the employees of belonging to a good organisation. The result of these and other initiatives was to move British Airways from being 'Bloody Awful, to Bloody Awesome' as one analyst put it!

4.8 Competitive energy

Another way of measuring the culture is to see how much energy is in the organisation. Energy can be generated by a compelling corporate ideology and an unrestricted climate. The four types of culture emerge, as shown in Figure A1.21.

If people throughout the organisation have a clear idea of the corporate ideology and strategy, and there exists a climate which encourages openness and initiative seeking, then you should have a high degree of

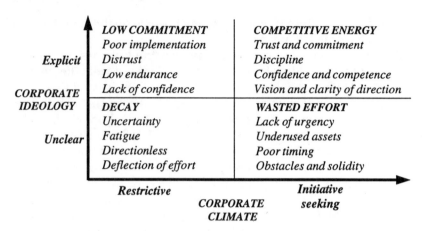

Figure A1.21 Competitive energy.

competitive energy. Sadly most do not. The worst ones have both an unclear ideology, and a restrictive climate which leads it to decay in an atmosphere of uncertainty and fatigue. Some have a restrictive atmosphere, although a clear ideology, but this leads to low employee commitment within an atmosphere of distrust, lack of confidence and low endurance. On the other hand those which have an open climate with lots of initiative, but an unclear ideology, end up with a lot of wasted effort in an atmosphere of under-used assets, lack of urgency and poor timing.

Understanding where your organisation is in this regard will help you decide if you want to increase communication (to clarify the ideology) or increase delegation, openness and management skills training (to free up the corporate climate). This is a diagnostic tool – it does not tell you what to do. But by understanding where you are, and where you want to go, you can then think clearly about what you need to do to get there! It helps to formulate the degree and components of a culture change programme.

4.9 Strategic Acceptance

Following on from the above is a matrix, shown in Figure A1.22, on which you can see what you have to do to improve strategic acceptance. The two variables here are the level to which the strategy is accepted and understood (i.e. is it just the board – if at all – or does the strategy fully and clearly permeate the whole organisation), and the quality of the strategy itself (either good or bad).

If you have a good strategy, but poor acceptance, then you need to communicate. On the other hand a widely accepted but poor strategy would need to be urgently reviewed and reformulated before the whole organisation charges happily over a cliff! Every company has a strategy, if you accept that strategy is action. If the action is undirected, or if the direction is known and accepted by only a few people, then you have a problem.

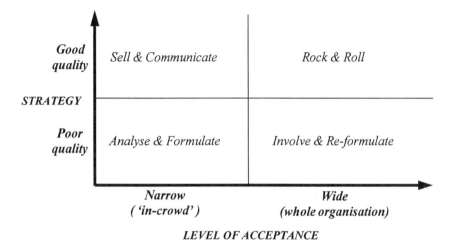

Figure A1.22 Strategic acceptance.

Depending where you are on the matrix will dictate the extent to which you have to rethink and involve others. Get the strategy right first in the minds of the people, and then Business Re-engineer!

4.10 Values versus strategy

Behaviour is driven by the strategy and values of the organisation. These are driven by the vision which the organisation has of itself and its future, as shown in Figure A1.23.

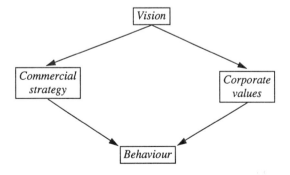

Figure A1.23 Linking vision, strategy and values.

The problems arise when the strategy is not consistent with the values. For example, a company which decides to pursue a low cost strategy (or LDC – see section 2.3 above) but does not have a cost-conscious approach will not do well. The importance that the corporate values match the strategic consistency cannot be stressed enough.

Too many organisations uphold values which do not match the strategy. One reason why earlier attempts to revive IBM did not succeed well was that although the strategy was to get the organisation to be more entrepreneurial, the values still dictated a bureaucratic approach (with any entrepreneurial idea having to go through a long process of hierarchical sign-offs). Too often one sees companies struggling to implement a cost leadership strategy, and yet one is overwhelmed by the opulent corporate headquarters, sleek executive cars and abundance of secretaries!

You can get an idea of what you want to change by analysing the values of the organisation and mapping them out alongside the strategy pursued. Four types of results can ensue, as shown in Figure A1.24.

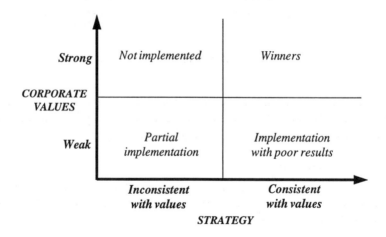

Figure A1.24 Implementation based on corporate values versus strategic consistency.

If your strategy is not being implemented, you need to see where it conflicts with the values held by the managers of the organisation, and work to change those values and remove the conflict.

4.11 Behavioural influences

At a more micro level there are nine key things which influence behaviour, shown in Figure A1.25. These are like levers which you can pull to get required results.

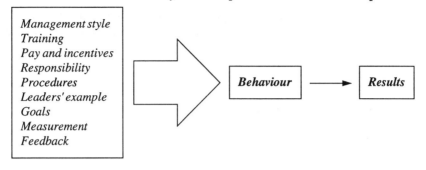

Figure A1.25 Influencing behaviours.

If you want to change results, you need to change behaviour, and if you want to change behaviour you need to understand the influence which the nine variables have on current behaviour. Once that is known, then you can work on how to change the influences! Again a way to measure the current impact and effectiveness of the influences is to design a 'soft to hard' questionnaire, as well as discreet one-to-one interviews.

4.12 Leadership styles

If one accepts that a leader's role is to get tasks achieved, and maintain a fundamental concern for the people achieving the tasks, then leadership style will revolve around concern for tasks and people.

The typical Anglo-Saxon approach is to be very task oriented, but not so people oriented – this normally results in a top-down 'tell' approach which may be good for crisis management but does not help encouraging initiative and the development of capabilities. On the other hand, a too people-oriented approach often results in a 'happy' organisation which achieves a fraction of what could be done. Four styles of leadership emerge, as shown in Figure A1.26.

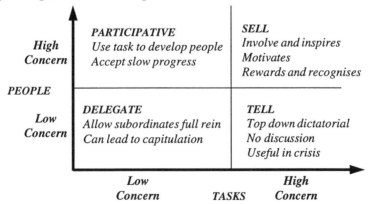

Figure A1.26 Basic leadership styles.

The best leaders are those who get the balance between these two concerns, and who understand which situation needs which particular style and adapt accordingly. A crisis situation will more often than not demand a 'tell' approach. A typical change programme situation will rely on a 'sell' approach.

4.13 McKinsey 7 S Framework

The 'McKinsey 7 S Framework' is a wider diagnostic tool developed by the world-leading consultancy firm McKinsey & Company, as shown in Figure A1.27.

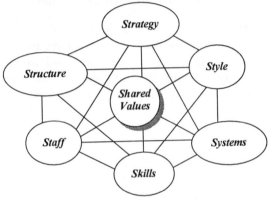

Figure A1.27 McKinsey 7 S Framework.

The framework shows the seven interactive variables within an organisation which have an effect on how the organisation operates and what makes it succeed or fail. An understanding of each variable, and the way that they influence each other and the overall organisation, can provide some unique insights which other tools cannot. It can also help one to understand how the three cornerstones of a successful organisation can be linked, as shown in Figure A1.28.

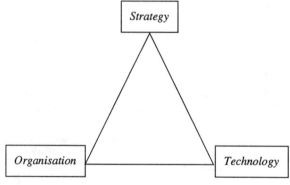

Figure A1.28 Linking the three cornerstones.

4.14 Opposition versus support

Any change programme needs to design a strategy to overcome opposition and engender support, as shown in Figure A1.29.

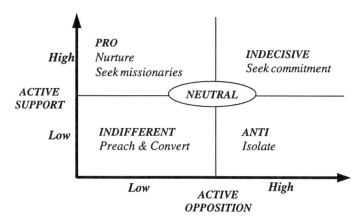

Figure A1.29 Opposition/support map.

The techniques outlined in Part 1, Chapter 4 can be employed to achieve this. However, before such techniques can be used, one must gain an understanding of who is for and who is against so that such techniques can be more effectively targeted.

4.15 Cultural behaviour

The opposition/support map (as shown in Figure A1.29) should, if applied to individuals, take into account what type of individuals are being targeted. Individuals may be in opposition for a variety of reasons, and thus need to be handled differently. A useful tool to help understanding of the dynamics involved, is the Cultural Behaviour Map – see figure A1.30. Opposition could be as much to do with the character type involved as with the fact that the stated 'opposition' is part of natural behaviour. For example, if a 'Good soldier' expresses opposition this needs to be considered more seriously than if a 'Rebel' does! Opposition from a 'Good soldier' would indicate that the proposed changes do not conform with the current company values.

4.16 The 'Three Rs'

Everyone in an organisation will go through the 'three Rs' shown in Figure A1.31 – recruitment, retention and removal (the latter either voluntary, involuntary or in a box!). Analysing each of the three (by asking the

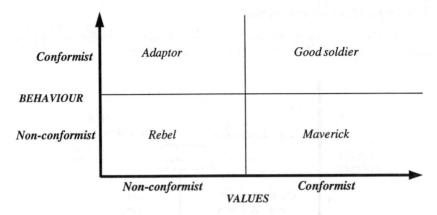

Figure A1.30 Cultural behaviour map.

employees themselves) will give a clear indication of how the organisation can be improved.

■ **Recruitment** sets the scene – how attractive is the company compared to competitors? What efforts are made to settle the employee in? What efforts are made to make sure that not only is the employee right for the company, but also vice-versa? How are refusals handled?
■ **Retention** can be helped by a whole host of processes and systems – the best question to ask is: do the employees turn up to work because they have to (to pay their bills) or because they really *want* to? What career prospects and training are offered? What systems of reward and recognition (other than straight pay) are employed? Does the

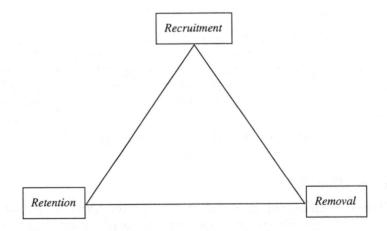

Figure A1.31 The 'three Rs'.

appraisal system merely mark people out of 10, or does it act as a living vehicle for people to identify their development needs, and for managers to understand the needs of their employees? What system is in place for employees to give their managers feedback on their leadership/management style? Both putting in a process that allows such upward feedback, as well as linking managers' appraisals to the feedback they get from employees is very difficult, but possible – and once in place produces good results. And on the other side, what disciplinary processes are there? Are they tight and respected, or loose and ignored?

∎ **Removal** is often an emotive and badly managed process. When people are made redundant, what effort is made to either retrain them for in-placement, or help them with out-placement? What are the procedures used to give someone the sack, or is it left to the whim of the immediate superior? Is it too easy, or even too difficult, to move someone onto a place (outside the organisation) where they can succeed? How many industrial tribunals have the organisation had to attend? When someone leaves voluntarily, what process is in place to learn why the employee is leaving? What process is there to try to keep the employee (apart from just offering more money)? What process is in place in time of sickness? And if, God forbid, an employee dies, what process is in place to support and console the family he or she leaves behind?

5. TOOLS FOR SHAREHOLDER ANALYSIS

5.1 Dynamic between income statement and balance sheet

The income statement and balance sheet are two basic financial reports which can be used to gauge the health of the company. From these two, one can construct the third important financial statement, the cash flow statement (sometimes called the source and application, or funds flow, statement). These together help to indicate the extent to which the shareholders are getting their returns. They provide key cash flow information and, together with future projections, show the level of shareholder value generated.

It is important to note that the two basic reports differ by nature – the income statement shows what has occurred over a *period* of time, while the balance sheet is a snapshot of the state of affairs at a *particular* time. Thus the income statement has an effect on a balance sheet which starts at the beginning of the period, and which is reported by a new balance sheet at the end of the period.

Let's look at some of the key things which one needs to understand in each.

5.1.1 *The income statement*

The income statement (or profit and loss – P&L – account as it is some-times called) shows the profitability of the business. Remember, *profit is not cash!* For example depreciation is shown as a cost, but it is a non-cash expense. Similarly, sales might generate negative cash if you need to pay suppliers before your customers pay you! Be that as it may, understanding the dynamics within the income statement is key.

The chief concern is to appreciate fully the relationship between sales and costs, and which costs are variable (i.e. go up and down directly with sales, such as raw materials), and which ones are fixed costs (such as a finance or marketing department). Once that is achieved you can work out the breakeven point and see how close you are to it.

You can gauge how successful you are by comparing your profitability to that of your competitors – both operational profit (Profit before interest and tax – PBIT) and earnings (Profit after tax before dividends are distributed). You can also compare with these of your competitors your 'P/E' ratio (price of the share divided by earnings per share), as well as your dividend yield (dividend divided by share price) and overall share yield (dividend plus capital appreciation of share, divided by share price). Like many ratios, the absolute is not as important as the comparison (either to past trends, or to competitors, or both).

5.1.2 *The balance sheet*

The balance sheet is simply a statement to show where the cash in the company has come from, and into which assets it is invested. On the one side are the assets, both fixed (such as land, buildings, etc.) and current (such as debtors, cash in the bank, etc.). This is balanced (or accounted for) by the liabilities and equity side of the balance sheet. Equity includes the cash that shareholders have put into the business (not to be confused with market capitalisation which shows what that investment is currently worth on the market). Equity also includes the amount of earnings retained after dividends have been paid. Liabilities include long-term bank loans, overdrafts and creditors (what you owe your suppliers at that point in time).

There are important dynamics to understand which exist between the income statement and the balance sheet, as shown in figure A1.32.

The circular dynamic, in its simplest form, goes something like this: cash (in the form of equity and debt) is raised to invest in assets. These assets are employed to generate sales, which (after meeting the operational, financial and fiscal costs) generate the profit. Some of this is paid as dividends, and some is put back into the liabilities and equity side of the balance sheet. It can then be used to buy more assets, or pay off liabilities. Actually it is a bit more complicated than that, as there are some direct dynamics as well as the basic circular one. Sales generate assets

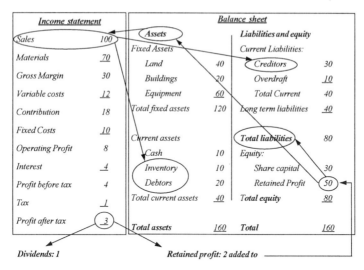

Figure A1.32 The dynamic between income statement and balance sheet.

(inventory which needs to be stored to generate the sales, and debtors who do not pay immediately) and they also generate liabilities (creditors who supply you). If these are not tightly controlled, although the business may be very profitable, if it is growing fast it might not generate any cash at all!

To serve the needs of your shareholders, you need to get the optimal dynamic within and between the income statement and the balance sheet. The outline above is very brief. One should appreciate that finance is more complex than a simple diagram. For example, various accounting differences (i.e. historical cost versus current cost accounting, inventory treatments of Last In First Out – LIFO – versus First In First Out – FIFO) can make large differences to the basic financial statements. However, the key thing is to understand the dynamic.

5.2 Key ratio analysis

Once the dynamic between the income statement and balance sheet are fully understood, a simple way of monitoring this dynamic is by looking at some key ratios. An example of this is the return on assets (ROA) ratio, which can be decomposed into constituent parts reflecting key areas of both income statement and balance sheet (see Figure A1.33).

The ROA is worked out first by dividing operating profit (PBIT – Profit before interest and tax) by total assets. The ROA itself equals operating profitability times asset turnover. Operating profitability is worked out

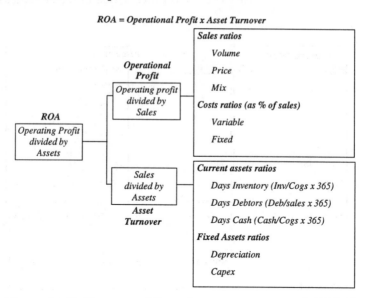

Figure A1.33 Decomposition of return on assets ratio (ROA).

by dividing PBIT by sales – this tells you how much operating profit you make for every £1 of sales. Asset turnover is worked out by dividing total assets by sales – this tells you how much sales are generated by every £1 invested into assets.

Both operating profitability and asset turnover can be further decomposed into other ratios such as percentage variable cost to sales, or how long it takes on average for your debtors to pay you (debtor days). The ROA ratio ignores financing and fiscal costs, and focuses purely on the operating side of the business.

The best use of this ratio is as a comparison, either with competitors or for year-on-year comparisons. By decomposing the ratio into its constituent parts one can get an idea of where the opportunities for improvement lie. ROA is also useful to get a broad feel whether or not debt is generating shareholder value – if the ROA is higher than the average interest cost, then debt is having a positive effect on the business. This is pretty much common sense – if you borrow money at a 10 per cent interest charge and put it into assets that generate a 15 per cent return, then you're onto a good thing. However, debt can get out of hand, so the amount of cash generated by the business and what that represents in terms of cover on the interest charge itself should also be taken into account!

So far we have looked at the two key financial statements and some ratio analysis. There are two further areas which need to be understood – cash flow and shareholder value. Both are linked.

5.3 Cash flow analysis

As the dynamic between the income statement and balance sheet shows, cash flow is affected by various parts of each statement. You need to understand the extent to which the business is 'cash rich' (i.e. generating more cash than is needed to support a growth in sales) or 'cash poor'. Filling out the figures for the various variables in Figure A1.34 will help answer that question.

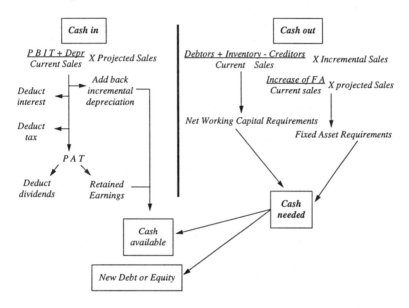

Figure A1.34 Cash flow analysis.

Essentially cash comes in from operations. To work out what cash is due in and what cash is needed to sustain the business, the following steps should be taken:

■ **Cash in** Take PBIT (Profit before interest and tax) and add back any non-cash expense (normally only depreciation, but there may be others). Divide this by the current sales to get the operating cash margin, and multiply this by the projected sales for the next year. This will give you the operating cash which you can expect to generate. Deduct from this amount the projected interest, tax and dividend payments, and add back any additional (i.e. incremental to last year) depreciation which will be charged next year. This gives you the amount of cash that the business will generate from the P&L in the following year.

■ **Cash out**. To work out the net working capital requirements, add the debtors to the inventory and deduct the creditors (you can use either the year end balance sheet or, better still, the average between year start and year end). Dividing this number by the yearly sales will give you the ratio of working capital requirement for sales, which multiplied by the next year's incremental sales will give you the amount of extra cash you need for next year's working capital (or the amount of extra cash which is generated). The fixed asset requirement is arrived at by dividing the year's increase in fixed assets (net of depreciation) by the yearly sales, and multiplying this ratio by the next year's projected sales. Adding the net working capital and fixed asset requirements will give you the total cash requirement for the business for the following year.

You finally arrive at the likely cash needed by deducting the cash requirement amount from the cash available amount.

This is a 'quick and dirty' figure only! It should be borne in mind that the projected sales assume current margins and projected non-cash operating costs and post-operating cash outflows. The balance sheet variables assume that the current dynamic between current/fixed assets and projected sales remains constant.

When considering a 'do nothing' scenario it is a useful tool, and can quickly give an indicative picture as to the likely financing requirements (from either debt or equity) of the future. It does not obviate the need for a more thorough cash flow prediction!

5.4 Shareholder 'value'

The 'value' to shareholders is often expressed in some form of financial way. However, there are a variety of ways to value a company, and great debate as to which is the right way. Frankly, the best thing to do is to understand how value is defined by the various approaches, and then understand the differences and implications of these valuations. The four broad approaches are outlined in Figure A1.35.

Let's consider each one, and the usefulness that they individually offer.

■ **Asset based valuation**. This gives an indication of the break-up value of the organisation, and (compared to the market capitalisation) the market/book value ratio. If an organisation's break-up value exceeds the market value, then the shareholders may (sooner or later) consider crystallising a gain. This value is used by corporate raiders looking for a fast buck!

■ **Market based valuation**. They often say an asset is worth nothing more than what other people are prepared to pay for it. So the market capitalisation (share price multiplied by shares outstanding) gives a

Asset based	*Market/Book value*
	Break-up value
Market based	*Direct quote*
	Price/Earnings ratio
Cash flow based	*NPV of future cash flows plus residual value*
Negotiation based	*Strategic fit*
	Scarcity value

Figure A1.35 Four ways to view value.

good indication of value. However, if you were to launch a bid to buy all the shares, the value would be driven up so market capitalisation is only of indicative use, and is best used for comparison with other valuation methods. Applying a straight P/E ratio (such as the sector average) also gives an indication, but differing accounting treatments can seriously blur this figure!

■ **Cash flow based value.** An increasingly accepted way of defining shareholder value is arrived at by discounting the future expected cash flows that an organisation generates by the cost of capital. This approach (often called SVA – shareholder value analysis) is very good for looking at future strategic options to show which ones generate the best value. It also shows what is generating and what is destroying value. It is dealt with in more detail below in Section 5.5.

■ **Negotiation based value.** An organisation may have an increased value to another as a result of strategic synergies or scarcity value. An example of such hidden synergy value is Nestlé's acquisition of Rowntree. The price paid by Nestlé was higher than many financial analysts concluded was 'reasonable' because the analysts underestimated the strength of the synergy between Rowntree's brands and Nestlé's distribution channels. Markets value a company based on what they believe a company offers to current shareholders. This may be lower than what it offers to others because of the synergies resulting from a merger with another organisation. So one question you need to understand is what could the possible value be to someone who could achieve these synergies (either a competitor, or another organisation within the business system).

You can see that value is not as objective as one would think. If you have a firm (and realistic) view of the various 'values' posed by each of the four approaches above, you'll have a good idea of the 'true' value. More important is to spot any 'value gaps' between, say, the market approach and another approach. This will show you any possible threats, as well as show that you might have a communication issue to deal with concerning the analysts and your shareholders.

So far we've looked at value purely in financial terms. There are other 'values' to consider, and these values need to be managed. One example is shareholder 'loyalty'. While shareholders of some Swiss chocolate firms know that the market value of their holding is understated, they are not likely to sell their shares for gain to an outsider – it is not for nothing that the AGMs of such companies are carefully stage managed, complete with plenty of delicious free samples for all to take home! The use of 'perks' to encourage shareholder loyalty (and give added value for the shares) are used by many firms, and include, for example, discounts for travel tickets (used by some ferry companies) and preferential terms for purchases (used by some retail companies). So the strategy of generating 'shareholder value' should be given a wider view than purely financial returns (although this will always be paramount).

5.5 Shareholder value analysis (SVA) approach

The basic premise of SVA is fairly simple. Its philosophy states that the shareholders have invested money in assets, and that the true value of that investment is the future cash generated by those assets, discounted back to the present by the weighted average cost of capital (WACC), to take into account the time value of money (i.e. if £10 is invested at 10 per cent to give a return of 10 pence in a year's time, then £10.10 in a year's time is worth £10 today).

Although the premise of SVA is simple, the practice is not! For those who wish to get more information, there are a few good books around: *Creating Shareholder Value – The New Standard for Business Performance* by Alfred Rappaport gives a good founding of the principles; *Managing for Value – A Guide to Value Based Strategic Management* by Bernard C. Reimann shows how the approach can be linked to other more conventional strategic approaches; *Valuation – Measuring and Managing the Value of Companies* by McKinsey consultants Tom Copeland, Tim Koller and Jack Murren also shows how the theory can be used. It is outside the scope of this book to cover all the 'ins and outs' of SVA. However, the outline which follows should give enough explanation to at least enable any understanding of how SVA is worked out, and how it can best be used.

Shareholder value is made up of four parts, three added together and one deducted, as shown in Figure A1.36. Let's look at each one of these components in turn.

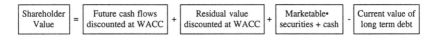

Figure A1.36 SVA analytical approach.

To work out future cash flows, you'll need to decide three key things, as shown in Figure A1.37.

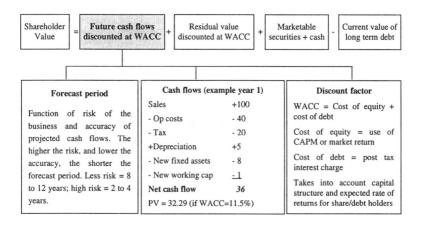

Figure A1.37 SVA approach: PV of future cash flows.

- Firstly, what is the most reasonable forecast period (residual value looks after the value generated after the last period in the forecast)?
- Secondly, what are the future cash flows within that period?
- And finally, what should the discount rate be to express the future cash flows in today's terms (i.e. time value of money)?

The *forecast period* is decided by the amount of risk in the forecast. The residual value calculation done later will pick up the longer-term value (i.e. generated in the post-forecast period). The *cash flows* are the post-tax operational flows after working capital and fixed assets are taken care of. Note that interest charge is not included in these flows, as this is picked up by the discount factor and the deduction of current value of debt.

The *discount factor* is the weighted average cost of capital (WACC) – in other words the weighted average of the return expected by shareholders and the post-tax interest cost. This is worked out by a series of formulas outlined in Figure A1.38. The cost of equity can be calculated using the CAPM (capital asset pricing method) formula. This assumes that two types of risk are involved in equities – the risk of the market,

Weighted Average Cost of Capital (WACC) =
Weighted cost of debt +Weighted cost of equity

Cost of Debt	
{long term rate x (1-tax rate)} x % of capital represented by long term debt	
Long term interest rate %	10%
Tax rate %	35%
% of capital as long term debt	56%
Weighted cost of debt =	3.6%

Cost of Equity	
{risk free rate +(beta x [risk free rate - return on market])} x % of capital as equity	
Risk free rate %	4%
Beta	1.4
Return on market %	14%
% of capital as equity	44%
Weighted cost of equity =	7.9%

WACC = 11.5%

Figure A1.38 SVA approach: use of WACC.

and the risk of the specific equity compared to the market. The latter is calculated by multiplying the market risk (itself equal to the market return minus the risk-free rate) by the company's 'beta' value. This 'beta' is worked out by analysts who take into account the relative volatility of the company's shares compared to the overall market. The best way to get a company's beta (short of doing a lot of historical analysis) is to phone up a city analyst or a business school and ask for the value. For example, the London Business School produces regular reports on company beta values.

The risk-free rate is frequently taken as the yield on long-term government bonds. CAPM is not the only way to calculate the cost of equity. One can be more simplistic by deciding what return equity holders should get, or one can be more complex and use another approach, the Arbitrage Pricing Theory (APT). However, CAPM is soundly based, and working on the assumption that it is the comparison of results gained (under varying scenarios) rather than a single absolute itself, then the theory is sound enough for general use.

It can be seen from this that the higher the amount of debt, the lower the WACC – however, one should still bear in mind the risk of the debt by looking at other variables such as interest cover represented by cash flow!

As stated earlier, the residual value calculation picks up the value of the post-forecast period which is generated. There are a variety of ways to calculate this, as shown in Figure A1.39. One can multiply the last period's earnings by an expected P/E ratio, or the equity by an expected MV/BV ratio. Or one can assume a break-up, and calculate the liquidation value (which is the most conservative approach). Or one can assume that the business will continue as an ongoing concern, and turn the post-tax operational cash flow (Profit after tax plus interest plus depreciation) into a perpetuity.

Whichever way is used, the resultant amount is discounted back to the present using the weighted average cost of capital.

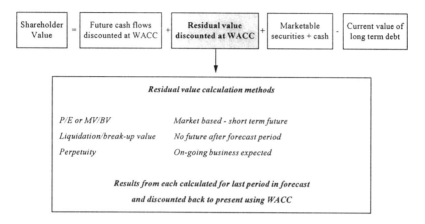

Figure A1.39 SVA approach: residual value.

As one can see the method chosen to calculate residual value differs according to the assumptions of those who are investing. If an exit from the investment is wanted, then most use a market-based calculation (such as P/E). So in this instance, the final earnings would be multiplied by the average P/E of the sector, and discounted back to the present using the WACC.

The most common approach is to use the perpetuity method by taking the last cash flow, deducting depreciation (which was added back) and ignoring working capital and fixed asset cash flow. This assumes that the fixed asset needs after the forecast period will be met by depreciation and that working capital will become balanced between short-term assets and liabilities. This amount is turned into perpetuity by dividing it by the WACC, and then by discounting the result to the present one gets the present value (PV) of the residual value.

Some people are initially uncomfortable with using a perpetuity as nothing lasts for ever. However, as the graph in Figure A1.40 shows, nearly 90 per cent of the value of a perpetuity is generated in the 15 years after the forecast period.

The remainder of SVA is calculated by adding existing cash assets, and deducting the present value of long-term debt.

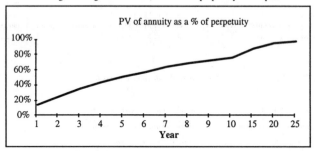

$$\frac{\text{Last period's post tax operational cash}}{\text{WACC}} \longrightarrow \text{Discounted back to present using WACC}$$

Assumes that the business has an on-going future past the forecast period, and that growth
will stabilise with no further incremental investment in working capital,
and that fixed assets replacement will be served by depreciation.

Although nothing lasts for ever, the use of a perpetuity is acceptable:

Figure A1.40 SVA approach: use of perpetuity for residual value.

An example showing the whole approach is in Figure A1.41.

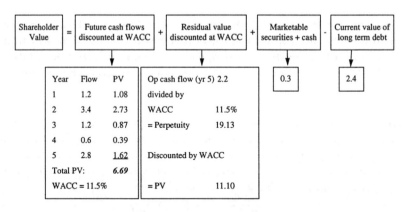

Shareholder Value	=	Future cash flows discounted at WACC	+	Residual value discounted at WACC	+	Marketable securities + cash	-	Current value of long term debt

Year	Flow	PV
1	1.2	1.08
2	3.4	2.73
3	1.2	0.87
4	0.6	0.39
5	2.8	1.62
Total PV:		6.69
WACC = 11.5%		

Op cash flow (yr 5) 2.2
divided by
WACC   11.5%
= Perpetuity   19.13

Discounted by WACC

= PV   11.10

0.3

2.4

Total Shareholder value = £15.69 million
Divided by 5.3 million shares = £2.96 per share

Figure A1.41 SVA approach: working example.

As you can see there are a lot of debatable assumptions behind this
approach. It is very number oriented, and will not appeal to intuitive,
'right brain' individuals. However, it is a very powerful tool. Its value as

an approach is not what the absolute value figure generated is, but how that figure compares either to other strategic options (calculated using the same SVA approach), or to other approaches in calculating shareholder value. As such it is a useful diagnostic tool to assist decision-making when faced with a variety of ways forward. There are some specialist software packages which can do the number crunching for you, such as Alcar's Value Planner.

5.6 Financial Strategic Options matrix

So far in considering the methods for shareholder analysis we've concentrated on analysing *cash* and *value* (and shown how the two are linked). A matrix which shows the strategic options facing a company can be employed using these two variables to highlight the financial strategic issues which should be considered.

By plotting these two variables against each other, four broad financial strategies emerge as can be seen in Figure A1.42.

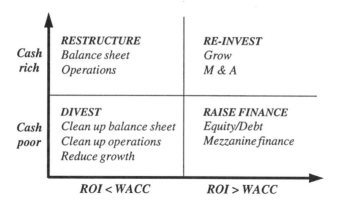

Figure A1.42 Financial strategic options.

The 'value variable' is measured by comparing the weighted average cost of capital (WACC) to the return on investment (ROI). ROI can be measured either by ROA (return on assets – profit before interest and tax divided by total assets) or ROCE (return on capital employed – the same as ROA, but with current liabilities deducted from total assets – sometimes called RONA, return on net assets). If the ROI is greater than WACC, then the company is generating positive value. You could also use the SVA approach as this variable, which is discussed more in Reimann's book *Managing for Value*. Do not worry too much which is used – either can do. The important thing is to understand what they show!

The cash rich/cash poor variable is worked out by using the approach highlighted in section 5.3 above. It should be noted that the cash flow analysed should be restricted to the current operating assets, and not include any future strategic changes being planned. So a bid for another company should be excluded, as this would muddy the waters – and by excluding such future assets, you'll be able to gauge the extent to which you can afford them in the first place!

In the best case, you have a cash rich concern which is generating positive value – so you need to think about increasing the business, possibly through mergers and acquisitions (M&A). If you are in this category, and the future looks stable, then the chances of Business Re-engineering being successful are low. Remember, the pain of the status quo should be greater than the pain of change itself! In the worst case neither cash nor value is generated, which means a radical shake-up, slowing growth and possible divestment. Depending on the position, the two other options are either to focus on the P&L and asset side of the balance sheet and sort out operations, or to look at the capital side of the balance sheet and sort out the financing of the business.

It should be stressed that this tool is of indicative use – life is generally more complex than a 2 by 2 matrix. However, it is a useful tool as it quickly shows the kinds of concerns that you should have regarding meeting the shareholder needs of the business.

5.7 Methods of forecasting

A lot of the work in analysing shareholders' needs, and the extent to which these needs will be met, will involve an element of forecasting. Although financial accounts are useful, they only reflect that which has already happened – and they do not show what the future holds. Forecasting the future is not easy – if it was life would be very boring! It is useful to understand the three basic approaches in forecasting, as shown in Figure A1.43. None of these are exclusive.

Some of the methods of forecasting shown in Figure A1.43 are complex, and it would be outside the scope of this book to show exactly how they are used – they demand a sound knowledge of mathematics, statistical analysis, financial accounting and economics. However, if you lack these skills there are people available in (or outside) the organisation who do have the skills. The important thing to understand is what the techniques can deliver, and to get a good balance between the three approaches.

■ **Qualitative**. This involves using normal market research techniques, asking the opinions of a selected group and using a sample to get a broad indicative view of the total. Thus any forecasting should include speaking to the people who have the most effect on the numbers! You can also talk to 'experts' such as market analysts, academics

Qualitative	*Research, Delphi, Experts*
Causal	*Regression, Econometrics*
Time series	*Moving averages, exponential smooth*

Figure A1.43 Types of forecasting.

and journalists – they all have opinions on what the future holds and (as they too would have done research) they can save a lot of time. It should be stressed that you should cast the net wide and then (together with other techniques) come to a reasonable conclusion.

■ **Causal**. This can be employed using econometrics (for a wide-scale application) or regression analysis (for a more focused application). For example, if, using straight regression, one can firmly prove a link between the company's sales and one or more variables which drive the figure, then regression is useful for future forecasting. Most financial calculators or PC spreadsheets can do this kind of analysis. It assumes that the historic causality remains constant, but if R^2 is higher than 90 per cent then this assumption is a fair one (although it should not be used in total isolation)!

■ **Time series**. If one has a good database over a decent length of historical time (say monthly figures over the past 5–6 years), and the business has not undergone any major change, then using time series decomposition is another useful way of forecasting. It can be used to show seasonality in sales movements, as well as to forecast likely future sales.

Although it is not vital for you to know the full science behind each one of these approaches, it is important to ensure that the teams doing the analysis undertake a balance of qualitative and quantitative approaches. If you get blank looks when you ask the people doing the analysis if they are using techniques such as regression or time series decomposition, then ask a local business school/consultant to come in on a short-term contract to beef up the quality of the job done, as well as pass on the skills to the team to do such analysis.

Many people rely on 'experts' either to help them forecast, or to pass judgement on their ideas. While there is nothing wrong with this, if used to the exclusion of other analytical techniques it can lead to wrong decisions. Experts have been known to be wrong! In 1837, the inspector of the British navy, Sir William Symonds, expressed the following opinion about the usefulness of ship screws: '... even if a screw had the force to propel the ship, it would be completely useless, because the ship could not be steered due to the screw's effect at the stern of the vessel.' Similarly, in 1839 the well known surgeon Alfred Velpeau wrote about anaesthesia: 'The elimination of pain in surgery is a wild notion. Aspiring to it is absurd at the present time. In surgery "knife" and "pain" are two words that will forever have to remain connected with one another in the patient's mind.'

6. SOME USEFUL PROCESS TOOLS AND TECHNIQUES

So far we've looked at some analytical tools and techniques which can be used to analyse the four typical key stakeholders in an organisation: customers, employees, suppliers and shareholders. These tools and approaches can be employed to improve the quality of the analysis needed to help you 'Know What You Want'.

There are a few other process techniques which I have come across which can be applied to help you gain an understanding of what is going on around you, as well as help you structure your thoughts. They can help the project and cross-functional process teams through some of their problems. They can help in driving change through, using skills such as negotiating and psychology. These are presented below, in no particular order.

6.1 The 'Johari' window

Two organisational development experts invented this matrix, and named it after their first names 'Jo' (Joe Luft) and 'Harry' (Harry Ingham). It may be found in other forms, but the example shown in figure A1.44 is among the simplest.

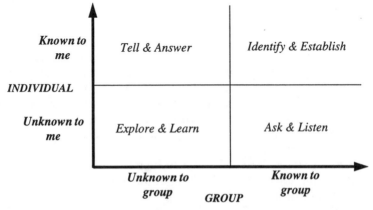

Figure A1.44 The 'Johari' window of knowledge.

Have you ever been to a group meeting where the debate goes round in circles, and people are struggling to understand each other? That is because in any group put together there will be things either known or unknown to individuals, and things either known or unknown to the group. Thus four areas of understanding need to be identified, with the first three dealt with quickly before one can begin to deal with areas unknown to both the group and the individuals. Many of the issues of Business Re-engineering will initially lie in this quadrant for the teams involved in the analysis during the first stage of 'Know what you want'.

When you form project teams, then, they should be aware of this matrix and use it to save them time and frustration!

6.2 Group dynamics

Forming teams should always include some team building and group dynamic training to ensure that the team understands the psychological implications of working together and so have a greater chance of success. The importance of this is discussed in detail in Part 1, Chapter 4.

Richard Weber identified that groups who perform well typically go through four stages, as shown in Figure A1.45.

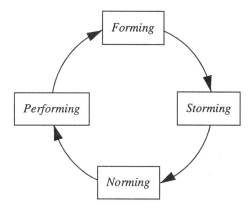

Figure A1.45 Group dynamics*.

Each stage is typified by different themes regarding interpersonal issues, group behavioural patterns, group tasks and leadership issues, as shown in Figure A1.46.

Many groups do not get past the 'storming' stage – they enter it, and because it is viewed as 'unnatural' they revert to the first stage: they become 'All gas, and no action!' Groups who receive some team building and group dynamic training will often perform better than those who do not. Before a group fully performs it is normal for some 'storming' to take place – this should be expected, and encouraged, rather than avoided.

Issue/Stage	Forming	Storming	Norming	Performing
Interpersonal	Inclusion	Control	Affection	
Group behaviour	Superficial, polite, ambiguity	Frustration, anger, attacks on leadership	Negotiation, agreement, cohesion	Growth, insight and collaboration
Group tasks/issues	Membership defined, introductions, formulating objectives	Decision making process, power and influence	Functional relationships	Productivity
Leadership	Dependence	Counter dependence	Inter-dependence	

Figure A1.46 Characteristics of the stages of group dynamics*.

The dynamic is iterative, and a group could go through it more than once. Those that do, end up performing better. The final stage of a group (not shown above) is 'Adjourning'. Typical behaviour includes having a celebration and forming longer-term relationships with reunions (such as school alumni).

6.3 'True' teams and 'false' teams

The matrix in Figure A1.47 is based on that used by Cigna International, which was developed by the Cigna Corporation in the USA together with Symmetrix, a Boston based consultancy. The story of Cigna International's re-engineering programme can be found in Part 2. Teams typically go through a stage of chaos before becoming 'false' teams. 'False' teams concentrate too much either on the relationships of the people involved (to normalise) or the tasks in hand (to perform). Only 'true' teams perform to their optimum, as they balance the needs of the individual and the needs of the task.

Teams need to be trained in team dynamics and understand the natural progression from chaos through 'false' to 'true' teams. Once they understand this progression then the sometimes dysfunctional behaviour which occurs (especially during the 'chaos' stage) can be treated in a more positive, understanding manner. Teams can be helped through the chaos and false team progression by active facilitation (as Cigna found in their re-engineering programme).

---

* Group Cycles reprinted with permission from NTL Institute. *Reading Book for Human Relations Training* (1982) edited by Lawrence Porter and Bernard Mohr, 'The Group: A Cycle from Birth to Death' by Richard C Weber, p68–71.

	FALSE TEAM	TRUE TEAM
High	High relationship focus Centred on social needs Confrontation avoided Good spirit, little action	Good performance Task, team and individual Happy, mutual respect Good action, good spirit
Low	CHAOS Typical starting point Ambiguous goals/process New faces What? Why? How? Who?	FALSE TEAM High task focus Centred on doing Co-operation limited Good action, poor spirit

CONCERN FOR NORMALISED RELATIONSHIPS

Low   **CONCERN FOR TASK ACHIEVEMENT**   **High**

Figure A1.47 Team performance and progression.

6.4 Facilitation

Facilitation was discussed in outline in Chapter 7. Figure A1.48 is based on the model used by Cigna International to help train their facilitators. Facilitators need to be able to play four key roles in helping teams.

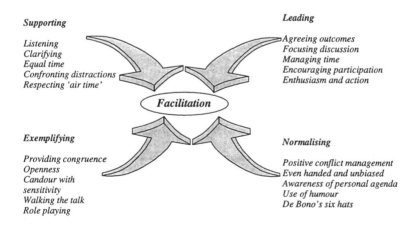

Supporting

Listening
Clarifying
Equal time
Confronting distractions
Respecting 'air time'

Leading

Agreeing outcomes
Focusing discussion
Managing time
Encouraging participation
Enthusiasm and action

Facilitation

Exemplifying

Providing congruence
Openness
Candour with sensitivity
Walking the talk
Role playing

Normalising

Positive conflict management
Even handed and unbiased
Awareness of personal agenda
Use of humour
De Bono's six hats

Figure A1.48 The art of facilitation.

It takes weeks to train a quality facilitator. Not only do they need to develop their interpersonal skills to fulfil the roles above, they also need to learn a whole variety of tools and techniques to help facilitate groups. An excellent publication on such techniques, which holds some 124 exercises for facilitators to use, is called *A Handbook of Structured Experiences for Human Relations Training, Volumes 1–4* (1984), edited by J. William Pfeiffer and John E. Jones, University Associates Publisher and Consultants. These are structured 'games' to help teams through the chaos and storming phases, and to help them build a good team.

Facilitation is not just about helping teams through team building exercises. They often have to help workshops through difficult discussions. Such discussions can often become acrimonious, as people's positions and views are threatened. A very simple technique which a facilitator can use is based upon Edward De Bono's six coloured hats, and is described in greater detail in the following section.

6.5 De Bono's six coloured hats

De Bono is a famous advocate for concepts such as lateral and water thinking. His six coloured hats (see Figure A1.49) help people to play roles and also keep the debate non-personal.

White hat	=	*'Paper' – factual, points of clarification.*
Red hat	=	*'Heart' – emotional, says feelings.*
Black hat	=	*'Judge' – judgemental, downside/practicalities.*
Yellow hat	=	*'Sun' – warm, good side of idea.*
Green hat	=	*'Grass' – grow, add to idea.*
Blue hat	=	*'Sky' – process, helicopter view (chairperson).*

Figure A1.49 De Bono's six coloured hats.

One of the practical problems of the first phase of Business Re-engineering is that functional managers are thrown together, often for the first time, to look at the organisation and start to come up with ideas on how to re-engineer it. Many ideas are thrown up, criticisms of functional areas occur (normally by those outside of the functions). Ideas are discussed, accepted or rejected.

The challenge is to keep such discussion away from what could be seen as personal attacks. The six coloured hats can be used to do this in many ways. For example, if an argument ensues about an idea, one can get the people who are for the idea to wear the black hats (to show the downsides) and those that are against to wear the yellow hats (to show the upside). This will help them to see the other point of view. Or one can get the group to take an idea and wear the green hats, to grow more idea out of it. Or if the discussion is getting too bogged down in detail, one can get those present to wear the blue hats and 'helicopter' back up. Using the hats is a humorous, cathartic and effective way to avoid acrimonious disputes.

6.6 Negotiation styles

Business Re-engineering typically involves a lot of negotiation. When negotiating or dealing with people it is advantageous if you can spot what kind of character type your opposite number tends towards, and then match his or her style. Carl Jung's analysis of human nature led him to identify four basic character types, within which are two opposites. We all tend to have elements of each character type within us, although some may be more pronounced than others. In extreme cases, some people tend towards one type almost to the exclusion of the remaining three. The four types are shown in Figure A1.50.

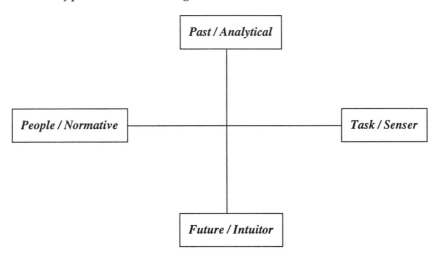

Figure A1.50 Negotiation styles.

In practice we all have elements of the four character types, but often a dominant type is obvious.

■ **People/Normative.** This type has high interpersonal skills, and tends to see a relationship as more important than a task. They are typified by people who like to have photographs of people around them (sporting groups, family, school groups, etc.). They will see situations in terms of the effect that the situation has on the people involved rather than the reasons for the situation happening. They value face-to-face communication rather than written, and like to start a meeting talking about personal things (such as common interests) rather than the task in hand. They are not very active, and adopt an easy going 'laissez faire' style.

- **Task/senser**. These are the opposite to the normative type. They are very task oriented, and do not give much thought to issues like the morale or happiness of those involved. They are very active, and spend a lot of time rushing about. Their offices are covered with bits of paper, 'To Do' lists, etc. They will happily answer a phone call in mid-conversation with someone else. They do not like long preambles, and are more interested in what needs to be done now rather than the reason why it needs to be done.

- **Past/analytical**. These people are very methodical. They are typified by the type of person who sits down next to a pad and pencil and straightens the pencil before speaking. Their office is clear of paper, and they are more interested in the reasons for a situation occurring than the future implications. They are very process oriented, typically conservative and want facts and figures rather than opinion and gut feel. They view people and tasks as necessary things to be managed, and are generally unemotional about them.

- **Future/intuitor**. These are the ideas people. They are often accused of having their heads in the clouds, but this is because they are looking forward and are very creative. Their office will have projected trend maps and pictures of nature. They are not worried about why something has happened, or its effect on the people and tasks today, so much as what the future implications will be. They are not very organised, and often flit between subjects.

It can be disastrous if you mismatch styles. A conversation with a senser using a normative style will be cut short very quickly. So identify the type of person you are dealing with, and match his or her style to get better communication.

6.7 Principled negotiation

One of the better books on negotiation is *Getting to Yes – How to Negotiate Agreement Without Giving In*, by Roger Fisher and William Ury. In it the approach of principled negotiation is detailed, which rests on four key things to do, as shown in Figure A1.51.

- **Separate the people from the problem.** Negotiations often dissolve into attack spirals, with those involved mutually recriminating each other. An important step is to strive to make the subject being negotiated as objective as possible, and to achieve a good relationship based

> *Separate people from the problem*
>
> *Focus on interests, not positions*
>
> *Invent options for mutual gain*
>
> *Insist on using objective criteria*

Figure A1.51 Principled negotiation.

on understanding (not necessarily agreement) of the various positions. Attacks on individuals should be avoided, or the risk is that the subject becomes so subjective and emotional no progress can be achieved. So keep people out of the subject and deal with it in an objective way.

■ **Focus on interests, not positions.** Negotiations often fail as each party has a stated position which, on the face of it, cannot be reconciled. To get round this, you should try to get a good understanding of why a party has a position (which is often a means to an end, rather than an end in itself). An understanding of people's interests will help you in the next step.

■ **Invent options for mutual gain.** There are many ways to solve a problem – by inventing a variety of options which can meet the interests of all concerned you put the pressure on those who sit in a stated position. You also open up the possibility of using the classic negotiating line 'If you could do x, then I could do y.'

■ **Insist on using objective criteria.** You can take a lot of heat out of a debate by basing the negotiation on agreed objective criteria (such as the market rate etc.). If these criteria are agreed well in advance, then this reduces the possible back-tracking on agreement later on!

The four principles above do not guarantee success, but they do help a negotiation get to a 'win–win' situation.

6.7 The use of rational bargaining overlaps (RBO)

In most negotiating situations, each side has a 'would like' aim, and each side has a 'walk-away'. The first thing to do is to be quite sure that you know what you want, and what your walk-away is (i.e. the point at which you will refuse). The next thing is to understand what the 'would like' and 'walk-away' is of the other side. If there is an overlap, then there is scope for negotiation. However, if there is no overlap, then you need either to work on the other side to bring their 'walk-away' down, or work on your own 'would like' to bring it within the range of the other's position. Figure A1.51 shows these two possible situations.

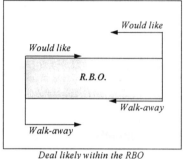
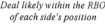
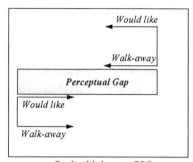

Figure A1.52 Rational bargaining overlap.

Doing an RBO analysis prior to a negotiation can help clear the mind and set an understanding for the kind of problems that may be facing you.

6.8 Selling techniques and SPIN®

Business Re-engineering involves 'selling' radical ideas. There are many selling techniques, but one which can be used well is called 'SPIN®'. A research group in the UK, Huthwaite, have evolved this very useful selling technique which is based on much research. They offer training courses in this technique. They followed many people on their selling trips to try to understand what differentiated the successful salesperson from the less successful ones. They found that successful salesmen asked many more questions and built up in their target client's mind the need for the service or product. Huthwaite then analysed the types of questions which were used and they fell into four broad categories (Situation, Problem, Implication, Need pay-off), remembered using the mnemonic 'SPIN®:

- **Situation Questions** are used to gain an understanding of where the client is and what his or her circumstances are;
- **Problem Questions** seek to identify what problems, difficulties, dissatisfactions the client sees in his circumstances;
- **Implication Questions** are used to build up the size of the problem and to get the client to understand all the implications of not solving the problem;
- **Need Pay-off Questions** are used to crystallise the need of the client and extend the perceived value.

The three steps in the use of SPIN® start with preliminaries, including introductions, matching styles and gaining control by asking 'May I ask some questions?' SPIN® questions are then asked, and when the needs of the client are clear, the next step is to demonstrate the capability to meet those needs. The final stage is to summarise and obtain some appropriate commitment. The approach is summarised in Figure A1.53.

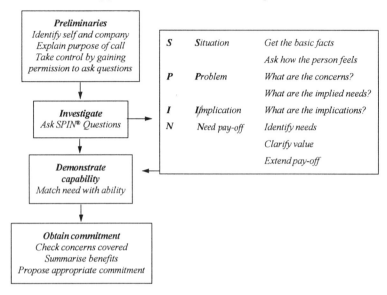

Figure A1.53 Selling techniques: asking questions!

Using SPIN® to 'sell' the need for change, and matching the need with agreement for a process, is a useful way to help drive change forward, especially in the earlier stages. It not only starts to build up dissatisfaction with the status quo, but also helps to get a clear idea of what process needs to be followed to get a re-engineering programme up and running. SPIN® is a registered trademark of Huthwaite Research Group Limited (UK telephone number: 0709 710081).

6.9 Military strategy and approaches

The word 'strategy' comes from the Greek word meaning 'the art of generals'. Business has adopted many quasi-military terms and approaches to help formulate strategy, which is not surprising when one considers that business is about competitive action, and the most competitive action known to mankind is war! The oldest (and some say the best) strategist who wrote down his approach was Sun Tzu, an ancient Chinese warlord. His work, *The Art of War*, is available today in hard and paperback, and well worth the read. His six principles, and what may be called their 'business' applications, are summarised in Figure A1.54.

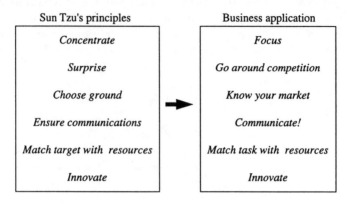

Sun Tzu's principles

Business application

Concentrate	Focus
Surprise	Go around competition
Choose ground	Know your market
Ensure communications	Communicate!
Match target with resources	Match task with resources
Innovate	Innovate

" Know yourself, and know your enemy,
and you can fight a thousand battles without defeat"

Figure A1.54 Sun Tzu's principles of war.

Selection and maintenance of the aim

Maintenance of morale

Co-operation

Administration

Economy of effort

Security

Surprise

Offensive action

Concentration of force

Flexibility

Figure A1.55 RMAS principles of war.

These principles of ancient Chinese strategy are similar to the modern-day principles taught by the Royal Military Academy Sandhurst summarised in Figure A1.55.

It's worth asking yourself how well the organisation is doing against each of these principles, and what could be done to improve matters. And when the re-engineering design and implementation plan is finished, quickly check back against these principles to see how well they are covered.

7. USING THE TOOLS AND SUMMARY

This appendix provides a whistle-stop tour of a whole variety of analytical and process tools and techniques which will help you 'Know what you want'. Some of the tools are diagnostic and some prescriptive. Many other tools and techniques exist, but the ones above are those generally found to be most useful.

It is important to realise that no one tool is a panacea. At the same time, although it is wise to use a variety of tools, there will be few (if any) situations when all of them are needed! To apply religiously all the tools in this appendix will result in paralysis through analysis, frustration and delay. So look at your situation, understand what the tools and techniques can and cannot do, and apply them in a controlled way.

Knowing what you want is only the first step in turning your visions into reality – don't forget that there are a few more steps to take before you get there!

Appendix 2

Project Planning
Tools and Techniques

1. INTRODUCTION

In Part 1, Chapter 3, an outline of a plan was briefly described, and then some of the key points of planning were highlighted. This appendix takes you through the plan outline in much more detail. But before you delve too deeply, and slavishly follow the proposed format below, a few cautionary points are worth noting:

- The outline below is about as detailed as you can get. If the project is complex, using many people (some full time, some part time) from across the organisation, then use it as much as you can. But if the project is fairly straightforward, use the simplified planning process described in Part 1, Chapter 3.
- Do not force people to go through what may seem to them as a very bureaucratic paper-based process. The outline below needs to be backed by some serious project planning training so that those involved can fully appreciate what you are trying to be achieve, and how they (as project team members) will benefit.
- There are many ways to skin a cat; there are many ways to produce a plan. As long as the objective is 'SMART', with the action as logical and clear as possible, and as long as the plan shows who does what and when, and comprises the optimal balance between time, cost and quality, then the actual format does not matter!

Below follows a suggested planning pro-forma, from page 1 through to the end. The very least a project manager should distribute is the Gantt chart and Work-to list, based on a sound PERT chart. The project plan acts as a contract, clarifying exactly what is expected. It also acts as a roadmap, which can be changed when reality steps in. It is easier to refine a detailed plan, than enter chaos with a poorly defined one.

2. PROJECT DEFINITION

This is the first section of the project plan. It sets the scene. As it is an important part of the plan, the project definition gets two pages to itself. The first page (Figure A2. 1) defines who is overall responsible for delivering what.

The project manager should be chosen with care. He or she should not be so senior that other duties will be a distraction from the project, nor so junior that he or she will be easily blocked by others more senior in the organisation who might be resistant to change. The project manager needs to be an opinion leader. If necessary he or she should be given some training in project management (which can be delivered in the planning phase, as discussed in Part 1, Chapter 7). He or she should be fully involved in preparing the plan, and should also be involved in building the project team. The project manager is the 'creator' of the project, and the 'author' of the plan, and should receive the full support and authority to get the project done.

Every project should have a 'sponsor' or 'project director'. Normally at top management level, this person acts both as a mentor to the project manager (offering guidance, advice and support), as well as being the representative of the 'client'. It is important for the project to identify who in the organisation the 'client' is. For example, a project to redefine the way products are launched might have the marketing and produc-

PROJECT NAME:		REF:
PROJECT MANAGER:	SPONSOR:	
OBJECTIVE:		
BENEFITS:		
DELIVERABLES:		

Figure A2.1 Project definition.

tion department as its clients. However, it should only have one 'client' representative, a role carried out by the 'sponsor' or 'project director'.

There is a distinct difference between a project objective and its benefits – many get them muddled up, with a muddled implementation as a result. An objective is a cause, the benefit is the effect. In other words, by way of example, it would be wrong for an airline to formulate a project with the objective of 'Cutting down departure delays' – this would more accurately describe an initiative (see Part 1, Chapter 2, section 3). The decrease of delays would be a *benefit* gained from a number of possible project *objectives*, which could include 'To buy 20 per cent more de-icing equipment by next winter', 'To recruit 10 per cent more check-in staff by next summer' and 'To train all check-in staff to increase productivity by 15 per cent by next July'. The project objective, therefore, is the summary action required to achieve a defined benefit. In the Framework for Success it is important to check that the 'objectives' are not simply the required benefits. At this stage you should focus on action, not results, and ask yourself *'So what's the action?'* But do not lose sight of the benefits, and quantify them. This will help in defining the measures of success.

The deliverables are also an important part of this overall project definition. Deliverables must be solid (i.e. you can kick them). For example, if the project objective is 'To train all check-in staff to increase productivity by 15 per cent by next July' with the benefit being reduced check-in delays and increased check-in productivity, then the deliverables could include a physical training package, a pre-booked location with all the necessary facilities, a documented schedule for staff training fully agreed by all involved, an agreed and signed off budget and the resources, qualified and prepared, to deliver the training. The project will then focus on getting the tools for implementation rather than an esoteric paper on how training could be increased. Some deliverables may not be apparent. For example, one deliverable could be 100 per cent management support for a new process. To turn a non-tangible such as 'support' into a tangible deliverable will involve asking the target population, possibly using anonymous questionnaires, the degree to which they support a new process. These questionnaires can then be summarised into a tangible report showing the findings. If the support is not there, then the project did not have a process in-built to gain the support in the first place.

Defining clearly the project objectives, benefits and deliverables will start to focus the mind of the project team on the action required. For example, if a deliverable is not only a new documented process, but also management commitment to implement it, then the project will have to include an element of training/workshops with the management concerned to get their commitment.

The second page of the project definition (Figure A2.2) deals with defining completion and success, as well as some other issues which the project should bear in mind. Every project should have a start and a defined end – if it does not, it is not a project! The definition of completion makes explicit when the project is deemed to be over. This allows those involved to understand when they will return to day-to-day activities or another project. It also prevents 'project creep' – if action is required after the project delivers, then either make it part of the day-to-day activities or formulate a new project.

The measures of success build mainly on the defined benefits. It is important to quantify these, and to have a monitoring system in place to ensure that the results are measured. At this stage it is important to focus on results not action. And if you can't measure it, you can't hit it. A definition of these measures will also focus the minds of the project team onto the process they need to ensure is in place to measure the success rate of their project. The measures can also be linked to bonus compensation for the team to assist motivation. One point to note is that the success of a project should not concentrate solely on the benefits – for example, the project could be successful in delivering its objective (i.e. increasing new de-icing equipment), but, due to outside factors (i.e. Air Traffic Control problems), fail to deliver the benefits assumed (i.e. reducing departure delays).

The constraints which face a project should be noted to assist the more detailed planning. These will invariably revolve around costs (which could be capped) and time (which could include a specified end date). It is also important to note what the impact of running the project will be on day-to-day operations as opposed to the end result of the project. A project could have far-reaching impact on daily operations in terms of needing resources, management time for input and the training needed, etc.

PROJECT NAME:	REF:
DEFINITION OF COMPLETION:	
MEASURES OF SUCCESS:	

CONSTRAINTS -   COST:
                TIME:
                OTHER:	

IMPACT OF PROJECT ON OPERATIONS:	
KEY DEPENDENCIES:	

Figure A2.2 Project definition – continued.

The final section of the project definition is to note any key assumptions and dependencies on outside circumstances. These can be summarised here, and described in more detail later in the plan. If these change during the course of the project it could indicate the reason for problems or the need to rethink the plan.

Although the project definition is the first thing to complete, it is important to note that the process for drawing up the plan is not a serial one, but an iterative one. In other words, some details of the project definition will probably be refined after completing the next few parts of the plan as more details and issues of implementation become clear.

3. WORK BREAKDOWN STRUCTURE

Once the definition is taken as far as it can be, the next step is to identify the detailed tasks that need to be carried out to achieve the objective and deliverables. A work breakdown structure (WBS) is really a pyramid of tasks broken down to detailed level, as shown in Figure A2.3.

This approach is counter-intuitive to the way most people plan in that it initially *ignores the timing and sequence of events*. Most people plan by saying 'First I'll do this, and then I'll do that, after which I'll do the other etc.' The problem with this approach is that it can miss concurrent activities, logic and some key tasks. Using a WBS guards against this risk. There are two ways to build a WBS:

■ **Top down**. This approach first details the types of activities which need to be undertaken. For example, a project might cut across various departments so the types of activities would be Marketing,

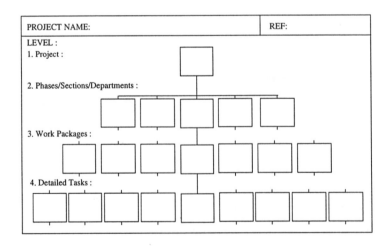

Figure A2.3 Work breakdown structure.

Finance, Production, etc. The next step is to list the types of activities within each area (which could be planning, preparation, roll-out, follow-up, etc.). The next level consists of the detailed tasks themselves, breaking them down into sub-tasks if need be. All of this is written onto 'Post-it' notes and the WBS can literally be built onto a wall. Using 'Post-it' notes allows them to be moved around if necessary.

■ **Brainstorm**. Another approach is to brainstorm with a group of people who have the knowledge of each area (and one or two who don't as they bring fresh eyes onto the structure). Everyone states all the tasks which they think need to be done, which are written down onto 'Post-it' notes and put onto the wall at random. Once all the ideas are exhausted, the 'Post-it' notes are organised into their WBS layers – some tasks will be subordinate to others. The gaps are then filled in by looking at each area. For example, a whole list of marketing tasks may be identified. When they are ordered in the structure, gaps may be apparent. If they are not one could ask questions such as: 'Are there any other Marketing tasks?' (to build sideways) or 'What does it take to get this task done?' (to build down) or 'What type of task is this, as it does not seem to fit with any others?' (to build up).

Depending on the circumstances, I personally prefer the second approach as it often yields better results in quality thinking, and gets people more involved (and thus enthusiastic). It can also be fun! It very much depends on the nature of the change being tackled and who is at the workshop.

Once the WBS is completed, it is best at this stage to write down the duration and effort onto the bottom layer of the 'Post-it' notes. Duration is how much elapsed time is spent for a task to be completed, and effort is how many person days are needed. These will come in useful when we build the timetable and assign resources.

It is also useful to colour code the lowest level 'Post-it' notes with a highlighter pen, colour coded against the second level. Thus if the second level of the WBS is by department, Finance could have a red dash, Marketing a green one, etc. This is useful to identify the type of tasks when they are reordered into a PDM network.

It is advisable to give each lower level task an alpha-numeric identification number – the letter can identify the type of task (i.e. 'F' for Finance) and the number can identify (together with the letter) the task itself. Such a coding structure helps if one is going to use a computer-based project planning application later on in the process (strongly recommended!).

By now you should have a pyramid shape of 'Post-it' notes plastered onto a wall. Each will have a task, with the top layers broken down into more detail below. The lowest level of 'Post-it' notes will also have a colour code to reflect the type of task, and the duration and effort needed for the task, as well as their own alpha-numeric code. Use pencils when writing out the 'Post-it' notes as some details may need to be changed!

The next step is to use the bottom line of 'Post-it' notes (i.e. all the identified, fully broken down and detailed tasks) to build a PDM network (or PERT chart as it can also be known).

4. PDM NETWORK (PERT CHART)

A PDM network, or PERT chart as it is sometimes called, is a graphic representation of what the work flow of the project looks like. PDM stands for 'Precedence Diagramming Method'. As its name suggests, it shows the tasks laid out by precedence.

The bottom layer of the WBS should now be rearranged and laid out across the wall showing the logical flow of events (hence the use of 'Post-it' notes!). Some tasks can start at the same time (and thus be laid out vertically one on top of the other), while others will depend on tasks finishing before they can start (laid out horizontally one after the other). Tasks do not happen in isolation, and they will have a relationship with another task(s). There are four basic types of relationship:

- **Finish – Start (FS)**. This is the most common relationship, and simply states that Task B cannot start until Task A is finished.
- **Start – Start (SS)**. This states that Task B cannot start unless Task A has started.
- **Finish – Finish (FF)**. This states that Task B cannot be finished until Task A is finished.
- **Start – Finish (SF)**. This is rarely used, and states that Task B cannot finish unless Task A has started.

Diagrammatic examples of these relationships are shown in Figure A2.4.

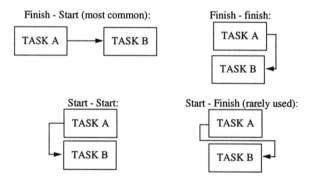

Figure A2.4 Example of task relationships.

It is common that such relationships are not so tightly defined. There may be either a lag in time between one task finishing before another task starts, or a lead time when a task can start earlier than the relationship defined. So these relationships can be adjusted using either 'lag' or 'lead' time.

Lag time is used more often than not. Lag time specifies a delay, while lead time specifies an overlap. An example of *lag time* is when we finish plastering the walls we can start the wall papering (i.e. Task A finishes, Task B can start – FS relationship). However, it cannot start immediately as the plaster must dry! We can have an FS relationship with a lag of two days. An example of *lead time* is when the wall is roughed out, we can start wiring the electrics (a straight FS relationship). However, we could save time if the electricians worked concurrently with the masons and started in the room a day before the masons finished. Task B (wire electrics) would have an FS relationship with Task A (rough out wall) with a one-day lead time. Lead time is sometimes call 'negative lag' time, as opposed to 'positive lag' time, for simplicity.

The diagram in Figure A2.5 gives a simple example of a PDM network.

Once you have arranged the 'Post-it' notes into a PDM network you can start thinking about working smarter – can the relationships be changed to save time, and when is the soonest that things can happen?

After fine tuning you can then work out the *critical path*. Simply put, a critical path is the longest path through a PDM network. If any delay occurs on this path, then the end date of the project will be delayed. In Figure A2.5 below the critical path goes from Task A, via Task C, through Tasks D and G to Task H. This path is ten days long, which is therefore the total project duration. Tasks A, C, D, G and H are critical – if any problems occur here the whole project timetable is in jeopardy.

The relationships are important, and should not be used just to move tasks about. Use lag or lead time for this. In the example in Figure A2.5,

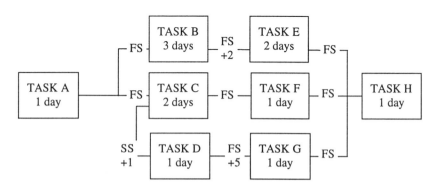

Figure A2.5 PDM network.

Task D has an SS+1 relationship with Task C, putting C on the critical path. The project duration would be the same if Task D had an FS+1 with Task A, releasing Task C from the critical path. Make sure the logic is well founded in order to simplify the critical path. The less tasks on the critical path, the less risk the project faces.

It is interesting to note that Tasks D and G are short – it is the relationship they have with other tasks which adds six days to their path. So just because a task is easy and quick does not mean that it is not critical! The other tasks have *float* – in other words there is time to spare. If delays occur on the non-critical path, then as long as the delay does not add an excess which makes the overall path longer than the critical one, there should be no problem.

Managing the critical path (and understanding where it is) is a key part of successful project management. Critical paths can move – for example, if Task B above is delayed by two days, then the project duration would be eleven days, and the critical path would now be Task A, through Tasks B and E to Task H. If it is delayed one day, then you have two critical paths and double the risk of not meeting the project deadline!

It is at this stage that most people give up in planning, due to the complexity of managing a PDM network! Thankfully there are simple-to-use software packages (such as Microsoft Project which can run in a windows environment) which takes some of the pain out of it all! This can not only draw up PERT charts, but can also help work out early start and early finish dates, as well as late state and late finish dates.

Early dates are worked out by doing a 'forward pass' through the project. So in the example above, if Task A (the start activity) began on 1 August, Task B and C can begin on 2 August. The early finish date for Task B would be 4 August, allowing Task E to start on 7 August (due to the lag time).

Late dates are worked out doing a 'backward' pass. If Task H must finish on 10 August, then the latest date Task B can start is on 3 August – in other words there is a one-day difference for Task B's early start and late start dates, which equates to the amount of float on Task B's path. And similarly, if the early and late dates on a task are the same then the task must be on the critical path.

As can be seen, this sort of analysis can be time consuming, so the use of software packages can really lighten the workload. The important thing to realise is that a project is made up of tasks which have dependencies. As long as you know what those dependencies are, which are critical and where the float time is, then when reality steps in and causes problems it should not take too long to understand if the problem is a big one (and thus needs management time) or a small one (and thus should not demand too much time to worry about).

The other thing to note is that successful project planning first starts with identifying the tasks, then calculates the duration of each task, and finally looks at the logical dependencies between them. From this, the detailed project timings can be worked out. It is *this* sequence which gives you your project timetable. Too often people begin planning with time, which can lead to false logic and delay once the project starts to roll.

If the project needs to be completed by a definite time, ignore this to begin with. The PDM network will tell you when you need to start if the end date is decided. Inevitably it tells you that you should have some time ago! At this stage you start pulling the levers of quality, cost and time. You can also start looking at clever ways of doing things, to change the process of the project itself by re-examining the relationships and tasks to see what time can be saved and what tasks can be dropped. Focus always on the critical path to begin with – it is pointless saving time on a float activity. Another option would be to see if the deadline can be moved – at least you will have a firmer base of knowledge to take such a decision.

Once the PDM network is acceptable as far as the time constraint is concerned, then you can start summarising the plan into a more digestible form. By the way, a PDM chart is another way of doing process analysis, used in business process re-engineering.

At this stage your project plan is a couple of sheets of definition, and a whole load of 'Post-it' notes splattered across the wall. This is not a particularly useful way to document things and it is time to summarise the tasks.

5. TASK SUMMARY SHEET

This summarises the lists of tasks and shows the time, duration and dependencies, as shown in Figure A2.6.

PROJECT NAME:					REF:	
No.	TASK	DESCRIPTION	BY WHOM	PERSONDAYS EFFORT	DURATION	PRECEDING TASK(S) & RELATIONSHIP

Figure A2.6 Task summary sheet.

A note about task numbers: most people would start at 1 and count up. Don't! Start instead at 010, and count up in tens. The reason for this is that if you want to insert a task, then you don't have to renumber them all. And remember to include an alpha prefix to identify the area of responsibility by making the number alpha-numeric. For example, the first task which the Finance department have to do would be numbered F010. Numbering tasks makes it easy later on for editing the plan or simply referring to the task in speech.

6. MILESTONE SUMMARY SHEET

It is useful to break the project up into a few key milestones. These should be of zero duration. For example, 'Deliver presentation' could be a two-day task, and should not be a milestone; 'Presentation ready for delivery' would be a better milestone. The milestones should be linked to the completion of key tasks mainly on the critical path. A summary sheet is a useful tool to assist later on in top-level management of the project progress, as shown in Figure A2.7.

PROJECT NAME:				REF:	
No.	DATE	DESCRIPTION / DELIVERABLES	DEPENDENT ON TASK(S)	RESPONSIBILITY	TYPE

Figure A2.7 Milestone summary sheet.

There are two types of milestone. If the milestone is linked to a task on the critical path it is 'critical'. If it is not linked to a task on the critical path then the milestone is 'planned' or 'non-critical'. Whilst a delay to a critical milestone will show an immediate problem which could affect the overall project timetable, a delay to a planned or non-critical milestone would highlight a potential problem. These milestones need to be communicated to everyone in the project: although these people will be individually committed to various parts of the project (and cannot be expected to remember all the details) they can have an overall understanding of the project structure by knowing the milestones.

7. EXTERNAL DEPENDENCIES

There may be external activities or events upon which the internal tasks in the project are dependent. As these are external to the project, they need not be planned or detailed. However, they do need to be summarised to remind the project team that there are activities outside the project which they need to be aware of. A suggested format is shown in Figure A2.8.

PROJECT NAME:			REF:		
No.	DESCRIPTION	DEPENDENT TASK(S)	RESPONSIBILITY	DATE	COMMENT

Figure A2.8 External dependencies summary sheet.

The column showing responsibility is key for establishing who to communicate with regarding any outside dependencies. It can also include a contact number and date for checking with those responsible.

8. RESOURCE SUMMARY

In the Task Summary sheet resources are allocated to each task. The resource summary sheet shows by resource who is doing what and when. It also shows any downtime such as holidays. Resource allocation can have a direct impact on task duration, possibly extending if it there are not enough resources or shortening it if resorces are more focused. A possible format is shown in Figure A2.9.

PROJECT NAME:						REF:		
NAME	SOURCE (i.e. Department)	CONTACT NUMBER	PROJECT ROLE	TASK NUMBERS	DATES NEEDED	TOTAL TIME NEEDED	COMMENTS (i.e. Holidays)	

Figure A2.9 Resource summary sheet.

The list of external resources should be as comprehensive as possible and also include resources outside the organisation which are used. Telephone numbers should be included to assist communication.

Make sure that the resources assigned to a project agree to what they are to do, and that (if applicable) their functional manager agrees to their inclusion, and to the extent of their inclusion, as well.

9. COST ESTIMATE

Once the tasks and resources have been decided you should be in a good position to estimate the costs for doing the work. The simple pro-forma shown in Figure A2.10 can be used to summarise the key points.

Once the costs are summarised, and before further planning is done (which at this stage is just summarising the plan into a few useful formats for day-to-day use), the cost should be compared to the original benefits – is the project worth it? The calculated costs should also be compared to the expectations of the senior management – the Framework for Success in Part 1, Chapter 2 is a great way of generating a whole series of detailed objectives (each supported by a distinct project) – but change has costs and sometimes there is a need to prioritise the timing!

PROJECT NAME:					REF:	
TASK	No.	COST	ORIGINAL ESTIMATE AS AT (/ /)	REVISED ESTIMATE AS AT (/ /)	PERSON RESPONSIBLE	EXPLANATION / ASSUMPTIONS

Figure A2.10 Cost estimate sheet.

10. PROJECT PROGRAMME/GANTT CHART

At this stage the bulk of the planning has been done. The key trade-offs between time, cost (including resources) and Quality have been made. A start date and end date for the project should have been calculated and agreed. It is time now to summarise the project into visual form to assist communication and project management. The project programme can be usefully summarised in a Gantt chart, which is a bar chart of activities using time as the scale. It can also list other items such as responsibilities, durations and dependencies between tasks. An example is shown in Figure A2.11.

Many people start with this form – to do so for simple projects is generally fine, but more complex ones should use the work breakdown – PDM – Task/Milestone/Resource Summary sheets first: the project programme will be a better product at the end of the day. Software project management packages are useful to produce such project reports as any changes can be swiftly entered, thus dispensing with time spent on drawing such charts up. One reason why such detailed planning is rarely done is due to the effort needed simply to produce the project plan!

While it may be useful to circulate the whole plan to all project team members, the next document is the best 'hymn sheet' for people to use on a daily basis to manage their time.

No.	Task/event	By whom	Duration	Preceding task(s)	AUGUST	SEPTEMBER	OCTOBER	NOVEMBER	DECEMBER	JANUARY
					2 9 16 23 30	6 13 20 27	4 11 18 25	1 8 15 22 29	6 13 20 27	3 10 17 24 31

PROJECT NAME: REF:

Figure A2.11 Project programme/Gantt chart.

11. WORK-TO LIST

This simple form can be used by project members (who may be split across the organisation's departments) to coordinate their actions and manage their time. An example is shown in Figure A2.12.

It is best to use week numbers (with projected dates for them) by counting up from the final week (which can be week 1). Thus a ten-week

PROJECT NAME: REF:

PROJECT WEEK NUMBER..................... PROJECTED DATE...........................

Task Type / Department	Task Number	Task Description	Start	Finish	Person Responsible

Figure A2.12 Work-to list.

long project would start in week 10. By having separate sheets for each week, the project plan can be neatly summarised into a booklet showing week by week who is doing what and when. This can be distributed to all involved.

12. AMENDMENTS

No plan survives first contact with reality. This maxim is often borne out by experience! However, if a plan is well thought out, then unless a total change in the assumptions occurs, it should be easy to adapt. The problem is that in a life span of a project several changes may be necessary – and then it is hard to remember what exactly is meant to happen. As the saying goes: 'When you're up to your neck in crocodiles, it's hard to remember that the original intention was to cross the swamp!' To facilitate control and aid communication, as well as to keep a record of who agreed what changes and when, it is useful to keep a log of any major amendments to a project plan. A suggested format is shown in Figure A2.13.

PROJECT NAME:				REF:	
No.	DESCRIPTION	REASON	EFFECTS	APPROVED BY:	DATE

Figure A2.13 Amendments summary sheet.

If the amendments are large, then it is simple to run off a new plan if project planning software is use. Remember to communicate with all involved – people may have planned the time in advance to meet deadlines, and they will need to understand the personal implications of what is being changed.

13. COMPLETION REPORT

A project should be signed off at its end. It is also useful to record how the project met its timetable and budget, and what lessons there are for the future. The completion report can also serve as a useful record for personal appraisal of the project manager. An example is shown in Figure A2.14.

PROJECT NAME:			REF:
Item	**DUE / COMMITTED**	**ACHIEVED**	**COMMENTS**
OBJECTIVE			
COST			
QUALITY			
COMMENT ON ACHIEVEMENT OF OVERALL PROJECT OBJECTIVES:			
LESSONS LEARNT:			
SIGN OFFS: PROJECT MANAGER:...................... SPONSOR:........................ DATE DATE			

Figure A2.14 Completion report.

14. SUMMARY

Getting to a plan which covers all the above pro-formas is hard work but very worthwhile. Remember the five 'Ps' of planning: Planning and Preparation Prevents Poor Performance. There are also simple but effective computer software packages that will carry out a lot of the hard work for you (such as working out detailed early and late start/finish dates for each task). An example is Microsoft's 'Project' – many others exist. The attractive aspect with such packages is that, once the plan is in, it is very simple to work out the impact of changes, and thus they are a useful sensitivity tool. They are also very useful for contingency planning. However, they do not obviate the need for some quality thinking up front.

The approach above is pretty exhaustive. Those untrained in project management techniques will find the approach difficult and not very enjoyable – they will not do well. So when the teams are formed, include some project management training with the planning phase. This will enable the project teams and their managers to learn new skills, to put them into immediate practice during the course, and to achieve a high-quality project plan. Remember, however, that if the project is simple and does not cross functional boundaries, then the minimalist approach in Part 1, Chapter 3 will be better.

Appendix 3

Information and Communication Technology

1. INTRODUCTION

This appendix is designed to give a brief overview of some of the information and communication technology available today, and the issues surrounding it, with relevance to Business Re-engineering. The technology, if applied well, can help organisations move from functional 'chimneys', through a matrix grid organisation, towards flexible, process-oriented teams organised like 'bubbles'. Technology, like the analytical, process and project tools and techniques described in Appendices 1 and 2, is just another tool. The technology in itself it does not achieve change. However, the technology can have a powerful effect when it is tied to a radical re-organisation which moves from hierarchies to teams focused on customers, and from functional management to process leadership. The appendix covers several areas:

- the challenge;
- from dumb to smart and on to client/server networks;
- electronic data interchange (EDI);
- document image processing (DIP);
- workflow software and groupware software;
- smart/intelligent agents and neural networks;
- when it all goes wrong;
- when it all goes right;
- the use of technology in the change process;
- where next – the multi-media communication 'revolution'.

These topics really only cover the minimum one needs to know to ensure that when a Business Re-engineering programme is being planned, you have the very basic knowledge to ask the right questions. The detailed 'nitty-gritty' about what some of these things actually are, and how they actually work, is not as important as how they can be used to help a company re-engineer itself. Once that is understood, then there exists a whole industry of providers and advisors who can ensure that the technological systems you need are put in place. And the main thing to remember is that 80 per cent of Business Re-engineering needs can be satisfied by relatively cheap off the shelf hardware and software. The key to re-engineering is not the technology, it is the ideas.

2. THE CHALLENGE

There have been many studies into the non-effectiveness of IT spend. For example, a report by Morgan Stanley calculated an $800 billion IT spend in the USA during the 1980s, with only a 0.7 per cent increase in productivity to show for it. What's gone wrong? Here are just a couple of thoughts:

- **Technology evolution.** When a new technology hits mankind, it does not immediately make an effect. Typically it takes about 30 years (i.e. just under a work generation) to gain critical mass. Electricity revolutionised industry, but not overnight. Computer technology has taken time to evolve from rarefied computer rooms on to desks at work, home and school. This has slowly enlightened previously unknowing users. Most workers and shapers of organisations did not grow up with the technology. The school children who have grown up with computer technology are not yet fully the workers and shapers of today.
- **Technology driven.** Computer technology appears like a black art to the computer illiterate. And those who have the art can tend to guard it and speak in another language. They can tend to be technologically driven. So companies can end up spending millions of dollars not really understanding what they are getting, being served by technological experts who don't really understand who they are serving. Computers in the past have typically just been used to automate *current processes* within functional hierarchies, rather than be employed to support radical new processes used by cross-functional teams. So many of the structural problems of the companies remained – the computers did not solve these problems, they just encoded them. However, as computer technology becomes more and more pervasive, and the communication between user and provider more and more frequent, so too does the understanding grow.

So the reasons for the 'failure' of information technology, and the fact that it is only recently that it is really having an affect, are more to do with attitudes than the actual technology itself. The real challenge facing any organisation is not in developing the technology – that part is easy. *The challenge is in changing people's attitudes to new ideas which embrace the technology* and apply it in a constructive and innovative way. And whether you use an inside IT department or an outside provider, make sure they have the ability to fulfil all the roles shown in Figure A3.1 as situations will differ.

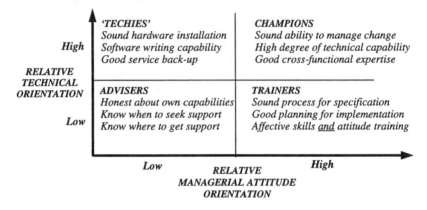

Figure A3.1 The roles of IT providers (internal or external).

The ideal IT provider should be a champion, with a good mix of 'techies' and 'trainers', but also honest enough about a situation to know when to be 'advisers' in order to seek additional support (either from specialist 'techies' or specialist 'trainers'). Make sure you start with defining the problem, not the technology!

3. FROM DUMB TO SMART AND ON TO CLIENT/SERVERS AND NETWORKS

Although computer technology represents a revolution for mankind, which will eventually have as great an impact as electricity in its effect, the technology itself has evolved. When computers first appeared in the 1950s it was reckoned that the total world market was four computers. Given the size and cumbersome nature of the computer at that time, and that the equivalent of today's PC would take up a building, they were probably right. However, mainframe technology evolved and computing power became the domain of the experts, locked away in a computer room, generating output for others to use, as shown in Figure A3.2.

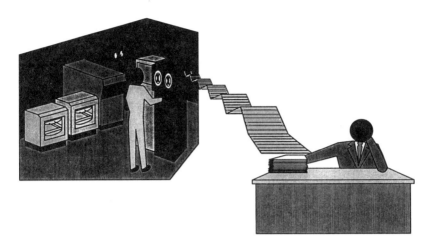

Figure A3.2 The era of the mainframe specialists.

It became apparent that users of the information needed more direct access, and so 'dumb' terminals evolved, which allowed users to access, and manipulate, data needed for making decisions. Soon, smart terminals allowed users to access data from the mainframe and process it on their own terminals, which freed up mainframe usage. Then the PC hit the scene, regarded at first by many as simply a toy (for use with games), or just a tool to speed up typing (with word processing). The rapid evolution of microchip technology allowed PCs to have the same computing power as previous mainframes. More pragmatic business applications like spreadsheets, database management and drawing software allowed people to use computers more productively. But PCs were initially stand-alone, and any output had to rely on the flow of paper. Soon, however, it became possible to link PCs through networks.

Client/server networks were the next natural evolution. This allows a more powerful PC with expanded memory (a server) to run a network of PCs (clients), as shown in Figure A3.3. People in different places, but locally grouped, can be linked on a Local Area Network (LAN) to share files and exchange documents. Software such as E-mail allows people to communicate by sending memos and letters electronically, without first having to print them off and send them via manual internal mail.

LAN technology is itself evolving. New LAN technologies, such as Ethernet and Fibre Distributed Data Interface (FDDI), allow up to ten times more information to be transmitted than traditional LAN networks.

The hardware evolution into client/server networks was also matched by a software evolution using much more user-friendly formats. Graphical User Interface (GUI) software such as that used by Macintosh,

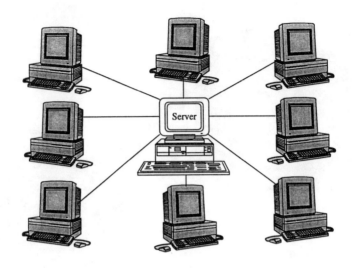

Figure A3.3 Client/server LAN assists communications.

or more recently by Microsoft's Windows (for use on IBM compatible machines), allows the user to work without having to memorise computer commands. A 'mouse' is used to point at icons, pictures and commands, as well as run more than one software package in separate windows on the screen. The use of *Windows, Icons, Mouse* and *Pull-down* menus (WIMP software) makes the transition for the computer illiterate more easy and intuitive. This evolution has done much to put computing power onto people's desks with better hardware and software (although it is reckoned that only 30 per cent of the software capabilities on peoples' desks are actually used).

LANs can also be linked together via Wide Area Networks (WANs) as shown in Figure A3.4.

Using LANs and WANs, information and communication technology can be linked to help organisations radically change the way they work. For example, the use of a satellite link can help communication and training in a geographically dispersed organisation. Many other possibilities exist. The case studies of National Vulcan and Banca d'America e d'Italia in Part 2 show how such technology can be used.

The linkages can be achieved through a variety of ways, from phone lines, mobile phones, satellites, hosts and Integrated Services Digital Networks (ISDNs). An ISDN allows 20 minutes of information previously faxed through a modem to be sent in a minute. Phone lines themselves are being revolutionised, with fibre optics allowing a vastly increased amount of data to be sent compared to using the more traditional copper wires.

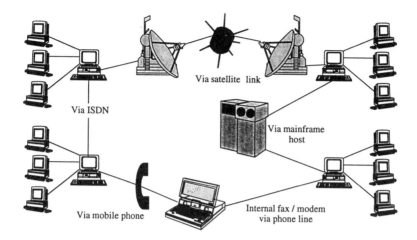

Via satellite link

Via ISDN

Via mainframe host

Via mobile phone

Internal fax / modem via phone line

Figure A3.4 LANs can be extended via WANs in a variety of ways.

The current mismatch between the analogue form of data (used on telephone wires) and the digital form of data (used by computers) is overcome using modems. This, however, slows the process down, and new LAN/WAN technologies, such as Asynchronous Transfer Mode (ATM), overcomes this.

There is an increasing use of ISDN for video conferencing on a PC using Windows technology. The evolution continues – with the result that the systems are faster, easier to use, more flexible and cheaper.

4. ELECTRONIC DATA INTERCHANGE (EDI)

Using LANs and WANs, data can now be transferred between organisations in a value chain (such as a retailer to a supplier, a distributor to a manufacturer). This can radically cut down time and costs and increase quality.

The example in Figure A3.5 below, a typical order process to a supplier, is just one of a variety of uses of EDI. We are surrounded by many others. These include the use of Automatic Teller Machines (ATMs) for cash withdrawals and balance enquiries; the ability to pay (and have credit checked) with a credit or debit card using Electronic Funds Transfer at Point of Sales (EFTPOS); the ability to manage stock control, reorder items and speed up customer service with bar-coded packaging and scanning tills which employ Electronic Point of Sale technology (EPOS). In Part 2, other examples of the use of EDI can be found in some of the case studies.

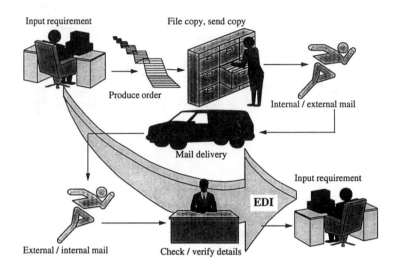

Figure A3.5 EDI can speed up process and reduce effort.

As helpful as EDI can be, it can also allow mistakes to occur at astonishing speeds. For example, a staff member of a well-known US bank mistakenly ran the same tape of payment instructions twice on the Clearing House Automatic Payments (CHAPS) system. This resulted in over $1 billion being erroneously paid out in less than 30 minutes. Despite such pitfalls, a recent European Union sponsored survey of EDI concluded that the new technology resulted in increased savings and customer service.

5. DOCUMENT IMAGE PROCESSING (DIP)

One of the problems facing an organisation which is re-engineering its processes is how to manage the transition from an information flow which is largely paper based to one which is managed by IT. In some circumstances, the use of document imaging can help. This can reduce the space and time allocated to managing paper records currently in use, and speed up the transition to the use of new IT systems by staff. DIP is applicable to organisations which are 'case based', although engineering diagrams and manuals also lend themselves to the technology.

Although DIP is a very useful technology and helps a transition, it is not automatically a panacea. National Vulcan, for example, did not use DIP to move from 10 million pieces of paper to a digital storage system. A new system was introduced with a new process, and this gradually eliminated the need for the paper documents on which the old process relied (see Part 2).

Three basic ways to scan documents using DIP can be employed, as shown in Figure A3.6.

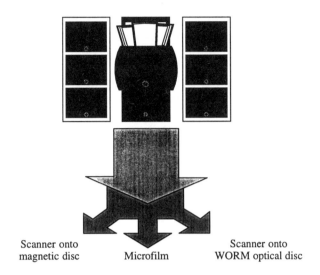

| Scanner onto magnetic disc | Microfilm | Scanner onto WORM optical disc |

Figure A3.6 DIP can save space and time.

Documents can be scanned onto PC hard (internal) or floppy (external) magnetic discs. They then simply become file items which can be sent via LANs/WANs. The scanning speeds can match fast photocopier speeds (up to four pages a second). Magnetic discs are slowly being replaced by optical discs, which look like CDs and can save 1,000 standard magnetic floppy discs (250,000 typed pages) worth of information. IBM has recently introduced an optical CD disc which can hold up to 1 million documents. They are relatively rare at the moment, and are mainly used for multi-media applications (see below) which demand a lot more storage space. Documents can also be scanned onto optical WORM discs. WORM stands for *Write Once Read Many*, and, as the name implies, once a document is scanned onto such a disc, the documents cannot be changed.

Both magnetic and optical storage of documents has a legal implication, because at the time of writing no test case has occurred which allows such stored documentation to be used in evidence in a court of law. This is because such stored data (even documents on WORM discs) can be tampered with. Microfilm, however, is allowed in courts of law. Documents are photo-reduced onto microfilm, which can be accessed using PC like terminals, or using PCs via an interchange unit. Current microfilm technology allows paper documents to be compressed into 2 per cent of the storage space: about 1,000 filing cabinets worth of documents (10 million A4 pages approx.) can be stored in a box under the end of a desk.

DIP will be around for some time to come, as paper still remains overwhelmingly the prime source of documented communication. DIP also exists in a wider environment, and as has already been mentioned the legal implications are complex. However, such an issue has been acknowledged by legal and governmental organisations. For example, in the UK, the current Criminal Evidence Act (introduced in 1968) is being re-examined by the Law Commission to be updated to cover the issue of computer records being used as evidence, In addition to this, recommendations for a code of practice are being developed by the Cranfield Imaging and Document Management User Group (CIDMUG) which consists of representatives from business, the computer industry, UK and EU government bodies, the legal profession and Cranfield University.

6. WORKFLOW AND GROUPWARE* SOFTWARE

Workflow software allows a previously manual process, with defined steps of information retrieval, manipulation and onward distribution, to be automated. The software manages the flow of work at each point of the cycle. Such software is usually adapted using off-the-shelf packages (flexible software which allows a high degree of adaptability to current/new processes), but bespoke software can be written. There are many examples of workflow software uses.

One example could be a letter from a customer who has one type of mortgage and wishes to change it to another, but would like a detailed account of what the new payment schedule would look like. On receiving such a request a staff member (depending on how the lending organisation is set up) would first need to access a mainframe to get the current balance of the mortgage, and then, using a spreadsheet, recalculate the new payment schedule. The next step might involve doing a current credit check on the customer to ensure the new request could be underwritten, and then finally a letter would need to be drafted and signed off. This could take hours, and sometimes days, in duration. Workflow software could fully automate the process and involve only inputting a few details to get the letter automatically drafted up, a process which can take seconds. If the letter needed input from another staff member, then the person could be automatically alerted, and the software would queue the work. Updates of work queues can be accessed in a matter of seconds by any person on the workflow.

Workflow systems can also incorporate 'smart' or 'expert' systems which take human skills and apply them automatically. For example,

---

* This term is derived from the combination of 'groupwork' and 'software'.

many mortgage underwriting transactions are very straightforward, as long as certain criteria are fulfilled. Smart workflow systems can do the underwriting automatically, allowing the underwriter in person to concentrate on the more difficult applications. The customer service is thus increased, with straightforward applications being processed very much faster, and more difficult ones getting a more personalised service.

Groupware software differs from workflow software in that it is not tied to a specific process, but allows different people working in different locations to communicate and work together (assuming, of course, that the hardware platforms are in place). There are many examples of groupware, in particular Lotus Notes. Lotus Notes is an off-the-shelf, flexible, software package which can be set up to meet the current information needs of an organisation. The package can be easily adapted to link into current mainframe databases, DIP databases and current LAN/WAN E-mail networks. It allows people to pass information on a subject, and also access any previously passed or stored information for reference. People in different locations can work on various parts of the same project and also be aware of the concurrent inputs of other people at the same time.

A variety of uses for groupware can be employed. For example, a cross-functional product development team can use groupware to act as the glue between their various activities, and so speed up the whole development process. Customer service can be speeded up, with immediate access to details regarding customers normally held across various parts of an organisation. There are numerous examples of how companies have used groupware to underpin their re-engineering efforts. Sun Alliance, for example, used Lotus Notes to improve the efficiency and service levels of its Broker Division (which deals with its full-time independent intermediaries). Price Waterhouse's consulting organisation used it to turn around a complicated multi-million proposal in four days, which needed four people working on it in three different locations. Despite hearing about the opportunity late, and being weeks behind the competition, Price Waterhouse won the job.

Groupware packages usually include a diary and meetings management system. Anyone who has tried to organise a meeting of several executives in different locations, with a variety of meeting venues possible, knows how long this can take. As long as people keep their diaries and movements up to date on the system, the software can check who is free when, book their diaries provisionally at the earliest opportunity, send an invitation via E-mail, book the venue, and then send confirmatory memos and the necessary working papers, again via E-mail. This can all be done in a matter of seconds, rather than the hours a typical manual approach would take.

Groupware in itself does not speed the processes up – it demands a whole new, sometimes disciplined, approach to sharing information and working together. However, once the re-engineering has been designed and the attitudes of those affected changed, groupware is a vital tool to allow an organisation to 'Do it'.

7. SMART/INTELLIGENT AGENTS AND NEURAL NETWORKS

One of the problems in managing such a growing and pervasive evolution of information and communications technology is information overload. Before we know it, we are all stuck behind a computer screen trying to make sense of it all, leaving the customer to struggle on alone! Smart/intelligent agents can help. These are software packages which can look at a variety of databases which are being continually updated, and then alert the user on any changes which needs particular attention, or filter out irrelevant data (to the user's specifications). Such software packages are often bespoke, but off-the-shelf packages are available, and they are being increasingly incorporated into other packages (such as Lotus Notes). They can take new data and automatically update the user's own database, as well as those of others he or she needs to interact with. The smart/intelligent agent can also be linked to diary systems to remind the user of meetings, and alert him or her to any new relevant data which may be needed for those meetings. They can run in the background on the PC/laptop, allowing the user to continue with any other work. They certainly help to overcome the information overload that can be faced by people using IT systems linked to a variety of databases and other users.

Neural network chips take the concept of smart/intelligent agents one step further. These are really 'intelligent' systems which can look at a whole load of data requests and patterns of occurrence and then 'learn' from the users what is important and what is not. They can 'teach' computers to work in a more intelligent and value added way. For example, a US bank's neural network realised that many credit card thieves first used the cards on very low transactions (such as a few dollars at a petrol station) several times in a day just to ensure that the theft had not been reported. They then used the cards for big ticket items. By the time the card was reported stolen, and corrective action for EFTPOS credit checks taken, the cards were disposed of. The neural network spotted this trend, from millions of pieces of information, and using smart/intelligent agents alerted bank staff about stolen cards even before the owners had realised the cards were lost.

The employment of neural networks and smart/intelligent agents is still very new. However, the potential to support a re-engineering programme, releasing staff to concentrate on serving customers rather than managing data, is huge.

8. WHEN IT ALL GOES WRONG

As IT and communication systems become more prevalent and underpin newly designed processes, the risk of failures must always be borne in mind. The systems are simply machines, but when they go wrong they can have a bad impact on the people who rely on them as shown in Figure A3.7!

Figure A3.7 ... and when it all goes wrong?

Although Murphy's law suggests there is no such thing as a fail-safe system, if a re-engineering programme is underpinned by new technology (and it should be), then make sure that the risks and possible things which can go wrong are fully understood and planned for. A 1993 UK government sponsored survey undertaken jointly by ICL and the National Computer Centre surveyed 850 companies. They found that a startling 80 per cent had suffered from computer breakdowns, and put the annual cost of such breakdowns at £1.5 billion. The main lesson is that the introduction of new information and communication technology must be accompanied by new processes to safeguard the systems and contingency plans to safeguard the organisation when the systems suffer from failures. A variety of disasters can occur:

- fire;
- power failure;
- viruses;
- hacking;
- hardware/software breakdown;
- network communication disasters.

There is no way of totally avoiding disasters, but there are contingencies one can put in place to minimise the risks and lessen subsequent damage. Most of it is common sense, but in the middle of implementing a complex Business Re-engineering programme with new IT systems, some of it can be overlooked which could be a costly mistake.

8.1 Fire

If a new network is being put into the building, take the opportunity to check and, if necessary, update the fire detection systems. Get the sprinkler systems checked as well. Ensure that file servers are well covered, and introduce additional extinguishers. If the worst does happen, ensure you have a disaster recovery plan. This could include a back-up file server in another building. Ensure staff back up data daily, and arrange for such back-up data to be stored at another location, ideally on another file-server/PC with the back-up happening over the wires automatically. Staff should also be encouraged to back up their own important data daily on discs and keep the discs in their briefcases/handbags. These back-ups will ensure that even if fire does strike and the computer system is destroyed, the data is not lost.

8.2 Power failure

Power failure is very rare, but can happen. There are a number of stand-by generators which can keep things running until the power is restored. Again, it depends on how crucial the running of the IT systems are. Check with the local electricity provider how long it would take them to restore power if it was lost (due to storms, cables being dug up, etc.), and see if you can last that long. If you cannot, take action. Although adding additional expense, take a positive decision regarding alternative power (even if it is not to put it in). If back-up power is not being put in, have a contingency plan about what to do if the systems go down, and make sure all users understand it.

8.3 Viruses

These are rogue computer software programmes which can be introduced (either on purpose or by accident) onto any computer system. They can vary in effect, from annoying (with stupid messages appearing on the screen) to disastrous (wiping out data, and destroying the operating systems of the computer). They come in lots of shapes and sizes, and some can lie dormant for a long time in the system before striking. They can either attack data files, or operating systems, or both. Ensure that each PC and network has built-in 'vaccine' software and virus checkers. Ensure that staff do not introduce discs from outside the building – a common source of viruses is people putting games onto their PCs. Ensure a strict policy of having no unauthorised software is understood by all staff, and that they understand the reasons for such a policy. If a virus is found, ringfence the computers being used, and take all the discs away for checking. Although inconvenient for those affected, discs are a quick way to spread viruses. Frequently check the file server and the network for viruses. And keep your virus checker software up to date. There are a lot of people out there who get their kicks by designing viruses which get around current virus checkers, and so computer systems rarely stay fully protected.

8.4 Hacking

Hacking occurs when unauthorised computer users gain access to data files and either lift data from them, or manipulate data in the files. Such hacking can occur either internally or externally. The use of passwords, which can be changed by those who own them whenever they want (suggest frequently), can deter hackers. There is also software available which denies subsequent access to a user who has failed to input the right password. Such software can also further deter hackers by sending them messages (such as those saying that their attempts to hack, and their location, have been identified and the authorities are being informed). If data is *very* sensitive and is on a network, see if it would be practical to lift the data off the system and keep it instead on a secured floppy/optical disc (backed up on another).

8.5 Hardware/software breakdown

Although very reliable today, hardware and software can suffer failures. At staff level ensure each user saves his or her work every ten minutes or so, and backs it up once or twice a day. If a failure does occur, at least not too much data will be lost. Make sure that you have a fast and responsive service agreement to look after such eventualities. These need not be from the same supplier which provides the equipment, although warranty agreements may prevent you from shopping around.

8.6 Network communication disasters

United Airlines still talk of the day they lost Seattle for several hours, as a roadwork gang dug up their ISDN cable. The problem with WANs is that, unlike LANs, you rarely control the environment in which they exist. Whatever method is used for linkage via WANs, make sure you ask the service provider what back-up system is available in the event of failure. Don't be fooled by claims of 'fail-proof' systems. They do not exist (mainly because even if *they* were 'fail-proof', the environment in which they exist is not). You can also prepare a contingency plan for switching to alternative means if failure occurs.

The points above are not exactly rocket science – but they frequently get forgotten in the chaos of change. Ensure that procedures and contingency policies are well communicated, possibly packaged under a 'Disaster Recovery' communication campaign. It is pointless having such plans and procedures if they are not regularly communicated!

9. WHEN IT ALL GOES RIGHT

The examples in Part 2 (especially National Vulcan, Cigna, BAI and Oticon) show how the use of information and communication technology can radically help to change the way an organisation works. It can also help change the way individual people work – the CEO of another of the case studies, Birmingham Midshires, has no office, just a laptop and a mobile phone. Here are just a few more examples of how the new technology can really 'liberate':

- The chairman of a European foundation for economic development which runs 158 local subsidiaries and staff of over 2,500 people leads the organisation using a mobile and laptop. He only spends 25 per cent of his time in an office, and keeps in touch using the technology.
- A leading German car manufacturer replaced the notepad and folder of sales people with a 'briefcase' office which had a laptop, printer and modem. Sales visits rose 20 per cent and the order process speed was increased by 70 per cent.
- A leading Swiss insurance firm issued all representatives with a laptop with in-built modem. The representatives can now offer clients not only bespoke insurance policies but, accessing a variety of databases, can also give advice on how to reduce the risks.

There is no doubt that information and communication technology can alter the way we work, and dramatically increase efficiency and customer service. But again remember the challenge is not so much the introduction of such technology, the challenge is changing the attitudes of those affected.

10. THE USE OF TECHNOLOGY IN THE RE-ENGINEERING PROCESS

The outline details above have concentrated on information and communication technology which help you to 'Do it'. Do not forget, however, that IT can help with the other stages of Business Re-engineering, 'Know what you want', 'Make a plan' and 'Monitor'. Traditional office software such as spreadsheets and relational databases can speed up analysis and subsequent reporting. Graphic and presentation software can increase the quality of inputs for a workshop. PC and overhead projectors can be linked to demonstrate future-state IT-enhanced processes. Process analysis and design can be sped up by the use of off-the-shelf software specifically designed to do such work (which can save a lot of time and effort preparing flow charts). If software needs to be designed to support a new process, Computer-Aided Software Engineering (CASE) tools can dramatically speed the process up, and improve the quality as well. And as has been mentioned in Part 1, Chapter 3, off-the-shelf project planning software can assist the development and delivery of quality project plans.

The use of such software within the change teams itself will help the organisation in its move towards a culture of IT-enhanced cross-functional teams coming together to solve problems and implement solutions.

11. WHERE NEXT – THE MULTI-MEDIA COMMUNICATION 'REVOLUTION'

The word 'revolution' is in quotation marks on purpose – the fact of the matter is what we are seeing is not so much a revolution as a speeded up pace of technological evolution. And those who have still yet to introduce PCs to their administrators and managers are going to find themselves a long, long way behind. If you want to make sure that the technology does not represent a 'bloody' revolution to your organisation, make sure it evolves with the changes.

Where are the changes leading us? Not surprisingly information technology (typically supplied by the computer industry) has been evolving close links with those who supply communication technology (such as phone companies). The linkages are now becoming wider. As computing power increases, along with disc storage space and PC screen resolution quality, then so too does the ability of PCs to play quality video-like images. And with video images now capable of being sent and stored digitally, it is not surprising to see the linkages between information and communication technology extended to television and video technology. The multi-media technology will allow people to use their laptops to hold conference video conversations with each other. It already allows multi-video conferencing (holding a conference with people in different places, but they are visible on their own TV screen). In just a few years, a laptop (and even palm top) will become a combined PC, TV, video, video camera, fax, and mobile phone all rolled into one. The ability for teams to communicate and cooperate on projects will be vastly increased, and 'face to face' communication will be increased. Managers will be able to spend more time leading and less time administrating. Organisations will be able to have more 'leaders' and less 'bosses' (see Part 1, Chapter 4, Figure 4.5).

Another new technology, virtual reality, will also have an increasing impact on organisations. Virtual reality has to date mainly been associated with games rather than any serious business application. That is beginning to, and will continue to, change. Design, marketing and training applications have been introduced. For example, potential Volvo customers can 'experience' a side-on collision which demonstrates the effectiveness of side impact bars. Some architectural practices offer clients the opportunity to 'walk though' a designed building to 'see' what it will actually look like in. Surgeons can practise their skills carrying out complex 'operations'.

The limit of information and communications technology seems to lie only in the scope of individual imagination, and the attitudes we have, to apply it.

12. SUMMARY

So what? The technological wonders of tomorrow can hardly be expected to make an effect on the organisation of today, if that organisation's attitudes are firmly entrenched in old traditional ways. If the organisation is functionally driven and hierarchically controlled then the technology outlined in this appendix will not be able to serve as much as it could. Adam Smith's and Frederick Taylor's principles of functional and hierarchical divisions of labour and tasks are all very well, but they were based on the assumptions of the technology and abilities of their day (many decades, and in some cases, centuries ago). Until organisations shrug off their old ways and re-engineer themselves, then the technology will remain at best just dreams, and at worst expensive paperweights. And as the technology marches on, and their competitors re-engineer to take advantage of it, those who will not change will simply fade away.

Reader's Feedback Questionnaire

We would appreciate some feedback on how useful you found this book, and any suggestions for changes to future editions. If you do not want to tear these pages out, feel free to photocopy them. Please tick the relevant boxes, add comments where you see fit, and post to Kogan Page Publishers, 120 Pentonville Road, London, N1 9JN UK (phone 071-278 0433). If you have other comments for the author, he can be reached via the publishers, or via E-mail on the CompuServe network (100322,1753).

Thank you very much for your feedback. We appreciate your input for future editions.

1. How useful was the overview in Chapter 1?

Extremely	Very	Mainly	A little	None!

Comments/Suggestions:

2. How practical were the ideas in Chapter 2?

Extremely	Very	Mainly	A little	None!

Comments/Suggestions:

3. How relevant do you feel the approach is in Chapter 3?

Extremely	Very	Mainly	A little	None!

Comments/Suggestions:

4. How useful are the techniques in Chapter 4?

Extremely	Very	Mainly	A little	None!

Comments/Suggestions:

5. How relevant are the measures outlined in Chapter 5?

Extremely	Very	Mainly	A little	None!

Comments/Suggestions:

6. How useful are the approaches described in Chapter 6?

Extremely	Very	Mainly	A little	None!

Comments/Suggestions:

7. How useful are the techniques described in Chapter 7?

Extremely	Very	Mainly	A little	None!

Comments/Suggestions:

8. How helpful are the 'starting points' in Chapter 8?

Extremely	Very	Mainly	A little	None!

Comments/Suggestions:

9. How useful are the case studies in Part 2?

Extremely	Very	Mainly	A little	None!

Comments/Suggestions:

10. How useful are the tools & techniques in Appendix 1?

Extremely	Very	Mainly	A little	None!

Comments/Suggestions:

11. How useful are the techniques in Appendix 2?

Extremely	Very	Mainly	A little	None!

Comments/Suggestions:

12. How helpful is the information in Appendix 3?

Extremely	Very	Mainly	A little	None!

Comments/Suggestions:

Bibliography

1. Copeland, T, Koller, T and Murren, J (1990) *Valuation – Measuring and Managing the Value of Companies*, John Wiley and Sons, New York, USA.

2. Fisher, R and Ury, W (1987) *Getting To Yes – How To Negotiate An Agreement Without Giving In*, Arrow Books, London, UK.

3. Hammer, M and Champy, J (1994) *Reengineering the Corporation – A Manifesto for Business Revolution*, Nicholas Brealey, London, UK.

4. Higgins, R C (1984) *Analysis for Financial Management*, Irwin Publishers, Illinois, USA.

5. Pfeiffer, W J and Jones, J E (1984) *A Handbook of Structured Experiences for Human Relation Training, Volumes 1–4*, University Associates Publisher and Consultants, La Jolla, California, USA.

6. Rappaport, A (1986) *Creating Shareholder Value – The New Standard of Business Performance*, Free Press of Macmillian Inc, New York, USA.

7. Reiman, B C (1989) *Managing for Value – A Guide to Value Based Strategic Management*, Basil Blackwell Ltd, Oxford, UK, in association with The Planning Forum, Ohio, USA.

Index